Praise for *The Reformations of Medicine*

In this engaging study, Ekaterina Lomperis deftly describes Martin Luther's new evangelical understanding of physical suffering and the role of medicine in alleviating it. Linking theology with pastoral care, she highlights those elements of the reformer's thought still relevant to Christian faith communities today. *The Reformations of Medicine* demonstrates the value of drawing from the past to address modern questions.

—Amy Nelson Burnett, Paula and D. B. Varner University Professor emerita, University of Nebraska–Lincoln

The Reformations of Medicine offers an innovative exploration of the intersection between religious belief and healing practices during the transformative era of the sixteenth century. Lomperis reveals how the Protestant Reformation not only reshaped theology but also reimagined nonmaterial dimensions of medicine. This book is an essential resource for every enthusiast of science and religion.

—Benjamin R. Doolittle, professor of internal medicine and pediatrics, Yale University School of Medicine

This book bridges the gap between early modern thought and contemporary questions about the relationship between religion and medicine. Using Martin Luther's religious understanding, Lomperis provides an excellent introduction to readers interested in the Reformation and its implications for suffering, healing, and medicine in its own context, as well as for contemporary society.

—Esther Chung-Kim, professor of religious studies, Claremont McKenna College, and president, American Society of Church History

Ekaterina Lomperis deftly breaks down barriers in this study, combining intellectual history and social history to clarify Luther's teachings on medicine, while also addressing divisions between modern medicine and faith healings. Her work is grounded in the breadth of Luther's thought, which places him firmly in his early modern context, while also illustrating how his doctrines of salvation and the Christian life were basic to the way he conceptualized health, divine providence, and monastic disciplines. A unique work that should be on the bookshelves of everyone interested in the early modern era and its ongoing significance for the modern world.

—R. Ward Holder, professor of theology, Saint Anselm College, and president, Society for Reformation Research

The emerging field of medical humanities has presented two gaps: one, a *longue durée* perspective on the discourse, and the other, connection between medicine, humanities, and works focused on religious-*cum*-theological matters. With *The Reformations of Medicine*, Ekaterina Lomperis offers a bold and groundbreaking account that fills both these gaps, with Martin Luther as the primary interlocutor. Readers will also appreciate the connection she makes between the world of the early Reformation with contemporary concerns and preoccupations. This book is written in a lucid style; readers will be glad to have chosen it. *Tolle lege!*

—Paul C. H. Lim, professor of humanities, Hamilton Center, University of Florida, and author of *Mystery Unveiled: The Crisis of the Trinity in Early Modern England*

An important contributor to both Reformation studies and the history of medicine, Prof. Lomperis offers a fresh perspective on Luther's engagement with Scripture and tradition, addressing head-on unhealthy theological misconceptions about sickness and healing. In a world impacted by pandemics and healthcare injustice, her proposal to draw upon Luther's own deliberations to reform modern medicine is both timely and necessary, providing the theological impetus for Christians to attend to both physical and spiritual well-being. This book should be read in congregations, hospitals, seminaries, and graduate schools!

—Kyle K. Schiefelbein-Guerrero, Grace Professor of Leadership, Lutheran Theological Seminary Saskatoon, and editor of *Church After the Corona Pandemic: Consequences for Worship and Theology*

Lomperis thoughtfully and, at times, provocatively argues that Luther's theology of suffering and his engagement with medicine offer valuable insights for contemporary medical ethics. By reexamining Luther's teachings and posing fresh questions to the past, Lomperis presents a more nuanced, faith-centered approach to medicine and modern healthcare.

—David M. Whitford, professor of Reformation studies, Baylor University

THE REFORMATIONS OF MEDICINE

THE REFORMATIONS OF MEDICINE

Early Modern Beginnings & Contemporary Possibilities

EKATERINA N. LOMPERIS

Fortress Press
Minneapolis

THE REFORMATIONS OF MEDICINE
Early Modern Beginnings and Contemporary Possibilities

30 29 28 27 26 25 1 2 3 4 5 6 7 8 9

Library of Congress Cataloging-in-Publication Data

Names: Lomperis, Ekaterina N., author.
Title: The reformations of medicine : early modern beginnings and contemporary possibilities / Ekaterina N. Lomperis.
Description: Minneapolis : Fortress Press, [2025] | Includes bibliographical references and index.
Identifiers: LCCN 2024040512 (print) | LCCN 2024040513 (ebook) | ISBN 9781506491172 (paperback) | ISBN 9781506491189 (ebook)
Subjects: LCSH: Luther, Martin, 1483-1546. | Medicine--Religious aspects--Lutheran Church. | Suffering--Religious aspects--Lutheran Church. | Healing--Religious aspects--Lutheran Church.
Classification: LCC BR333.5.M66 L66 2025 (print) | LCC BR333.5.M66 (ebook) | DDC 261.8/3210882841--dc23/eng/20250109
LC record available at https://lccn.loc.gov/2024040512
LC ebook record available at https://lccn.loc.gov/2024040513

Cover design: Ashley Muehlbauer
Cover art: Christ as Apothecary, 1602, National Germanic Museum Nuremburg. Sourced from Science History Images/Alamy Stock Photo.

Print ISBN: 978-1-5064-9117-2
eBook ISBN: 978-1-5064-9118-9

To my family

CONTENTS

ACKNOWLEDGMENTS

I was first introduced to Martin Luther's thought as a master's student at Harvard Divinity School, over fifteen years ago. My late advisor, Ron Thiemann, encouraged my desire to study Reformation traditions deeply and engage them creatively. I am grateful to the faculty of the University of Chicago Divinity School, where I subsequently pursued my doctoral work in theology and the history of Christianity. Willemien Otten and Dwight Hopkins modeled for me the highest standards of historical and theological vigor. I learned from my doctoral advisor, Susan Schreiner, the importance of early modern scholarship's rigorous traditions and the confidence to forge my own intellectual path. I will always be grateful for her scholarly brilliance, courageous thinking, and friendship. I am thankful for my colleagues and our many conversations at the meetings of the Sixteenth Century Society & Conference and the Conference on Medicine and Religion, which have helped shape the vision for this book.

At different stages, this project has been supported by many grants and fellowships, including those from the National Endowment for the Humanities, the Martin Marty Center for the Advanced Study of Religion, and the Louisville Institute. I am grateful to my institution, George Fox University, for two summer research grants that helped bring this project to completion. My deans, Roger Nam, MaryKate Morse, and Tammy Dunahoo, have been exceedingly supportive of my work, including this project. I express my appreciation to my research assistants and George Fox University's Portland Seminary students, Maria Hearing and Louie Hogan, for their help and linguistic expertise. My research assistant, Sarah Lee, with dedication helped me bring the manuscript to completion. My editor at Fortress Press, Laura Gifford, has been outstanding, consistently offering flexibility and valuable feedback.

I am grateful to my extended family in my native country of Moldova for their support. My husband and children have walked alongside me with unwavering encouragement, support, and patience. My young daughters invented their own game of "finishing the book," as I was working long hours on finishing mine. I dedicate this study to my family, whose creative approach to life's challenges embodies the ethos of this book.

INTRODUCTION

IN 1520, LESS than five months prior to his excommunication, Martin Luther published a programmatic address, *To the Christian Nobility of the German Nation Concerning the Reform of the Christian Estate.*[1] Among other matters, this treatise outlined his proposals for reforming the curricula of two of the three higher faculties of late medieval universities—theology and jurisprudence. Regarding the remaining third higher faculty of medicine, Luther merely stated that he would leave the task of reforming medical education to physicians themselves.[2] This brief remark had once been interpreted as indicative of Luther's theological disinterest in the practice of medicine. Indeed, few in Luther's vast body of works extensively discussed medicine. Additionally, in his private remarks uttered in informal settings and later published as his "Table Talk," the older Luther purportedly scoffed at invasive and overly controlling medical treatments to which he was subjected by doctors. On one occasion, while commenting on a strict diet prescribed by physicians, which allegedly left patients exhausted to the point of death, Luther grimly concluded that "to live medically is to live wretchedly."[3]

Given Luther's seeming lack of enthusiasm for medical practice, it is unsurprising that until now there has not been a major study exploring his theological approach to medicine. Previously, Richard Toellner argued that Luther perceived medicine as ultimately irrelevant for theology, resulting in the Reformation's lack of influence on medical education at the University of Wittenberg.[4] While Toellner's conclusion that new Protestant ideas failed to affect the Wittenberg medical faculty was later refuted by Vivian Nutton and Mitchell Lewis Hammond, scholarly investigations into Luther's own theology of medicine have been remarkably scarce.[5] A notable exception is Johann Anselm Steiger's 2005 study, *Medizinische Theologie: Christus medicus und theologia medicinalis bei Martin Luther und im Luthertum der Barockzeit.* However, Steiger's important work primarily focused on Luther and the subsequent Lutheran tradition's use of medical imagery and metaphors in theological expositions of Christology, soteriology, and theological anthropology, rather than on medicine itself.

This book interrogates Luther's religious vision of physical suffering, healing, and medicine, with particular attention to his instructions regarding their proper use. While extended engagements with medicine are indeed sparse in Luther's works, his lectures, sermons, and treatises contain a multitude of scattered and often brief remarks on bodily afflictions, pursuits of physical healing, and the practice of medicine. This book identifies and analyzes such remarks within the broader context of Luther's thought. Luther's lectures on the Old Testament contain a particular wealth of such troves and will thus be the primary, albeit not the sole, focus of my study. When examined together, these glimpses reveal a remarkable underlying theology of medicine and the pursuits of physical healing, which, as I will demonstrate, reflect new Protestant spiritual concerns.

Martin Luther's teachings on the healing and protection of the body also bring to light a previously underappreciated dimension of his theology of suffering, a pivotal theme in his thought. Unlike his engagements with medicine, Luther's theology of suffering has stimulated a long tradition of academic exploration, which has remained vibrant throughout recently published works. In addition to the earlier well-established research on Luther's "theology of the Cross," primarily centered on the suffering of Christ, newer studies have highlighted affective, pastoral, and polemical dimensions of his theology of human suffering.[6] For example, Susan Karant-Nunn showed that Luther sought to challenge certain expressions of medieval affective piety and remold his audience's emotional responses to death and suffering in light of Protestant religious instruction.[7] She offered a hermeneutic of the Reformations as a "reformation of feeling" reflecting the importance placed by its religious leaders on eliciting proper emotions in response to afflictions.

Furthermore, Ronald Rittgers's remarkable recent study argued that Luther and his followers undertook a "reformation of suffering," intending to reshape inherited medieval Catholic religious understandings and lived piety of suffering in light of their Protestant soteriology.[8] According to Rittgers, Luther came to understand a true Christian (*Christianus*) as a "Crosstian" (*Crucianus*) who, while not intentionally pursuing suffering, obediently submitted to afflictions, when they inevitably arose. Rittgers further demonstrated that, in a break with a medieval perspective on suffering as a form of penance for sin, Luther wanted "Crosstians" to willingly embrace suffering as a divine gift, testing and strengthening their faith, mortifying their sinful nature, and conforming them to Christ.[9] Finally, Vincent Evener contended that, under the influence of late medieval mysticism, Luther believed that Christians were to accept suffering, including from disease, as a divinely imposed transformational experience mortifying their self-will. True Christian teachings had to proclaim such suffering as necessary for spiritual discernment, the reception of true doctrine and faith, and a pious life pleasing to God.[10]

However, this vigorous tradition of scholarship, stressing the essential role attributed by Luther to suffering in matters of Christian faith, transformation, and piety, has inadvertently sidelined his views on the possibilities of stopping suffering through healing: in particular, the healing of a suffering body through medicine. While Luther's fierce critique of self-imposed physical afflictions, such as through monastic ascetic practices, has been well-documented, the emphasis on his strong theological affirmation of unchosen calamities might suggest that Luther's positive view of suffering implied its unqualified acceptance and even embrace. On the contrary, I will contend that, at least in response to instances of physical suffering, Luther advocated and even mandated active outward resistance, including through the use of medicine, which he saw as divinely established means for healing.

Furthermore, I will argue that Luther's instructions regarding the proper use of medicine and the pursuits of healing were informed by his theology of means and especially his original theology of idolatry. I will explore Luther's views on supernatural healings and show that he regarded medicine and healing miracles of faith as two different channels communicating God's physical healing to the sufferers, although God preferred to heal through medicine, not miracles. Luther based his theology of medicine on his exegesis of the Bible, which, I will demonstrate, he read as narrating a sacred history of medicine, beginning with the tree of life in the garden of Eden and continuing through the present day against an ongoing spiritual battle for human health between angelic and demonic forces.

"Might it not be that only theology can save medicine?" philosopher of medicine Jeffrey Bishop famously asked in the concluding sentence of his seminal study, which detailed multiple crises of modern medicine.[11] Posed over a dozen years ago, this invitation to engage modern medicine theologically still awaits a comprehensive scholarly conversation. The few existing works approaching medicine with a theological lens have primarily pursued this by exegeting biblical passages, drawing on early Christian approaches, or leveraging perspectives particular to the Catholic or Eastern Orthodox traditions. Historical Protestant thought has remained underutilized. While I do not aim to use Luther for the "salvation" of medicine, it is my intention to constructively reimagine some of his insights to serve as spiritual resources for addressing pressing challenges in the use and practice of contemporary medicine. Although these spiritual resources would most directly speak to reforming engagements with medicine by Christian communities of faith, I hope that their contributions will ultimately benefit the broader state of health care and public health. Thus, this historical study also contributes to the intellectual enterprise of "theological humanism," aiming to use religious traditions to enhance human experience in a pluralistic society.[12]

Chapter 1 will discuss major medieval theological approaches to medicine and healing as the background against which early modern Protestant attitudes subsequently emerged. The chapter will argue that in late medieval Europe these approaches were permeated by soteriological concerns. In addition to Christian faith, the late medieval Church stressed the necessity of avoiding sin, accomplishing virtuous works, and participating in the church's sacramental system in order to eventually merit salvation. The pursuit of healing and the practice of medicine were laden with opportunities for performing both sinful and virtuous deeds, and, therefore, could either endanger or advance the healers' and their patients' pursuits of salvation.

Chapter 2 will investigate Luther's theological interpretations of human bodily suffering, including due to diseases and injuries, self-imposed ascetic practices, violence inflicted by others, and deprivations caused by external circumstances such as imprisonment or famine. I will demonstrate that Luther viewed health as a divine gift and blessing, but not as a sign of divine approval. I will further reveal the soteriological stakes behind Luther's critiques of intentionally subjecting the body to suffering through ascetic practices, as manifested in his lectures, sermons, and even, I will contend, visibly through his own body. I will show that in his mature lectures on

Genesis, Luther developed a spacious and multifaceted hermeneutics of physical suffering that encompassed diverse biblical themes and interpretations of its origins, significance, and implications. According to Luther, experiences of physical suffering could serve as an essential tool for spiritual transformation, a mark of authentic faith, an opportunity for Christian witness to the unbelieving world, and, occasionally, as painful divine discipline and bitter medicine for sin.

I will demonstrate that for Luther, while internally recognizing and welcoming the spiritual benefits of afflictions and enduring them well, Christians also ought to outwardly resist suffering by piously utilizing available means. In fact, in his lectures on Genesis, Luther claimed that it was a sin for Christians to recklessly endanger their bodies or to ignore faithful opportunities to alleviate their physical suffering and provide for their bodily needs. I will contend that Luther's famous theological dialectic between the "inner" and "outer" person helps elucidate the perceived tension between the dual emphases on internal acceptance and external resistance to suffering in his theology. By allowing for a variety of reasons for suffering and requiring an outward resistance to afflictions, Luther's theology of physical suffering invited, or at times commanded, the use of medicine and healing means.

Chapter 3 will explore Luther's theology of physical healing and medicine. I will argue that Luther's instructions regarding the proper use of medicine were grounded in his theology of means and, especially, in his overarching concern with idolatry, conceptualized as trust erroneously placed in created means rather than in their divine creator. Luther found in Old Testament narratives surprising examples that illustrated the necessity of utilizing medicine, yet without placing the hope for healing in its use and instead relying on God alone. According to Luther, the same affective disposition should also apply to using non-medical means of healing. The emotional detachment from medicine was both theologically necessary to avoid idolatry and rational, since, for Luther, medicine's healing power was supplied by God.

I will contrast Luther's teachings on medicine with an alternative early modern Protestant approach put forth by a pioneering Radical Reformer, Andreas Bodenstein von Karlstadt. Karlstadt shared Luther's religious concern with misplaced trust but comprehended its implications in a fundamentally different way. I will further demonstrate that Luther understood divinely provided miraculous and natural medical healings as occurring according to a similar pattern: both were animated by God's healing power, subsequently channeled through different kinds of created means, and both required vigilance against idolatry. In conclusion, I will discuss Luther's vision of the spiritual warfare for human health, waged between the demonic and angelic forces since the inception of human history.

Chapter 4 will discuss how Luther constructed a sacred history of medicine, based on his reading of the book of Genesis. Medicine had its divine origin beginning with the tree of life in the garden of Eden, which Luther viewed as yielding medicinal fruits enabling perpetual youth. However, in a break with the dominant preceding tradition that linked the origin of disease to Adam and Eve's disobedience, for Luther, not the fall but the flood was the historical point of emergence of most human illnesses and bodily ailments, which have since been multiplying and growing more severe. The chapter will also discuss Luther's theological vision of women's reproductive suffering based on his interpretation of the third chapter of Genesis.

Chapter 5 will propose strategies for utilizing Luther's theology of medicine, physical suffering, and healing as spiritual resources to address pressing challenges in the use and practice of contemporary medicine. In response to a lack of spiritual interpretations engaging suffering in clinical contexts, Luther's thought can contribute to developing a balanced theology of suffering, sensitive to both the historically unprecedented possibilities and the persistent limits of modern Western medicine. Luther's approach encourages the intentional and persistent use of medicine while remaining spiritually equipped to face the possibility of incurable suffering and attentive to the formative role of the experiences of afflictions.

In response to the religious tradition conceiving of medicine as spiritually inferior to miraculous, divine healing, especially characteristic of some expressions of the rapidly growing global Pentecostal-Charismatic Christian movement, I will argue that Luther's theology can disrupt the hierarchy between "natural" and "supernatural" cures. This hierarchy may leave religious practitioners feeling spiritually defeated or distressed when faced with a seeming lack of divine intervention to heal them or others. It could also negatively affect such Christians' health outcomes due to delayed or limited use of medical interventions. I will show that Luther's theological model suggests that it is spiritually unwarranted to reject or delay medical treatment while expecting divine healing. For Luther, both natural and faith healings were supplied through different created means by the same divine source, with God's "preferred" method being the use of medical means.

While some Christian faith communities have been reluctant to use medicine, others have embraced a broader cultural reliance on it as the primary conqueror of suffering, provider of comprehensive well-being, source of reassurance amid health uncertainties, and even defeater of death against biological odds. In response, I will contend that Luther's theology of idolatry can challenge Christian communities of faith to recognize and reconsider such quasi-religious perceptions of medicine. By explicitly divorcing physical well-being from righteousness, Luther's thought provides tools to confront the new American cultural "healthism," which positions individuals as moral agents ultimately responsible for deserving the good of health through virtuous health behaviors. This problematic approach presents physical well-being as a due reward for health-controlled living, while rendering health failures as character failures on the part of "undeserving" populations. Furthermore, in the United States, medicine has consistently demonstrated a "preferential option" for the white rich and has been marked by the rising health care costs and eroding health equity. Despite the deepening crisis of health care equity, a strong religious-like cultural attachment to the "rescue fantasy" of medicine has fostered tenacious resistance to reforms that would explicitly introduce greater limits or more regulated access to certain interventions, with the goal of improving their overall accessibility. The idea of limiting medical interventions potentially available to oneself, even if it would lead to a greater access for others and would not adversely affect one's own prospects of recovery, can be existentially threatening in a culture that holds a quasi-religious perception of medicine. Luther's conception of idolatry calls on Christians to critically examine their potential unacknowledged idolatries of medicine perceived as the primary source of protection and restoration of their vital needs. Luther's theology invites a reformation of Christian spiritualities of medicine, liberating faith communities to advocate for a more just and equitable health care access.

In this book, I adopt a traditional historical periodization, referring to the period that began in 1450 and encompassed the sixteenth-century Protestant Reformations as "early modern." I describe the fourteenth and the first half of the fifteenth century as the late Middle Ages. It must be noted that historians have debated the elements distinguishing "early modern" from "late medieval" and acknowledged that "early modernity" had been defined based primarily on the events of Western European history. Recognizing these challenges, I use the designation "early modern," conscious of its blurred boundaries and of its reflection of Western European historiography as merely one among many approaches to structuring the global pasts.

This book's references to the "medieval Church" pertain to the medieval Catholic or Roman Church, as it was known by its contemporaries. While this shortcut reference is common in Western scholarship, it must not obscure the existence of "the other" medieval church: the Eastern (Orthodox) Church with its center in Constantinople, which, since the "Great Schism" of 1054, had been officially separated from the Roman Church of the West. My use of the word "evangelical" reflects its appropriation by early modern reformers to describe their movement as focused on the gospel or the good news *euangelion* of justification by grace through faith alone. The term displays a certain historical continuity but also deviates from the current meanings of "evangelical" Christianity in North America, traced to the pietist and revival movements of the mid-eighteenth century.

"Physical suffering" or the "suffering of the body" in this study refers to experiences of physical pain or distress caused by disease, injury, or other adverse bodily conditions, including deprivations such as hunger or imprisonment. This reflects both Luther's own understanding of the meaning of the "suffering of the body" and contemporary typologies, distinguishing physical from other forms of suffering. Current literature also differentiates between the categories of "pain," describing the body's neurological response, and "physical suffering," encompassing its other dimensions and implications, including psychological, social, and metaphysical or spiritual. Although Luther operated within a drastically different conceptual framework, he, too, recognized the complex nature of suffering, and his theological discussions of physical suffering consistently included its nonmaterial dimensions. At the same time, in Luther's context, biological factors, such as disruptions in brain chemistry, were neither known nor recognized as contributing to the development of mental illness, which was construed in non-material or even spiritual terms. Therefore, this book will not consider Luther's engagements with mental disorders unless his own interpretations explicitly linked them to experiences of bodily pain or distress.

Luther's methods of biblical exegesis raise serious questions from the perspective of historical-critical biblical scholarship or other contemporary hermeneutical methods. His unwavering commitment to using the doctrine of "justification by faith" as the hermeneutical key to the entire Scripture is, at best, dubious. While mindful of these concerns, this book aimed to understand how Luther used biblical texts to develop a new Protestant theology of medicine, not to critically assess the validity of his hermeneutical approach. The same goal of representing Luther's own method and theology has also informed my general rendering of his assumptions about the authorship, significance, and history of the Bible. For instance, for Luther, the Hebrew Bible was certainly the "Old Testament," which recorded actual historical events and spoke directly to the Christian church. I used inclusive language for humans and have sought, as much as possible, to avoid using pronouns in reference to God. However, in cases when such avoidance was infeasible while rendering Luther's exegesis, I used masculine pronouns, given that for Luther such use carried theological significance.

Throughout this study, I have sought to maintain the posture of a guest to the early modern intellectual milieu, intending to encounter it on its own terms. This posture became more difficult to maintain when Luther's theology expounded beliefs and assumptions that were unfair and harmful. While Luther's more extreme and out-of-line attacks on his theological adversaries were not part of this book's discussions, I have dealt with his uncharitable polemics when exegeting certain biblical narratives that engaged medicine or physical healing. This included Luther's caricatured presentations of the views held by his theological opponents, most prominently Catholics and Radical Reformers, who were also the subjects of his personal attacks, which were frequently unnuanced and vile. The hateful import of theological ideas must be denounced. The instances of Luther's ferocious condemnations of Israelites' presumed behaviors should be especially acknowledged and reprehended, given their oppressive and violent implications for the history of antisemitism.

While Luther was one of the more inflammatory (one might say, vicious) sixteenth-century controversialists, religious polemics of that era embraced argumentative discourse and personal offenses that would be considered incendiary in the twenty-first century, yet are commonly encountered when studying early modern thought. This book extends an invitation to the religious and medical worlds of Luther and other early modern Reformers as they perceived, constructed, and experienced such worlds. Overall, my goal has been to present early modern theologies in ways that are never apologetic or defensive, not always sympathetic, but consistently true to how their authors themselves understood what was at stake behind their engagements with physical suffering and healing. As a historian, it is my hope that if Luther were to read this book, he would find it perhaps a critical but consistently fair account of his intended spiritual reformation of medicine.

The sixteenth century began an age of great transformations in both medicine and religion. It was marked by the emergence of modern anatomy, which gradually changed medieval medicine, predominantly informed by the theoretical precepts of natural philosophy, into scientific, evidence-based medicine. The sixteenth century also ushered in a period of tumultuous religious reformations, characterized by the emergence of Protestantism to become the third major global expression of Christianity as well as by reforms within Catholicism. Much like in our own era, many inherited aspects within medicine and religion were increasingly challenged, becoming unsustainable and eventually replaced by new forms of knowledge, beliefs, and practices. Much like in our own era, in the words of William Bouwsma, there was a "growing inability of an inherited culture to invest experience with meaning," as the massive reformations of religion and medicine demanded new interpretive models.[13] Luther's early modern theology of physical suffering, healing, and medicine speaks to medical and religious anxieties of our own era, attempting to make meanings of our rapidly changing realities by both denouncing and holding on to our pasts.

1

THE EARLY MODERN REFORMATION OF SALVATION

WHAT DID THE founder of the Protestant Reformation, Martin Luther, seek to reform about medicine? To answer this question, we must first understand what he sought to reform about religion. The responses to why the Protestant Reformation began in the first place usually encompass some of the following historically accurate observations. By the sixteenth century, there was growing popular discontent over the rather worldly financial ambitions of the medieval Church, manifested in, among other things, its selling of indulgences, which drew theological criticisms even from within its own ranks. Indulgences promised their buyers a remission of punishments for sins, either during this life or in purgatory, feared by late medieval imaginations as the place of final and painful spiritual cleansing. High church officials had the reputation of being wealthy and greedy landlords who oppressed their peasants. The practice of purchasing ecclesial offices resulted in one's spiritual estate being seen primarily as a source of income. This commercialization also promoted priestly absenteeism especially from remote parishes in less desirable locations.

In many communities, clerical drinking, gambling, fighting, and engaging in sexual relationships, despite supposed celibacy, was commonplace, with priests in some regions having their own designated entrance to a local brothel.[1] While attempts at cleaning up these "irregularities" were regularly undertaken by reformers from within the medieval Church, little had changed on the ground, and popular opinion concurred that the Church had fallen into a deep moral crisis. The use of the Latin mass and the Vulgate translation of the Bible made them unintelligible to parishioners and to many clergy, who, especially in rural areas, commonly learned their duties by apprenticeship and lacked formal education. This reduced religious services to ritualistic ceremonies centered on the Eucharist, which compounded a growing point of discontent for many among a laity increasingly hungry for a personally meaningful faith and religious experience. In addition, the rising national consciousness of European political rulers resisted the financial and political influence extended into their lands by the papacy in Italy, thereby stirring desires for a national church that they could control.

However, while these factors certainly contributed to the growth of the Protestant reform movement, and help explain its rapid expansion, none of them provided the initial spark that set this movement in motion. The Protestant Reformation was, first and foremost, a theological event. It might sound strange to contemporary readers that a major historical occurrence—which ended medieval Christendom, redefined the map of Europe, eventually leading to the formation of modern European states, and instigated numerous social, economic, and cultural changes—was ignited by a controversy over a religious doctrine. Yet, the foundational reason that propelled the third main expression of global Christian faith into existence was a theological dispute about salvation.

This chapter will examine the central soteriological beliefs of late medieval Christianity. In light of these beliefs, I will highlight spiritual dimensions of medieval practices pertaining to physical suffering and healing, including the devotional significance of the experiences of pain, the use of religious practices to halt the spread of the plague, and the blurred boundaries between natural, religious, and "superstitious" or magical healing. I will show that the medieval Church's instructions regarding medicine were permeated by soteriological concerns, demanding acquired righteousness for salvation. Impious misuse of medicine was sinful and could endanger the pursuits of salvation for both healers and their patients. In contrast, charitable medical practice could be spiritually meritorious and therefore soteriologically beneficial. Finally, I will discuss Martin Luther's challenge to late medieval teachings on salvation, which also entailed a challenge to the religious approaches to medicine.

Late Medieval Teachings on Salvation

The late medieval Church did not have an officially defined doctrine of salvation. Roman Catholic soteriological dogma was formally delineated after Luther's death, at the mid-sixteenth century Council of Trent, aiming to affirm the unity of Catholic teachings against the Protestant challenge. Prior to Trent, major late medieval theological schools—including Franciscans, Thomists, and Augustinians—offered competing understandings of various elements involved in salvation, theologically termed "justification." At the same time, despite these debates, late medieval theologians shared a unified understanding of the core theological presuppositions about justification, which was promulgated by the Church. This shared understanding defined salvation as a process, whose outcome in this life remained uncertain. In order to be saved, Christians needed to acquire righteousness by having their faith formed by love. This formation occurred through participation in the Church's sacraments and the performance of spiritually meritorious works, seen as essential human contributions toward meriting salvation.

Medieval thought conceptualized salvation as a journey, starting from birth and typically continuing past death into purgatory. Each Christian was a *viator*, or traveler, toward the ultimate goal of being declared righteous by Christ on judgment day.[2] The first milestone in this journey was the sacrament of baptism, which, in medieval Europe, was administered to all Christian infants shortly after birth. At the 529 Council of Orange, the belief in original sin became an established part of Western Christian doctrine. The medieval Church taught that all were born in a state of sin, but baptism removed the guilt of original sin and restored the baptized person to a state of grace. It was necessary for salvation to die while in a state of grace.

However, baptism did not eliminate from the soul original sin's lingering effects, known as concupiscence. Concupiscence would push baptized Christians to sin, making them fall from a state of grace back into a state of sin. In restoring Christians to a state of grace, a paramount role belonged to the Church's sacraments, especially penance and the Eucharist. A key element of penance was confession, which, to be truly efficacious, had to be heartfelt, fully acknowledge all committed transgressions, and stem from genuine contrition over sin, not simply the fear of punishment. Confession was followed by priestly absolution and the performance of works of satisfaction for sin. While only proper confession and absolution were required to restore the penitent to a state of grace, the works of satisfaction served as a form of earthly punishment and restitution offered to God and the neighbor for the offense of sin. In the words of Thomas Aquinas, they were "the payment of the temporal punishment due on account of the offense committed against God by sin."[3] Penance was a prerequisite for partaking of the Eucharist, which infused the spiritual virtue of *caritas* (or love) into the Christian soul, thereby allowing a believer to acquire spiritual merits and grow in righteousness.

The precepts of the New Testament were treated by medieval Catholic thought as establishing the new moral law. The images of Christ as judge and the new lawgiver, who made the moral requirements of the Mosaic law even stricter, permeated religious imaginations. From the perspective of medieval faith, acquiring literal righteousness as stipulated by Christ was essential for salvation. After all, in Matthew 5:20, Christ unambiguously stated to his followers that "unless your righteousness exceeds that of the scribes and Pharisees, you will never enter the kingdom of heaven."[4] At the same time, the Church was well aware that even most Christians sincerely contending for holiness would still die without completely attaining it. In light of this, the concept of purgatory was gradually developed. Those who died in a state of grace but without fully acquired righteousness went to purgatory as a spiritual place of final cleansing from sin, in preparation for the final judgment.

The belief in the necessity of acquired righteousness for salvation also naturally translated into placing soteriological importance on avoiding sin and performing good works. In the spiritual realm, accomplishing works of virtue allowed Christians to earn so-called spiritual merits, which could be condign or congruous. Condign merits were fully deserved, while congruous ones were "weaker" merits, which God graciously credited as such. Late medieval theological schools debated the nature of merits and spiritual conditions allowing to earn them. For example, late medieval Franciscans, including Scotists and Nominalists, taught that it was possible to earn weaker, congruous merits even while in a state of sin, a position disputed by Augustinians. For Augustinians, in order to attain congruous merits, it was necessary to be in a state of grace; sinful human beings could never deserve fully condign merits. Augustinians maintained a pessimistic view of human nature and taught that virtuous deeds only became meritorious because they were mercifully accepted as such by God.[5]

The relationship between human free will and God's sovereignty constituted another point of soteriological debates among late medieval thinkers. Augustinians contended for a continuing literal affirmation of the doctrine of predestination, as taught by Augustine and, in 529, accepted as the Church's official position at the Council of Orange. For example, without disputing the need for sacraments and acquired righteousness, the renowned fourteenth-century Augustinian theologian Thomas Bradwardine insisted that God's election of some for salvation was the ultimate defining factor in justification. Bradwardine attacked as a revival of Pelagianism the Nominalist position that earning merits could precede the reception of grace. Later, in the fifteenth century, another important Augustinian thinker and Martin Luther's mentor, Johann von Staupitz, similarly emphasized Augustine's teachings on the bondage of the human will. While affirming the importance of earning weaker, congruous merits in a state of grace, Staupitz strongly rejected both the possibility of receiving spiritual merits in a state of sin and the reality of condign merits.[6]

In contrast, late medieval Nominalists interpreted predestination for salvation as God's mere foreknowledge of an individual's future merits and use of grace. For these theologians, the Augustinian view on predestination was overly deterministic.[7] Instead, Nominalists stressed both divine and human freedom, and humanity's inherent moral potential. A prominent representative of this school of thought was the fifteenth-century theologian Gabriel Biel, who held a high theological anthropology and regarded individuals as partners cooperating with God in the enterprise of salvation. Following another prominent Franciscan, Duns Scotus, Biel conceived of grace as being purely an "enrichment of nature that is pleasing to God's will."[8] Biel's soteriology emphasized that if people did what was within themselves, God would not deny them God's grace. This saying, which was initially intended as an encouragement for monks, for Biel, came to signify the ability of individuals to succeed in pursuing virtue due to their own works. According to Biel, sinners could earn God's first dispensation of grace by their own efforts, even while still in a state of sin, and receive congruous merits for doing what was within them.[9]

At the same time, as medieval thinkers debated these soteriological elements, they shared a foundational conviction that human contribution through the accumulation of spiritual merits was a necessary dimension of salvation. They also agreed that repeated participation in the Church's sacraments of penance and the Eucharist was essential, since, through this participation, Christians received *caritas* and were restored to a state of grace. While espousing different views on the possibility of merits in a state of sin, medieval thinkers maintained a consensus that, in a state of grace, good works would be divinely counted as meritorious. This made virtuous deeds important for salvation. As Heiko Oberman explained, late medieval soteriologies perceived *iustitia Dei* (God's justification and/or righteousness) as being distinct from and following *iustitia Christi* (Christ's justification and/or righteousness). In earthly life, Christians were assured of receiving "Christ's righteousness" as *caritas* infused into the soul through sacramental participation in a state of grace. However, the reception of the "righteousness of Christ" did not guarantee the eventual reception of the "righteousness of God" or God's justification to be rendered to (or withheld from) the sinner on judgment day. The ultimate divine justification would depend on how a Christian *viator* had chosen to utilize Christ's righteousness, as evident by their own acquired righteousness. A medieval Christian's hope was to eventually merit eternal life as a due reward for their moral efforts in a state of grace.[10]

In light of this, the medieval soteriological outlook excluded the possibility of having subjective certainty regarding one's salvation.[11] The Church recognized that devout Christians would experience doubts about whether they would ultimately be saved or damned to hell. Such doubts were praised as "pious" since they manifested as honest acknowledgment of one's persistent moral imperfection and continuing need of contending for righteousness. Hope in God's mercy was supposed to assuage anxieties of Christian *viators*, while humility and "pious doubts" were necessary to encourage their avoidance of sin and pursuits of virtue.

Medieval Catholic theology espoused an elaborate typology of faith, with its various kinds playing distinct soteriological roles.[12] For example, common people, ignorant of many matters of doctrine or scripture but piously trusting that the church's teachings were true, possessed what was termed "implicit" faith. This form of faith was contrasted with the "explicit" faith possessed by learned individuals, which presumed a deeper, more intricate understanding of the doctrines of the Church. Furthermore, one's cognitive acceptance of the teachings of the Catholic Church produced an "unformed" faith, which was not soteriologically efficacious. In order to contribute to salvation, unformed faith had to be gradually formed by love, understood as the sacramental virtue of *caritas*, which was infused into souls at the Eucharist and outwardly expressed through works of virtue. For late medieval Christians, faith had to work together with humility inspired by pious doubts, fear of God's righteous judgment, and hope in God's mercy. Apart from humility, fear, hope, and love, faith was utterly inadequate for meriting eternal life. After all, as James 2:19 clearly taught, even demons, on their way to damnation, possessed faith but shuddered.

Medicine and Salvation in Medieval Theology

Concerns with salvation permeated medieval religious approaches to medicine. In November 1215 at the Lateran Palace in Rome, Pope Innocent III opened the Fourth Council of the Lateran. It was a grand and ecumenical gathering that included representatives from the Eastern Orthodox church and European political rulers alongside numerous Catholic religious leaders. Lateran IV, as the council came to be known, had shaped the theology and practices of the Catholic Church for centuries to come. Having decreed on numerous matters, from adopting the doctrine of transubstantiation as the official understanding of the Eucharist to requiring Jews and Muslims to wear distinct clothing, in its canons twenty-one and twenty-two Lateran IV addressed medicine.

Although the main point of the council's twenty-first canon was to mandate at least yearly confession for all adult Catholic Christians, it also offered an implicit affirmation of the craft of skilled doctors. The canon instructed priests to emulate the prudence and discernment of adept physicians in diagnosing and treating the wounds of human sin during confession. While canon twenty-one elevated the work of physicians, canon twenty-two emphasized the precedence of spiritual over physical wellness and restoration. It also reaffirmed the traditional belief in a potential connection between sin and disease, having stated that,

> *As sickness of the body may sometimes be the result of sin—as the Lord said to the sick man whom he had cured,* Go and sin no more, lest something worse befall you—*so we by this present*

> *decree order and strictly command physicians of the body, when they are called to the sick, to warn and persuade them first of all to call in physicians of the soul so that after their spiritual health has been seen to they may respond better to medicine for their bodies, for when the cause ceases so does the effect. This among other things has occasioned this decree, namely that some people on their sickbed, when they are advised by physicians to arrange for the health of their souls, fall into despair and so the more readily incur the danger of death. If any physician transgresses this our constitution, after it has been published by the local prelates, he shall be barred from entering a church until he has made suitable satisfaction for a transgression of this kind. Moreover, since the soul is much more precious than the body, we forbid any physician, under pain of anathema, to prescribe anything for the bodily health of a sick person that may endanger his soul.*[13]

Thereby, canon twenty-two established two principal religious directives for physicians, both of which were reflective of medieval soteriological beliefs. The first one charged physicians with the duty to admonish their sick patients to seek penance prior to using medical help. Confession could serve as a spiritual remedy against bodily sickness, in case it was caused by unrepentant sin. Moreover, it was critical for a seriously ill Christian to receive the last rites to be restored to a state of grace, since dying in a state of grace was necessary for salvation.[14] The second directive prohibited physicians from prescribing treatments that might be beneficial for the body but would be considered sinful by the Church. This reflected the medieval concern with sin as directly jeopardizing the pursuit of salvation. Unlike temporal bodies, human souls never died; it was better to remain physically ailing but spiritually well.

The twenty-second canon of Lateran IV exerted a pervasive and enduring influence on theological engagements with medicine in the Middle Ages. It was subsequently incorporated into Pope Gregory IX's 1234 canonical collection known as the *Decretales*, which compiled, modified, and harmonized previous pontifical legislation to produce an updated and unified authoritative Catholic jurisprudence. The canon's inclusion into the *Decretales* confirmed its binding status as part of canon law. Furthermore, Darrel

Amundsen demonstrated that multiple medieval religious writings conveyed teachings and concerns similar to those expressed in the twenty-second canon.[15] Moreover, the medical instructions of Lateran IV were explicitly reflected in medieval medical literature, such as the treatise *De Cautelis Medicorum* attributed to Arnald of Villanova.

The principles of the twenty-second canon were repeatedly cited by high and late medieval homiletical texts and confessional manuals, assisting priests in leading penitent physicians to acknowledge the entirety of their transgressions. These texts and manuals revealed widespread misgivings about physicians' alleged lack of religious commitment and, consequently, their moral deficiencies. A medieval proverb illustrated this suspicion by claiming that "out of three medics, two were atheists" (*tres medici, duo athei*). Medieval penitential instructions and homiletical exhortations sought to establish moral boundaries around doctors' work in order to protect their patients financially, physically, and spiritually. Such rules of professional conduct were concerned with physicians' competence, payment, and integrity. They warned against concealing effective treatments in hopes of extending a patient's illness for financial gain, experimenting on patients, treating them rashly or negligently, failing to gain or maintain appropriate professional competence, or neglecting to seek counsel from other physicians when unsure about treatment.

Additionally, medieval confessional and homiletical literature shared the worry of Lateran IV that physicians were prone to disregarding spiritual considerations to promote their patients' physical recoveries. A thirteenth-century sermon by Jacques de Vitry warned: "God says keep vigils; the doctors say go to sleep. God says fast; the doctors say eat. God says mortify your flesh; the doctors say be comfortable."[16] Treatments and regiments considered spiritually transgressive by the Church included certain sexual behaviors, such as advising patients to practice masturbation or engage in extramarital sexual activity. Another category of prohibitions targeted dietary advice. For instance, doctors were forbidden from encouraging their patients to consume intoxicating beverages or to eat meat or other forbidden foods during Church-designated fasts. The belief in the spiritual implications of physicians' actions also fueled medieval anxieties over Christian patients being treated by Jewish or Muslim doctors, over whose practices the Church did not extend its religious control. Consequently, the medieval Church regularly forbade Christians from seeking treatment from non-Christian physicians, although in reality this prohibition was frequently violated, including by religious leaders themselves.[17]

The Church's efforts to morally police the work of medical practitioners were driven by spiritual concerns not only for the souls of patients but also for those of Christian physicians. In addition to hurting their patients physically or spiritually, physicians' negligence, abuse, greed, and neglect of the Church's teachings would damage their own spiritual state. The thirteenth-century Dominican Humbert de Romans summarized this sentiment in his sermon: "Above all let them [physicians] beware of doing aught in their art against God in themselves or in others, lest whilst they heal bodies they kill souls, others' or their own."[18] With its emphasis on avoiding sin and acquiring righteousness as essential for justification, medieval thought recognized a strong connection between medicine and salvation. The practice of medicine was laden with numerous opportunities for committing or leading others to commit spiritually transgressive actions, endangering the healers' and their patients' pursuits of salvation.

Natural, Spiritual, and Superstitious Healings

While the Church sought to regulate physicians' actions in order to protect their own and their patients' pursuits of salvation, it recognized that patients also bore moral responsibility regarding their use of medicine. A sermon titled "Sick Fools" by the German priest and professor of theology Johann Geiler von Kaiserberg offers an example of a prominent admonition to exercise discernment when looking for healing. In composing this sermon, Geiler heavily relied on a satirical poem "The Ship of Fools," written by his lifelong friend Sebastian Brant.[19] "The Ship of Fools" was one of the most popular (and widely plagiarized) works in fifteenth-century German literature, having undergone three editions over the span of five years. The poem identified and mocked typical vices and "follies" of its contemporary Germans, including the shortcomings of patients and physicians in verses thirty-eight "Of Patients Who Disobey" and fifty-five "Of Knavish Medicine," with the former becoming the foundation for the message of the "Sick Fools."[20]

Just as other late medieval works communicated the importance of the religious dimensions of medicine to physicians, Geiler's sermon underscored its primacy for patients. It highlighted the traditional medieval connection between sin and disease, and stressed the necessity of the patient's devotion and supplication for divine assistance. Neglecting to first consider the spiritual causes of illness and ignoring the spiritual aspects of healing could result in the inability to secure healing through medical means or even worsen one's condition. In particular, Geiler taught that,

> *There are many people who do not consider that they should avoid sins which often are a cause of disease. They constantly seek for health from the physicians and seldom or never call on the Lord God. Therefore, that often happens that they become all the sicker.*[21]

Geiler identified and attacked seven misguided behaviors exhibited by the sick. Five of these behaviors were unwise, but not necessarily sinful. They included showing disdain for medicine, misleading the physician, disobeying the physician's advice or following it belatedly or incorrectly, and, finally, "seek[ing] medicine and advice from old women or those who have never learned medicine."[22] Geiler distinguished these actions from the two concluding wrongdoings, which, in addition to being foolish, were also spiritually transgressive. These were seeking "medicine and health from witches and exorcisoresses of the devil" and "neglect[ing] one's duty to God—to make use of medicine and not desire the help of God."[23]

It is notable that two out of the seven "follies" committed by the sick involved seeking healing from ill-equipped women. Medieval concerns about the spiritual and physical harms potentially arising from women practicing medicine were motivated by misogyny coupled with economic self-interests.[24] From the end of the twelfth century, universities gradually displaced monasteries as centers of medical education. That shift had significant implications for women's participation in learned medicine. Since university education was inaccessible to women, their perceived legitimacy as healers was significantly curbed. Furthermore, over the course of the twelfth and thirteenth centuries, medical and surgical practitioners became organized into guilds. Guilds attempted to limit medical or surgical practice to their members by invoking the need to protect patients from incompetent medical charlatans. It was not uncommon for guilds to appeal to the Church to discipline perceived charlatans through its courts and the threats of excommunication. Many of these alleged charlatans were women whose lack of formal medical training placed them outside the guild system. In addition, the medieval European worldview was permeated by a sense of magic routinely happening on life's most mundane levels.[25] Purported practitioners of harmful black magic, including occult healing practices, were again overwhelmingly women.

While Brant's original poem scorned "old women" in general as unsuitable healers, Geiler's sermon drew a distinction between incompetent women-healers and the "witches and exorcisoresses of the devil." The first type misled the sick out of ignorance, but the second did so with malicious spiritual intent. It might be challenging for a twenty-first-century reader to grasp subtle distinctions between magical, superstitious, miraculous, and natural forces in medieval healing.[26] For example, while uses of some herbs or animals were considered acceptable, others would be regarded as spiritually transgressive occult practices. Medieval theologians developed criteria for distinguishing between "natural" and illicit "superstitious" means of healing. These distinctions determined the perceived religious legitimacy of a healing method, even if in practice a potential lack of such legitimacy was frequently disregarded. For example, in his monumental work, *Summa Theologiae,* Thomas Aquinas provided the following strategy, by drawing on Augustine's teachings:

> *When things are used in order to produce an effect, we have to ask whether this is produced naturally. If the answer is yes, then to use them so will not be unlawful, since we may rightly employ natural causes for their proper effects. But if they seem unable to produce the effects in question naturally, it follows that they are being used for the purpose of producing them, not as causes but only as signs, so that they come under the head of a compact entered into with the demonic . . .*
>
> *Hence: There is nothing superstitious or wrong in using natural things for the purpose of causing effects which are thought natural*

> *to them. But if in addition there be employed certain cyphers, words, or other vain observances, which clearly have no efficacy by nature, then this is superstitious and wrong.*[27]

In other words, according to St. Thomas, an assessment of means used in healing required examining their causal effect. If healing were to be brought about by powers naturally inherent in a particular instrument, its use would be considered spiritually legitimate. However, if the instrument lacked the natural capacity to produce a healing effect, then its effectiveness would be attributed to externally supplied, demonic powers. Theologically and philosophically, this method allowed for a distinction between religiously legitimate and superstitious, magical, pagan, or occult healing practices.

Nevertheless, in reality, when applied to medieval medicine, this coherent philosophical reasoning did not fully apply. During that era, not only did folk medicine frequently employ practices that could be described as magical, but even university-trained physicians relied on means that we would now consider superstitious. In his classic study, *Magic in the Middle Ages*, based on his analysis of medieval healing manuals, Richard Kieckhefer demonstrated that, in practice, the boundaries between "naturally inherent" and externally supplied healing powers were often blurred.[28] For example, even when preparing a "natural" herbal remedy, apothecaries tended to observe various spiritual and religious taboos and rituals. The choice of ingredients was influenced by their symbolic as well as natural properties. Moreover, treatments were often performed with attention to the activities of heavenly bodies. Finally, healing handbooks frequently recorded medical recipes and prescriptions in obscure, arcane languages, suggestive of mysterious occult writings. Medieval healing manuals appeared to be more concerned with using all available means to increase the efficacy of their eclectic remedies and drug formulas than with establishing their spiritual legitimacy through a philosophical analysis of the causal relationship between their inherent and manifested healing powers.

Moreover, from the perspective of the medieval Church, not all means of healing that were not "natural" would be considered superstitious or religiously illegitimate. Central to medieval culture were devotional pursuits of physical cures through seeking the spiritual assistance of saints.[29] Christian beliefs about sainthood evolved significantly throughout the history of Christianity, including during the Middle Ages. The late Roman system of social patronage heavily influenced an emerging perception of saints as benevolent mediators between humans and God. In medieval Christianity, saints could be both living and deceased. Postmortem, owing to their lives of exceptional holiness, saints bypassed the painful time of cleansing from remaining sin in purgatory. They went straight to heaven, where they could directly intercede for the needs of the living. Due to their righteousness, saints acquired a wealth of spiritual merits far exceeding what they themselves needed for their salvation. Therefore, they could spend their excessive merits on assisting living petitioners.

In his classic study of saints in late medieval Western Christianity, André Vauchez noted that premodern popular imaginations firmly connected expressions of sainthood with the saint's embodiment.[30] It was believed that saints' bodies exhibited a spiritual energy known as *virtus*. Even after their passing, because of the presence of *virtus*, saints' remains were considered incorruptible and even emitting a pleasant odor. Folk beliefs endowed such incorruptible remnants, known as relics, with miraculous powers. Starting as early as the fourth century CE, public desire for relics and their miracles became so strong that bishops became involved in dividing existing relics and distributing them to newly Christianized areas. This new practice of the division and distribution of existing relics in response to their increased demand contributed to the development of theologies arguing that even a small relic contained the fullness of a saint's miraculous power.[31] Although in popular imagination a relic's marvelous abilities could be manifested in a variety of wonders, in the Middle Ages the miracles of healing were the most frequently sought ones.[32] Eventually, elaborate classifications of healing saints evolved within medieval devotional landscapes, assigning a particular saint to nearly every kind of disease.

Moreover, initially, saints' wondrous powers, including healing ones, were also associated with the geographical locations of their passing. However, over time, as the relocation of relics became widespread, the devotional focus shifted from the places of the saints' deaths to shrines that housed their remains and that were often based elsewhere. In the Middle Ages, this spiritual importance of shrines gave rise to the practice of pilgrimage.[33] Pilgrimages ranged from lengthy journeys to internationally renowned shrines to shorter local trips that often coincided with a particular saint's feast days. Beyond their religious significance, pilgrimages also played a significant economic role by fostering infrastructure development, trade, and even the commerce of relics.[34] As Robert Swanson underscored, the medieval use of saints, relics, and pilgrimages were also politically influenced processes. Official decisions pertaining to saints, including canonization, were ultimately controlled by the papacy and affected by a range of practical considerations beyond purely spiritual ones.[35]

However, from the fourteenth century onward, the once-prominent role of pilgrimages in the medieval devotional landscape began to decline.[36] Vauchez attributed this decline to a growing conviction that saints' healing powers could be accessible through intercessory practices beyond physically touching their actual relics, for example, through devotion to saints' images or religious vows. Therefore, wondrous healings were increasingly sought from a distance, eliminating the necessity of travel. Ronald Finucane described this phenomenon as a gradual late medieval transition from "shrine-cures" to "home-cures."[37] Indicating this new development, late medieval miracle records compared to earlier centuries reported an increase in healings among populations previously unable to journey on a pilgrimage, such as children and women suffering from pregnancy complications.[38]

In addition to the slow waning of pilgrimages, Late Middle Ages saw three other significant developments regarding saints, bodily suffering, and healing.[39] First, there was a growth in various expressions of devotional cults centered around objects associated with the Virgin Mary and Christ, including the Eucharistic host, the so-called *arma Christi* (images of the instruments of the Passion, such as the cross, nails, or the crown of thorns), and the images of the physical heart of Christ. These objects evoked the broken body and underscored the strong devotional aspects of suffering in late medieval religion.

Second, a typical medieval appeal to saints in heaven commonly proceeded according to a spiritual "exchange model."[40] A sick petitioner approached the diseased saint in prayer, vowing certain devotional acts, such as offering votive gifts or embarking on a pilgrimage, in exchange for healing.

If a petitioner was incapable of taking a vow, it could be done on their behalf by another person. While the sick interceded for assistance, the saint was not obligated to fulfill the request. Therefore, the "spiritual exchange" model did not guarantee healing to the supplicant and medieval religious texts emphasized that miracles, while real, were not to be assumed or expected. Pilgrimages to shrines, increasingly less common, were now primarily undertaken by those who had already experienced miraculous cures and needed to fulfill their vows. Keeping one's word given to the saint was paramount, and late medieval shrine records included cautionary tales of those who failed to uphold their end of the bargain and whose disease had returned.

At the same time, compared to the previous centuries, in the Late Middle Ages, the "exchange model" became less transactional. It added a new dimension of expressing affection toward the saints and their holiness and seeking their assistance with both physical and spiritual concerns. As Vauchez summarized this new trend:

> *From the 1300s, the relationship between the faithful and the saints began to lose its "mechanistic" and automatic character. The* virtus *of the servants of God was no longer seen only as a collection of mysterious forces acting in a privileged place; the contract between the faithful and their heavenly protector continued to be based on the principle of "a fair exchange," but became more personalized in devotion, and sometimes acquired a new affective, moral or religious dimension. The miracles requested were essentially cures, but other sides of life came within the sphere of influence of sanctity, the effectiveness of which was more often defined in terms of protection and even salvation.*[41]

The late medieval connections between sainthood and bodily suffering also manifested in the era's third major development: the emergence of "living saints," or mystics capable of unusual bodily experiences.[42] Sometimes, these saints' bodies exhibited marks, wounds, and scars known as *stigmata*, resembling those of the crucified Christ. Stigmatization was legitimized by the Church as an authentic embodied expression of Christian devotion. Besides stigmata, "living saints" displayed visible alterations of their bodily functions during intense mystical experiences known as raptures. Unlike the contemporary eschatological use of the term *rapture* by fundamentalist Protestants, medieval raptures were experiences of mystical union with the divine, considered the culmination of the soul's spiritual ascent. During a rapture, a mystic would visibly lose all bodily sensibility and mobility, as their soul was believed to be fully carried away in a union with God.

The ability to forgo natural ways of caring for one's own body, such as eating or sleeping, for unusually prolonged periods functioned as another potential embodied indicator of sanctity. A prominent example was the fourteenth-century Italian mystic St. Catherine of Siena, who became famous for her progressively austere asceticism. According to her confessor, Raymond of Capua, as a teenager, St. Catherine survived on a diet of bread, water, and raw herbs.[43] While also practicing other forms of bodily mortifications, by the age of twenty, she gave up bread and eventually almost entirely forwent eating and drinking. In his book, *Life of St. Catherine of Siena*, Raymond claimed that the extent of St. Catherine's dietary abstinence was unprecedented in the history of the church. For Raymond, that testified to her special spiritual status. In particular, since her ability to forfeit basic nourishment could not be explained by natural reasons, it must have been supernaturally supported by "the fullness of spirit."[44] Due to the prominence of her asceticism and charitable works, St. Catherine became an influential spiritual and even political counselor, involved in efforts to resolve political dissensions in Italy and in persuading Pope Gregory IX to move the papal residence from Avignon back to Rome in 1377. St. Catherine's fame inspired many ascetic imitators.[45] In the Late Middle Ages, deliberately subjecting one's body to physical suffering became an important aspect of devotion in monastic, mendicant, and even some lay religious settings. This included the attempted use of physical suffering as a means of healing, particularly during the Black Death.

Pain as Medicine for the Black Death

In the history of European Christianity, the Late Middle Ages witnessed many developments that paved the way for the overarching religious reforms of the sixteenth century. In the history of medicine, this era similarly set the stage for the subsequent reformation of medical knowledge and the emergence of the scientific method.[46] However, the path to both reformations lay through a series of crises. Just as the late medieval Church struggled with the commercialization of spirituality, financial abuses, clerical moral laxity, and an increasing inability to meet the religious needs and desires of the laity, so too did late medieval medicine face a succession of major disease outbreaks that it was not capable of adequately addressing.

Late medieval medicine operated with limited and often inaccurate ideas about the human body and its disorders. The education of physicians, who constituted the medieval medical elite, primarily consisted of training in "library medicine" within university halls. Doctors predominantly learned from a small number of ancient authoritative texts trusted to correctly describe the composition and functioning of the human body. In 1315, in Bologna, Mondino de Liuzzi performed the first public dissection for educational purposes. However, this practice did not become common in medical education until the mid-sixteenth century. While in certain cases late medieval medicine was able to bring relief as well as treat some conditions, overall, its capacity to cure diseases or curb their spread was rather modest.

It is in this context that mid-fourteenth-century Europe was struck by recurrent pandemics of a disease referred to in its contemporary sources as pestilence or plague (*pestis* or *pestilentia*). This pandemic was later called the Black Death, however this term had not originated until the sixteenth century.[47] Most historians now postulate that the Black Death was likely the bubonic plague or a mixture of bubonic and pneumonic plagues, although the exact nature of the disease and whether it could be identified with modern bubonic plague has been debated. The plague was brought to Europe in 1347 by fleas infecting black rats that lived on Italian ships returning home from Crimea. It is hypothesized that the rat fleas transmitted the pathogen to humans once the ships carrying the rats reached Mediterranean ports; a human-to-human transmission could also have been possible. The plague struck Constantinople in the summer of 1347, followed by the Italian cities of Sicily in October, and Genoa, Venice, and Padua the following winter. From Italy, it rapidly reached the territories of France, Spain, Portugal, and England, spreading throughout the Holy Roman Empire, of which Germany was a part, between 1348–1350. The Black Death became a global pandemic, affecting Eastern Europe, Western Asia, and North Africa. In the West, it continued to return virtually in every generation from its first outbreak until its mysterious disappearance from Europe in the eighteenth century.

The Black Death was estimated to be one of the deadliest pandemics in known history, having killed between thirty and as high as fifty percent of European populations. In affected individuals, its symptoms normally surfaced within six days after the initial infection. They included high fever (from 103 to 104 degrees Fahrenheit), nausea, and limb and lower back pains. These initial symptoms were followed by excruciatingly painful swellings of lymph nodes in the armpits or groin, known as *buboes*. The individual case mortality was estimated at sixty percent.[48] In late medieval Europe, it was exacerbated by widespread malnutrition, which weakened immunity and increased susceptibility to infectious diseases. Plague proved especially deadly in urban areas, where overcrowded living quarters offered few opportunities for effective quarantine. In addition, many urban neighborhoods were infested by rodents and routinely contaminated with feces of humans dumped on the streets and of animals freely roaming around. These pervasive unsanitary conditions of medieval city dwelling made the spread of the disease virtually unstoppable.

The economic impact of the plague was profound. It disrupted trade, commerce, and production, exacerbating existing economic hardships and leading to intensified marginalization of minority groups. In addition, the threat of death and severe physical suffering wrought by the Black Death struck at the core of late medieval communal fabrics, damaging traditional familial and societal ties. This is how a witness to the first major plague pandemic of 1348 described its catastrophic effects:

> *[O]ne who did not see such horribleness can be called blessed. And the victims died almost immediately. They would swell beneath the armpits and in their groins, and fall over while talking. Father abandoned child, wife husband, one brother another, for this illness seemed to strike through breath and sight. And so they died. And none could be found to bury the dead for money or friendship.*[49]

The frightening reality of the plague led to the increase in apocalyptic sentiments and interpretations of the plague as God's punishment for human sin. Consequently, it fueled the growth of penitential practices, including individual and communal liturgical processions. Particularly in German-speaking lands, this included the rise of the movement of flagellants—pilgrims who severely whipped their bodies as a form of collective penance seeking to appease God's wrath manifested in sending the plague. When medicine was helpless in curbing the plague's spread, late medieval Christianity not only provided frameworks for interpreting its meaning but also an outlet for action, attempting to halt the devastation of pestilence through religious means. The medieval religious response aimed at alleviating the severe physical suffering inflicted by the plague came as an imposition of another form of severe physical suffering upon one's own body.

The logic behind this use of physical suffering to bring physical healing was theological. As discussed earlier, the sacrament of penance, in addition to genuine contrition, confession, and priestly absolution, involved the penitents' subsequent performance of the works of satisfaction for sins, in lieu of temporal punishments for their transgressions. In late medieval Catholicism, a full forgiveness of sin required making reparations before God for the committed offense. Not just penance, but salvation, too, required a contribution of human works. The flagellants' self-imposition of physical suffering as a penalty for sins and an attempt to secure divine forgiveness, healing, and salvation from plague were impulses thoroughly grounded in medieval soteriological outlook.

Spiritually Meritorious Medicine

Was caring for the sick a Christian—and perhaps soteriologically significant—obligation? For medieval thinkers, a primary scriptural warrant for the soteriological import of caring for the sick was Matthew 25:31–46. In this parable, the Son of Man, ascended on the throne, separates the righteous from the unrighteous as sheep from goats. He rewards with eternal life those who performed various works of charity, including visiting him in his sickness. In response to the objections of the righteous, they are reassured that serving the least of the King's brothers was akin to serving the King himself. Conversely, those who failed to offer food, drink, clothing, or a visit to "the least of these" in prison or on the sick bed, thereby refused to serve the King and would suffer his condemnation to eternal punishment.

Taken at face value, Matthew 25:31–46 appeared to imply that visiting the sick was not merely a praiseworthy work of charity but an actual divine requirement for justification. This posed a challenge for the late medieval social structures of healing. Learned physicians charged high fees, thus making their services available only to the affluent, rather than to "the least of these" among the sick. At the same time, for a medieval audience, Matthew 25:31–46 also raised the question of whether it could be morally permissible to refuse care to some of the sick, and, if so, what the criteria should be for choosing whom to treat.

The teachings of St. Thomas Aquinas provided a theological "middle ground" to mediate between the biblical mandate to care for the "least" of the sick and actual medical realities. In question nine of article thirty-two of the *Summa's* secunda-secundae, St. Thomas used 1 Timothy 5:8 and Augustine's *On Christian Doctrine* (1.28) to argue that works of mercy ought to first benefit those who were more closely united to the benefactor. At the same time, for St. Thomas, other factors, including the potential beneficiary's righteousness, needs, and role in the community also had to be taken into account in making the determination of whom to serve.[50]

Further in question seventy-one, St. Thomas specifically interrogated the issue of moral professional obligations of lawyers and physicians, both known for demanding steep payments for their specialized knowledge.[51] Article one inquired whether a lawyer had a moral duty to represent lawsuits brought by the poor, a question that St. Thomas stated applied similarly to whether a physician was obligated to treat the destitute sick. According to St. Thomas, given the impracticality of lawyers or physicians assisting everyone in need, they should prioritize whom they served based on criteria such as time, place, and personal connection.[52] A physician was ethically obliged to care for someone only if there were absolutely no other sources of help available. Nevertheless, for St. Thomas, if a physician chose to treat a person whom he did not have a moral duty to treat, he would be offering a praiseworthy work of mercy.

In subsequent article four, St. Thomas examined a related question of whether it was ethical for a lawyer and, by extension a physician, to require payment for their services. St. Thomas affirmed that both were entitled to charge fees, as long as their fees were fair. Demanding an inflated payment would constitute a sin against justice.[53] At the same time, St. Thomas stressed that if these learned individuals chose to serve the poor gratuitously, by forgoing human compensation they were striving for a divine reward.

St. Thomas placed visiting the sick within his typology of seven corporal almsdeeds, or works of mercy, alongside feeding the hungry, giving drink to the thirsty, clothing the naked, harboring the harborless, ransoming captives, and burying the dead.[54] With his characteristic fondness for detailed definitions and typologies, he described almsgiving as an exterior effect of charity. He subsequently defined visiting the sick as a corporal act of almsgiving addressing a person's special need arisen from an internal cause. Although St. Thomas used the term "visiting the sick" (since this was the wording in Matthew 25), he clarified that the meaning of this work of mercy was not simply to pay a visit but also to provide care and healing.[55]

According to St. Thomas, visiting the sick constituted an act of a corporal or physical (as opposed to spiritual) alms, because it directly responded to an ill person's bodily needs. Therefore, as a work of mercy helping the body, healing the sick, while appropriate for particular situations, was generally inferior to any of the seven spiritual alms, including prayer, counseling, reproof, instruction, consolation, forgiveness, and forbearance.[56] At the same time, while conveying physical benefits to the recipients, serving the sick also produced spiritual benefits for the almsgiver. For example, it could move the sick to offer prayers on behalf of the healer. For St. Thomas, this should not be interpreted as "purchasing" a spiritual benefit through a material deed. Such purchase would be theologically and philosophically impossible, since, according to St. Thomas, "spiritual things infinitely surpass corporal things."[57] Furthermore, provided that the work of mercy, including healing, was genuinely performed out of love for God and neighbor, it earned the almsgiver soteriologically essential spiritual merits.[58] In sum, serving the sick also served their caretakers' own spiritual needs.

These conclusions of the *Summa* influenced subsequent medieval religious approaches to charitable medical treatment. Amundsen has shown that confessional manuals endorsed St. Thomas's criteria for prioritizing the provision of medical care based on pre-existing relational or other connections. Moreover, by referencing the *Summa*, medieval penitential handbooks taught that physicians were morally obligated to treat poor patients free of charge only if withholding such treatment would result in the patient's death. At the same time, without spiritually mandating charitable medical provision in most cases, the handbooks encouraged it as meritorious, and, therefore, advancing the physicians' salvation.[59]

In conclusion, medieval approaches to physical suffering and healing revealed deep religious dimensions. They encompassed a diversity of healing pursuits: some were deemed acceptable such as seeking assistance through saints or devotional objects, while others were denounced as superstitions. The practice of medicine was viewed as having spiritual implications grounded in medieval soteriological beliefs, demanding acquired righteousness for salvation. Impious practices and misuse of medicine, failing to conform to the church's doctrinal and moral teachings, were sinful and could hinder the pursuits of salvation for both healers and patients. In contrast, charitable medical practice could be spiritually meritorious and therefore soteriologically beneficial. In the sixteenth century, the Protestant Reformation challenged the medieval connection between acquired righteousness and justification, thereby disrupting the religious dimensions of medieval approaches to pain and healing. New spiritual perspectives on suffering and medicine emerged, rooted in the reformation of salvation initiated by Martin Luther.

Martin Luther's Reformation of Salvation

Martin Luther (1483–1546) was born the eldest son of Hans, a likely illiterate farmer turned an affluent copper miner, and Margarethe Luther in the Saxon town of Eisleben of the Holy Roman Empire. Having improved his own financial standing, Hans was determined to propel his gifted son further up the social ladder, for both his own and his family's benefit. In the sixteenth century, opportunities for social mobility were increasingly available to capable sons of economically successful commoners. Hans invested heavily for his offspring to receive formal education by attending three Latin schools in the area. These focused on the "trivium" of grammar, rhetoric, and logic, and Martin later described them as purgatory and hell. At the age of seventeen, Martin enrolled in the University of Erfurt, one of the most prestigious German universities of his time, where four years later he earned a master's degree. According to his father's wishes, he subsequently entered the higher faculty of jurisprudence, preparing for a respected and financially lucrative career as a lawyer.

However, on July 2, 1505, Luther was returning to the University after visiting home when he found himself caught in a terrifying thunderstorm in an open field.[60] Years later, his supporters viewed this episode as providentially reminiscent of the biblical conversion of Saul in the book of Acts. On the road to Damascus, Saul was brought down by light from heaven flashing around him. Like Saul, Luther saw next to him a lightning bolt striking the ground. In fear for his life, he cried out to Saint Anne, the known protector from thunderstorm dangers, "Help! Saint Anne, I will become a monk!" Luther's life was spared. It might have been a moment of a rash promise, uttered in great distress, but Luther considered it a vow.

Upon safely returning to Erfurt, Luther dropped out of the University and sold his books. Fifteen days later, following a farewell dinner with friends, he walked across town to knock on the door of the Observant Monastery of the Hermits of Saint Augustine. His friends were incredulous, and his father was outraged at the waste of his hefty investment in his son's education and future.

Luther certainly had options as to which monastic order to join. At that time in Erfurt alone there were fifteen monastic houses. The Order of Augustinian Hermits was a mendicant order, meaning that its members combined the cloistered life with active ministry in the city as ordained priests. Within the late medieval monastic landscape, this dual spiritual estate as a monk and a priest technically made Luther, like other members of mendicant orders, a "friar" (or a "hermit"), although, in his writings, Luther frequently simply called himself a monk. As monks, friars vowed chastity, poverty, and obedience to the monastery's prior, dedicating themselves to the pursuit of Christian spiritual perfection through structured daily rhythms of prayer, liturgy, and rigorous spiritual disciplines. As priests, their duties outside the monastery walls encompassed preaching, pastoral care, combating heresy, and providing religious instruction.[61]

The responsibility for religious instruction also meant that medieval mendicants played a significant role in university education, with many renowned medieval scholars emerging from their ranks. St. Augustine's Hermits in Erfurt were recognized for their intentional intellectual orientation and contributions to philosophical and theological studies, producing several well-reputed theologians of late medieval Germany. They were also known for their dedication to piety and religious devotion, being part of the "Observant" movement within late medieval monasticism. In contrast to "Conventuals," Observant groups sought spiritual renewal of monastic life that they believed had become overly lax and lost much of its intended spiritual vigor. Having left behind his worldly life, Luther did not seek an easier path to fulfill his hasty vow. He chose a monastery known for its strict adherence to monastic rules and rigorous religious commitment.

According to the Augustinian rule, Luther spent a year and day in the monastery as a novice, studying the order's teachings, practices, and way of life. During that first year, he was given the freedom to change his mind and leave at any time. He stayed. A year later, Luther donned his black Augustinian habit, symbolizing the death of his old self, and took his monastic vows, binding himself officially and unbreakably to the order for the rest of his life. Two years later, he was ordained as a priest. Luther's deep commitment to his vows was shown by the fact that even after he was released from the order in 1519 against his wishes, he continued to regard himself as an Augustinian brother. He did not remove his habit until October 1524, by which time the Reformation was well underway.

As an Augustinian friar, Luther's intense devotion, keen intellect, and administrative skills did not go unnoticed. Following the directives of his superior and mentor Johann von Staupitz, he returned to university studies. In 1510 Luther accompanied Staupitz on an important trip to Rome, advocating for politically and ecclesially sensitive matters concerning his order. Eighteen months later, he completed a doctorate in theology and assumed a professorship of the Bible at the recently established University of Wittenberg. Soon he was also appointed minister of the Wittenberg church and district vicar of the Augustinian order, responsible for overseeing eleven Augustinian monasteries in Saxony. Although he abandoned for good the prospects of a worldly career, Luther's stature as a young ecclesial leader was rising.

Despite his successes, Luther wrestled with profound feelings of spiritual inadequacy and of being unable to ever accomplish enough good works to earn God's approval. As discussed earlier, in order to be efficacious, late medieval Catholic penance required a full confession of all sins committed, paired with genuine contrition over breaking God's law. Penance, followed by partaking of the Eucharist, restored Christians to a state of grace, enabling them to acquire spiritual merits through virtuous deeds in hopes of attaining salvation. From a medieval perspective, a pious friar lived in a state of higher perfection compared to lay Christians and even regular priests. An Observant monk's path was not easy, given its rigorous devotional requirements. But in a religious world fraught with soteriological uncertainty, the journey of a devout friar offered greater reassurance and hope for attaining righteousness and meriting salvation. A choice of the faithful monastic life was supposed to alleviate the fears of those anxious about the eventual fate of their souls.

Nevertheless, Luther's monastic dedication did not bring him spiritual relief. Acutely sensitive to his persistent moral imperfections despite his best efforts, Luther led a life of intense devotion, and yet could not escape the sense of God being angry with him for his sins. He struggled with the fear of unrecognized sins that would invalidate his confessions. His inner turmoil extended to feelings of resentment and even hatred of God as the judge of sinners, whose standards of righteousness required for salvation seemed impossible to meet, no matter how hard he tried.

With the medieval tradition, Luther took literally Christ's clear admonition that "unless your righteousness exceeds that of the scribes and Pharisees, you will never enter the kingdom of heaven" (Matt 5:20). While observing Jewish law already presented grave challenges, Jesus's teachings, such as those expressed in his Sermon on the Mount, elevated God's moral standards to an ostensibly unattainable level. Marital fidelity required effort, but Christ's equating a lustful look with adultery made consistent adherence to God's law exceedingly difficult. His warning against anger and quarrels, likening them to murder and threatening divine condemnation, raised the bar even higher. And yet, as a faithful Catholic, Luther was compelled to believe that works of virtue were essential to salvation. He knew that on judgment day, each Christian's moral accomplishments will be assessed, leading to justification or eternal condemnation. Luther struggled to understand how gospel could be considered "good news."

By 1518, after intense wrestling with Scripture, Luther arrived at his "Reformation breakthrough."[62] In his own words, the Holy Spirit gave him his evangelical discovery "in the cloaca," perhaps while on a toilet, although he could also be referring to a study room located just above it, in the monastery's high tower.[63] Luther's insight came while pondering in the cloaca the meaning of the phrase "the righteousness of God" in Romans 1:17. According to Paul, "the righteousness of God" was revealed through faith, as was also stated in Habakkuk 2:4, "the one who is righteous through faith will live."

From the perspective of late medieval theology, this was a puzzling assertion. The righteousness of God was revealed to medieval Christians through God giving a due reward to virtue and due punishment to sin. Furthermore, faith did not make Catholic Christians righteous, but they acquired righteousness through faith formed by love. Luther agonized over the meaning of this passage, until one day he arrived at his "Reformation breakthrough." In his own words,

> *At last, by the mercy of God, meditating day and night, I gave heed to the context of the words, namely, "In it the righteousness of God is revealed, as it is written, 'He who through faith is righteous shall live.'" There I began to understand that the righteousness of God is that by which the righteous lives by a gift of God, namely by faith. And this is the meaning: the righteousness of God is revealed by the gospel, namely, the passive righteousness with which merciful God justifies us by faith, as it is written, "He who through faith is righteous shall live." Here I felt that I was altogether born again and had entered paradise itself through open gates.*[64]

Luther's "evangelical discovery" was that the merciful God bestowed his righteousness upon sinners through faith, rather than demanding that they acquire literal righteousness with the help of their own efforts as a condition for meriting salvation. Therefore, Christians were justified because of their faith, not on account of their faith and works, just as the New Testament repeatedly and explicitly affirmed. Luther knew from experience that human sin ran too deep for even most devout Christians to fulfill the moral precepts of the New Testament and attain righteousness truly measuring up to God's standards. For Luther, this realization did not imply that Christians could live immoral lives or misinterpret their salvation as a license to sin, against which the apostle Paul also cautioned. True faith, Luther argued, transformed hearts, making them obedient to God and leading to lives outpouring with virtuous works of love and service to the neighbor. These works would be produced freely out of love and gratitude to God and a genuine conformity to Christ, not out of fear that if one were not sufficiently good, they would be damned to hell.

Martin Luther as a Biblical Interpreter

Since the thirteenth century, Western medieval thought has traditionally been categorized into three main expressions of theological traditions: scholastic, monastic, and vernacular. By the time of his Reformation discovery, Luther's education and experience positioned him at the intersections of all three. Although Luther eventually rejected major dimensions of medieval religious thought, he was nevertheless shaped by late medieval exegetical approaches and as a reformer retained some of their major dimensions. Luther's theological production was inseparably tied to his exegesis of Scripture. He extensively studied the Bible as a student, grappled with it as a friar, taught it as a professor, debated its interpretations as a Protestant polemicist, and regularly preached on it as a priest and pastor in Wittenberg and beyond.[65]

As a professor and doctor of the church, Luther took extremely seriously his stated responsibility to exegete and teach the Bible. During his own intellectually formative time as a student, Luther was trained in the scholastic interpretive tradition. The tradition belonged to university settings and was facilitated by Latin as a *lingua franca*, fostering scholarly discourse across linguistically diverse parts of Christendom. The scholastic approach strictly followed a rigorously defined method of argumentative reasoning, designed to prevent logical fallacies and to preserve the truth. Medieval scholars interpreted Scripture according to its four "senses" or meanings—literal, allegorical, moral (ethical) and anagogical (eschatological). In Latin Christianity this distinction between several complementary meanings of the Bible was first developed by Augustine. Augustine authored the pioneering work of Western Christian hermeneutics, *On Christian Doctrine*, where he also articulated an overarching exegetical principle for understanding the Bible. According to Augustine, the goal of Scripture was to teach love of God for God's own sake and love of neighbor for God's sake. A biblical passage should be understood literally, according to its plain meaning, if its message aligned with this goal. However, if its literal sense seemed to condone violence, immorality, or otherwise contradict the above principle of ordered love, then a passage should be interpreted allegorically.

Augustine's hermeneutical approach, distinguishing between different meanings of Scripture, exerted enduring influence throughout the Middle Ages. Unlike contemporary academic study of religion, late medieval scholarship did not separate biblical and theological studies. Theology was supposed to expound the teachings of Scripture, while guiding principles for biblical exegesis were outlined in the foundational Christian doctrines and dogmas of the medieval Church. In order to ensure harmony between these binding doctrines and the Bible, scholars frequently applied an allegorical approach, especially to passages that presented a challenge. The "literal sense" of Scripture was considered its lowest meaning, and particularly in interpreting Old Testament texts it was often set aside in favor of Christianized interpretations. In addition to studying the Bible, theology students devoted considerable time to exegeting important medieval works, notably Peter Lombard's *Four Books of Sentences*. Additionally, scholastic exegesis actively interacted with and drew upon other medieval theological writings, patristic thought, canon law and certain classical authors, most prominently Aristotle.

As a reformer, Luther criticized aspects of his scholastic training, particularly the excessive time spent learning from medieval summas (which he thought would have been better invested in studying the Bible) and the intellectual authority of Aristotle, whose relationship to Christian theology he once compared to that of darkness to light. However, Luther's scholastic education equipped him with a vast knowledge of the history of Christian exegesis. The principle of "sola scriptura," which later came to be associated with Luther, did not imply one's "sole" authority of interpreting Scripture in isolation from the exegetical traditions of the church. In contrast,

Luther's lectures on the Bible contained numerous both positive and critical references to patristic and medieval interpretations of particular passages. Especially prominent were his appeals to the writings of Augustine, who always remained the leading influence on his theology. While Luther criticized what he saw as the excessive use of allegory in scholastic exegesis, he did not completely abandon this interpretive strategy. Significantly more so than medieval thought, Luther stressed the importance of the "plain" meaning of Scripture. However, for Luther, the "plain" meaning of Scripture was not simply its "literal" sense but the one that, in some way, communicated Christ and the gospel.[66]

Luther's hermeneutical approach was also influenced by the medieval monastic tradition, which, in contrast to the scholastic method, stressed spiritual formation over intellectual analysis. His daily routine as an observant friar included an established pattern of devotion, with the study and meditation on Scripture being its integral part. This concern for the Bible as a tool of spiritual development, not merely a source of doctrine, continued to characterize academic exegesis of Luther the reformer. He also paid sustained attention to the practical applications of the Bible for daily Christian life. Finally, Luther's thought reflected certain emphases of vernacular theologies that were produced outside of academic or monastic settings. Vernacular authors lacked formal theological training and wrote in their native languages, as opposed to Latin. Although Luther, as a professor and a priest, remained outside this tradition, he shared with it an appreciation of mysticism, which deeply influenced his theology of suffering.

Moreover, Luther's reform program benefited from his exposure to the humanist intellectual program, emphasized in the curricula of the Universities of Erfurt and of Wittenberg. Humanists stressed the importance of reading ancient primary sources in their original languages, the study of which they concurrently promoted. As a friar and a doctor of the church, Luther was fluent in Latin, the language of the medieval academy. He began studying Hebrew the year he formally joined the Augustinian order and gained considerable fluency by the onset of the Reformation. He also learned Greek with the help of his colleagues Philip Melanchthon and Matthew Aurogallus at the University of Wittenberg.

In addition to employing his linguistic training and talents as a Bible interpreter, Luther utilized them to produce a German translation of the Bible, which had earlier been accessible primarily through its Latin Vulgate translation created by Jerome in the fourth century. When confined to seclusion at the Wartburg Castle in 1521, Luther used the Vulgate Latin and Erasmus's Greek edition to translate the New Testament into German over the course of eleven weeks. Later, he added his prefaces to the individual books of the New Testament and rearranged their order according to what he thought was their importance in conveying the gospel, with the epistle to the Romans appearing first. It took Luther significantly longer to complete the Old Testament translation due to his extremely busy schedule and vast responsibilities as a Reformation leader, his newly developed kidney and gallbladder issues, and his struggles with accurately rendering the tone of certain Old Testament texts, particularly the book of Job. Luther eventually published his Old Testament translations in several installments over twelve years, culminating in the release of the so-called "Luther's Bible" in its entirety in 1534. However, contrary to what the name might suggest, the "Luther's Bible" was not the product of Luther's sole labors. It was refined through ongoing consultations with a team of scholars that Luther assembled, with whom he held extensive discussions about the appropriate German rendering of difficult or key passages.

Beyond its religious significance, Luther's translation of the Bible was recognized for its literary contributions, considerably shaping the development of modern high German literary language. While there were some limited German translations of the Bible previously available, unlike Luther's, they did not use a unified German language understood across the different dialects of German-speaking areas of the Holy Roman Empire. Furthermore, unlike previous renditions, Luther prioritized conveying scriptural messages in commonly spoken language and metaphoric expressions native to German, rather than strictly preserving the wording and syntax of original texts.[67] His contemporary printers made fortunes from selling his translation; Luther himself never asked for royalties. While the Bible had previously been accessible only by extremely limited educated publics of the Holy Roman Empire, it was estimated that by the year of Luther's death, forty percent of German-speaking Protestant households owned a copy.

While Luther preserved continuity with certain aspects of late medieval exegetical traditions, he also broke away from them in significant ways. The "Reformation breakthrough" resulted in Luther experiencing what he saw as a form of exegetical enlightenment, when, in his own words, to him "a totally other face of the entire Scripture showed itself."[68] Luther began to see the teachings of justification by faith permeating the whole Bible. For Luther, Genesis already made God's plan for salvation clear, proclaiming that Abram "believed the Lord, and the Lord reckoned it to him as righteousness" (Gen 15:6). The apostle Paul stated in his letter to Ephesians that Christians were saved through faith, not of themselves as a result of their works, but as the divine gift, so that no one may boast (Eph 2:8–9). While the Catholic Church encouraged Christian "pious doubts" with regard to their spiritual standing with God, Luther stressed that Romans 5:1 explicitly reassured the church that they "are justified by faith" and "have peace with God through Lord Jesus Christ." And what could Christ mean when he claimed in Matthew 7:17–18 that it was the goodness of a tree that made its fruit good, while its corruption made its fruit evil? Medieval theology taught the opposite: it would be the good fruit understood as virtuous works that would ultimately make the tree a better one, just as one would acquire righteousness through performing righteous works.

For Luther, Paul's epistle to the Galatians dealt the final blow to any past, present, or future theologies attempting to link salvation to human works. He emphasized that the entire purpose of this letter was to defend the doctrine of justification by faith and refute the false teaching that salvation also required the works of the Jewish law. While medieval Catholic leaders promulgated what they saw as the new law of Christ, distinct from the Old Testament one, Luther stressed that the overarching theological objection remained the same. Both Paul's Jewish Christian antagonists and Luther's medieval Catholic opponents required a contribution of human works for salvation, contrary to Paul's claim that "a person is justified not by the works of the law but through the faith of Jesus Christ" (Gal 2:16). The only notable Scriptural challenge to justification by faith was posed by the epistle of James. Luther criticized the epistle of James for its shortcomings in communicating the gospel as being "an epistle of straw" compared to other New Testament writings. He saw his criticisms supported by the ancient questioning of the letter's authenticity and its historical difficulties in securing its eventual place in the biblical canon. Nevertheless, Luther acknowledged that some of James's concerns could be reconciled with the message of salvation by faith. At the same time, for Luther, James's supposed argument for the necessity of works for justification would collapse in the face of the unified biblical testimony found across its multiple books from Genesis to Galatians.

Luther's insistence on justification by faith alone also entailed a rejection of the medieval belief that acquired (or literally attained) righteousness was necessary for salvation. However, Luther did not dispute the traditional connection between righteousness and salvation; rather, he reframed it. For Luther, salvation indeed required righteousness, as Scripture clearly taught, but not one's own righteousness (which would be unattainable); rather, the righteousness of Christ. In place of the medieval concept of acquired righteousness, Luther offered his own category of an imputed one. Sinners were justified not based on their own attained righteousness but on account of the righteousness of Christ imputed (or credited) to them through faith. Christ covered sinners with his righteousness, akin to a hen sheltering her chicks under her wings during a storm. When God looked upon sinners, he saw not their remaining sins but the full righteousness of Christ imputed to them.

In order to illustrate the imputation of righteousness, Luther used his contemporary legal analogy regarding ownership in marriage. Although modified and expanded, the medieval legal system retained many principles from ancient Roman law, particularly from the Code of Justinian. Ancient Roman law required a strict separation of owned goods between spouses. It generally prohibited gift-giving between a husband and a wife, due to concerns that it could easily lead to conflict or even divorce.[69] Despite this prohibition, each spouse had full use (referred to as "possession") of the other's property during the marriage. Consequently, while married, a husband's property became his wife's possession and vice versa.

For Luther, this principle elucidated the union of a Christian with Christ, which he, following a New Testament metaphor, described as a heavenly marriage between the church as the bride and her divine groom. In this union, Christ's property was righteousness, fully available to the church as her possession. Conversely, the church's property was sin, of which Christ accepted a full possession and which he bore on the cross. This, in Luther's words, a "joyous exchange" happened when a sinner entered a union with Christ. This exchange enabled sinners to be justified as righteous, not by their own merit but due to Christ's righteousness, of which the sinners had the full possession.

This concept also explained Luther's paradox of a justified Christian's moral status as being simultaneously sinful and righteous. Christians remained sinful with their own sin but also became righteous with the imputed righteousness of Christ. However, this dual status did not negate the necessary moral transformation in the Christian life. On the contrary, for Luther, the union with Christ will be healing Christians from their sin and promoting their growth in literal righteousness. Their love and service to the neighbor must pour out as both a fruit and a testimony to their salvation. In this regard, Luther agreed with James that faith without works was dead.

A hallmark of Luther's theological break with late medieval Catholicism was his rejection of its elaborate typology distinguishing between different forms of faith.[70] For Luther, Christian faith was trust in God's promises, including the incredible promises to forgive, restore, and justify by grace those who repented and believed. Faith clung to God's benevolence expressed "for us." Luther saw the essence of Christian faith as radically receptive and relational. It rendered believers to be pure recipients of God's gift of salvation, without giving anything back in return. Faith also related believers to Christ, by enabling their participation in and union with him.[71] Based on Galatians 4:6 and Romans 8:15–16, Luther inseparably linked faith to the work of the Holy Spirit, who produced it supernaturally in human hearts. By faith, Christians saw God as their merciful father, not as their stern judge and, like little children, called out to him "Abba! Father!"[72] The internal testimony of the Holy Spirit reassured Christians in the security of God's love for them.

In addition to the Holy Spirit's internal witness, for Luther, faith was also confirmed by the external testimony of God's Word, on which it had to firmly rely. Luther was acutely aware that sustaining such unwavering reliance required intentional spiritual attention and vigilance. Christians would have to resist the erosion and distortions of their trust, instigated by the devil, the world, and, crucially for Luther, by their own minds. God's chief promise of salvation by faith alone certainly contradicted human ideas of justice, which required meriting something in order to receive it. According to Luther, Christians would inevitably be tempted to doubt God's Word, as God's promises would always seem irrational to human reason that had been negatively affected by sin.

Luther read the Bible as full of narratives illustrating the challenges involved in maintaining such authentic and resolute faith against external assaults and internal doubts. For example, Abraham trusted God's tremendously disruptive call to abandon his family, land, and the religion of his people. Later, he believed God's incredible promises to bless humanity through his descendants. Luther emphasized that Abraham's trust in God's Word did not come easily for the patriarch but was born amid his wrestling with sins, hesitations, and fears. For Luther, Abraham modeled to the Christian church the significance and implications of faith lived out as trust amid difficult circumstances and ultimately rewarded by divine justification.[73]

Likewise, for Luther, Noah presented a great example of faith.[74] Luther stressed that in his generation Noah and his household were the only ones whom God considered to be righteous and intended to save from the flood. Watching Noah day after day diligently building a giant boat, his neighbors must have considered him insane. Luther imagined that "the world regarded Noah as exceedingly stupid for believing such things; it derided him and without a doubt also made his structure the object of ridicule."[75] Luther's Noah had to maintain unwavering trust against the world's skepticism and his own inner doubts. He had to keep believing God's Word that he had received divine approval and election for salvation in the face of humanity's impending destruction.

In response to Luther's overarching emphasis on faith, Luther's Catholic opponents accused him of prideful spiritual assumptions regarding justification. The medieval Church praised doubts about one's salvation as pious, showing a healthy and candid lack of presumption about one's acquired virtue. In contrast, Luther found such doubts crushing. From his personal experience, he agreed that a morally attentive and spiritually honest Christian could not deny the continuing persistence of sin in their lives, despite their best efforts. However, for Luther, this realization would trap Christians in perpetual uncertainty regarding their standing with God. How could a Christian experience the true peace that surpasses all understanding, as described by the New Testament writers, if their spiritual destiny was uncertain and partially dependent on their never fully adequate efforts to live righteous lives? How could a Christian love with their heart, mind, and strength the God who in return might condemn them to eternal torments in hell?

Luther's Catholic opponents blamed him for spiritually sanctioning and implicitly encouraging moral latitude. They predicted that Luther's vehement divorce of virtuous actions from soteriological motivation would ultimately undermine the incentive for ethical behavior, plunging society into an immoral abyss. In contrast, for Luther, Catholic teachings, which stipulated the pursuit of salvation as a justly earned merit, could never yield in its followers the love of God with all their heart, mind, and strength. Instead of love, these teachings would encourage fear and even resentment of God, if one acknowledged, in accordance with the medieval use of Ecclesiastes 9:1, that all were in the hands of God, yet no one knew whether love or hatred awaited them.

Ultimately, for Luther, adding good works to faith in order to merit salvation would rob the church of the possibilities of experiencing and manifesting Christ-like sacrificial love, which was shown by Jesus laying down his life solely for the benefit of others. In contrast, as medieval Catholic Christians were putting forth their best efforts to cooperate with grace, they themselves needed their acts of charity to form their faith by love in order to avoid condemnation and receive justification as their due reward. How could Christians truly love like Christ if, in every good deed performed and every act of love toward neighbors, there was an undeniable dimension of clear spiritual self-interest?

In sum, Luther denounced medieval teachings on justification as contradicting Scripture, fostering spiritual anxiety and even anger at God, and ultimately promoting fear-based service to the neighbor, which would invariably exhibit a degree of self-interest. In contrast, what Luther saw as the true message of the gospel granted Christians true freedom. This was the freedom from the overwhelming burden of having to merit one's salvation as well as the freedom of knowing and loving God as a merciful father and savior. At the same time, this liberty also bound Christians in Christ-like loving service to their neighbors, but solely for the sake of the neighbors' benefit, not their own justification. As Luther emphasized, while Christians did not need their own good works, their neighbors certainly did.

Luther's rejection of the necessity of virtuous deeds for salvation disrupted the medieval religious approaches to healing and medicine, tied to soteriological understandings. As a reformer, Luther developed a new approach to physical suffering, healing, and medicine that was thoroughly grounded in Protestant theological concerns. Luther's reformation of salvation necessitated a spiritual reformation of medicine.

2

MARTIN LUTHER'S REFORMATION OF PHYSICAL SUFFERING

ON APRIL 15, 1530, on Good Friday, Luther strode into the halls of Coburg Castle, a formidable medieval fortress perched atop a hill, commanding a view of the town of Coburg below. That night was the eve of Easter coinciding with the Eve of the Diet of Augsburg, the last early modern attempt at bridging theological chasms between the Catholic and Lutheran camps. Nine years had elapsed since Luther's excommunication, and he continued to remain under the Imperial Ban, making impossible his open attendance at the meetings of the Diet. The following day, in the castle chapel, before an honorable audience of Lutheran princes, court officials, and leaders of the reform movement, Luther delivered what would become his seminal sermon on the subject of suffering.[1] Drawing loosely from a synthesis of passages from Matthew 27, Luke 23, and John 19, the "Sermon on Cross and Suffering" sought to prepare and encourage his listeners in anticipation of the inevitable tribulations Luther believed would arise from the presentation of the Protestant confession to the Catholic emperor.

As a poignant illustration, Luther invoked a popular medieval legend of St. Christopher, carrying Christ the child across a tumultuous river. While, from the outset, Luther assured his audience that St. Christopher never performed any such deed and never even existed, Luther nevertheless found the story edifying in its exposition of Christian suffering. St. Christopher was endowed with great strength and stature. Initially he found the child on his back to be light, delightful, and certainly easy to carry across the waters. However, as he was getting into the deep, the child began to feel increasingly heavy. Then the turbulent currents arose, roaring and foaming, threatening to overwhelm the saint, with the child pressing an increasingly unbearable weight on his shoulders. On the verge of drowning, St. Christopher firmly grasped his wooden staff—referred to by Luther as a "tree"—until he finally emerged, with the child still on his back, on the other side of the river. This is why the saint was called Christopher, which meant Christ-bearer.

Luther preached that all Christians were called to emulate St. Christopher when they found themselves navigating the trials of faith and bearing the yoke of the gospel through tumultuous waters. When first experienced, Christian faith appeared inviting, pleasant, and effortless to carry. However, in the life of any believer, a time would inevitably come when the bearers of the seemingly lightweight Christ would find themselves in deep waters of tribulations. The delicate and beautiful Christ on their shoulders would feel heavy and burdensome. In the middle of the tempest, Christ-bearers must cling to the tree of God's promises with unwavering faith. Paradoxically, Luther contended, the divine assurances promising peace and comfort also promised suffering for those who entrusted themselves to Christ. As believers received Christ in faith, they received him fully, together with his suffering, which manifested in various forms, including physical afflictions.

The profound spiritual wrestling with suffering reverberated throughout Luther's thought during his entire career as a reformer. It has been noted that the depth of his interest in suffering and its impact on the subsequent generation of pastors was unmatched among early Protestant theologians.[2] This interest and impact had not gone unnoticed by scholars, with numerous studies having since explored Luther's approach to divine suffering (known as his "theology of the Cross") and, relatedly, his theological and pastoral responses to human adversity. At the same time, Luther's theological interpretations of physical suffering as a distinct form of affliction have not received adequate scholarly attention. This chapter will investigate Luther's exegesis of the suffering of human bodies, including due to diseases and injuries, self-imposed ascetic practices, violence inflicted by others, as well as deprivations caused by external circumstances, such as imprisonment or famine. I will trace the development of these themes across several of Luther's milestone writings on bodily suffering. I will pay particular attention to his interpretations of afflictions in lectures on the Old Testament that revealed and encapsulated key aspects of Luther's engagements with suffering in his mature thought.

The chapter will show that Luther viewed health as a divine gift and blessing but not as a sign of divine approval. Following this, I will reveal the soteriological stakes behind Luther's critiques of intentionally subjecting the body to suffering through ascetic practices, as manifested in his lectures, sermons, and even, I will contend, visibly through his own body. I will demonstrate that in his mature lectures on Genesis, Luther developed a spacious and multifaceted hermeneutics of physical suffering that encompassed diverse biblical themes and interpretations of its origins, significance, and implications. Luther believed that experiences of physical suffering could serve as an essential tool for spiritual transformation, a mark of authentic faith, an opportunity for Christian witness to the unbelieving world, and, occasionally, as painful divine discipline and bitter medicine for sin.

I will argue that for Luther, while internally recognizing the inevitability of afflictions and welcoming their spiritual benefits, Christians also ought to outwardly resist suffering by piously utilizing available means. In fact, in his lectures on Genesis, Luther taught that it was a sin for Christians to recklessly endanger their bodies, ignore opportunities to alleviate their physical suffering, or neglect faithful ways of providing for their bodily needs. I will further contend that Luther's theological dialectic between the "inner" and "outer" person illuminates the tension between the dual emphases on internal acceptance and external resistance to suffering in his theology. By acknowledging various reasons for suffering and advocating for outward resistance to afflictions, Luther's theology of physical suffering often invited or even commanded the use of medicine and other healing means.

Martin Luther's Theology of Health

Luther consistently spoke of good health as God's gift, for which Christians should offer prayers of supplication and gratitude. In 1529 he composed the *Small Catechism*–an abridged version of his renowned *Large* one, intended to aid the heads of households in providing simple instructions in faith. There, in his commentary on the Lord's prayer, Luther explicated the meaning of the request to "give us today our daily bread." According to Luther, this daily petition was offered not merely for bread, but for all of the body's essential needs, among which he counted good health.[3] Similarly reflecting this sentiment, his commentaries on John 16:23 offered an expanded version of the Lord's Prayer, asking God to "give us our daily bread, good weather, and health."[4] In his treatise, *Fourteen Consolations*, Luther enthusiastically lauded the divine blessing of enjoying a strong, alert, and healthy body, particularly a male one![5]

At the same time, Luther noted that despite its importance, the blessing of health often remained taken for granted, abused, and overall unacknowledged as a special divine gift.[6] He repeatedly criticized this perceived tendency in his various works, including the lectures on Ecclesiastes, on the Psalms, and the sermons on the Gospel of John. For instance, in the 1530 lecture on his beloved Psalm 118, Luther posed a question of whether, if faced with a choice between preserving health or acquiring an empire, anyone would choose the latter. The answer to this hypothetical dilemma, of course, should be to choose health over power, honors, and wealth, thus underscoring health's paramount value. Yet, most Christians failed to recognize the privilege of daily enjoying a well-functioning body. Luther admonished Christians for routinely neglecting to thank God for their healthy hands, feet, legs, noses, or fingers. He taught that the opening verse of Psalm 118 to "give thanks to the Lord, for he is good"

> *should be in the heart and mouth of every man every day and every moment. Every time he eats and drinks, sees, hears, smells, walks, stands; every time he uses his limbs, his body, his possessions, or any creature, he should recall that if God did not give him all this for his use and preserve it for him despite the devil, he would not have it.*[7]

Thus, Christians who neglected to acknowledge God's role as the ultimate giver and protector of physical well-being were guilty of ingratitude. Their ingratitude frequently persisted until the day when their physical well-being was suddenly threatened or lost. For many, this would become the time of transformation, turning them to God in prayer in recognition and appreciation of God's good gift of health and his power over it. Consequently, for Luther, disease, injury, or another bodily impairment could also serve a positive, spiritually formative function.

At the same time, Luther also cautioned against interpreting physical wellness as a sign of God's favor or his reward for using one's body well. While good health was always a divinely granted blessing, it did not necessarily indicate divine approval. Sometimes, prosperity, including physical well-being, may serve as a divine test to see whether, in highly favorable circumstances, Christians would maintain humility, obedience, and the fear of the Lord. On other occasions, the divine distribution of material blessings may seem inexplicable or random to human understanding and our sense of justice. As Luther observed in his lectures on Genesis, God "scatters his blessings, gives gold, silver, fruits, peace, and good health even to the unthankful and the worst men."[8]

For Luther, a historical illustration of God's seemingly indiscriminate distribution of material blessings, including to the undeserving, was shown by the case of the residents of Sodom and Gomorrah, which he discussed in his lectures on Genesis 15:2–3.[9] From a contemporary standpoint, Luther read the story of Sodom as a biblical case against the prosperity gospel, outlined hundreds of years before its actual emergence in the twentieth century. Luther's sodomites enjoyed a prosperous land, peaceful existence, abundant wealth, and good health. Their healthy bodies were not troubled by plagues or diseases. They reveled in an abundance of food, freely indulging in gluttony and becoming intoxicated with wine at their public feasts.

Luther cited Ezekiel 16:49–50 to accuse the Sodomites in misusing their prosperity by becoming prideful, immoral, and oppressing the poor and needy. However, before they fell into actual sin, the downfall of Luther's sodomites began with a theological misinterpretation. Because of their prosperity and freedom from major afflictions, Sodom's residents assumed that they were good people leading good lives that had earned God's favor. Furthermore, having presumed God's love and approval of their actions, based on their external circumstances, the sodomites became complacent about the security of their well-being and began misusing their wealth and health. Eventually, Luther's sodomites no longer showed reverence for God or love for their neighbors. The arrogant sodomites obliviously persisted in their sin until one day God annihilated their unsuspecting city. Sodomites' theological hermeneutical mistake stood as a cautionary tale against misinterpreting good fortune, including good health, as a sign of divine approval or a license to misuse one's blessings against others.

Furthermore, just as the presence of good health did not imply divine approval, its absence did not indicate divine displeasure either. In his 1539 programmatic work on ecclesiology titled *On the Councils and Churches*, Luther outlined his seven marks of the true church.[10] While the first six marks (the Word, baptism, communion, absolution, ordination, and worship) were in continuity with the preceding medieval ecclesiological tradition, the last one signaled a radical departure. Luther asserted that the true church must be marked by suffering. According to Luther, just as God was hidden in the suffering of Jesus, so the glory of the true church had to be concealed within her suffering, thereby initiating Christ. This suffering, characterizing the true church, also included the physical afflictions experienced by her members. For Luther,

> *One recognizes the holy Christian people outwardly by the relic of the Holy Cross, that it must undergo all the misfortune and persecution, all sorts of tribulation and evil (as the "Our Father" prays) from the Devil, world, and flesh; . . . outwardly poor, scorned, ill, weak, suffer, so that it can be like Christ, its head.*[11]

The outward suffering, poverty, and weakness of the true (evangelical) church, concealing its glory, contrasted with the manifested appearances of the visible magnificence and glory, intentionally displayed and emphasized by the medieval Catholic church. This juxtaposition underscored a central theme in Luther's ecclesiology: the true church was a communion of suffering saints, not a powerful, triumphant institution. For Luther, the distinction between the false (Catholic) church of glory and the true (evangelical) church of sufferers also stemmed from the reality that the suffering of the latter often came from persecution by the former. Evangelical bodies bearing suffering from displacement, imprisonment, malnourishment, sickness, and torture displayed the marks of the true church.

Luther recognized that his religious opponents likewise experienced suffering. As theological controversies were unraveling in the 1520s, Luther distinguished between authentic and "counterfeit" suffering. Unlike authentic suffering, which was essential for spiritual formation, counterfeit suffering offered no such benefits. Authentic suffering was externally inflicted on a Christian and had to be the kind of suffering that, even while realizing its spiritual benefits, one would gladly be rid of. In contrast, "counterfeit" suffering was frequently self-chosen and self-imposed.[12]

Self-Imposed Physical Suffering

In the course of his career, Luther increasingly differentiated between the suffering sent by God and self-chosen suffering, which he believed his theological antagonists erroneously sought out and embraced. In particular, Catholic monastic communities remained a constant target of his critique for their alleged self-infliction, undue abuse, and especially their misinterpretation of the theological significance of bodily pain.[13] Once himself a devout friar, zealously mortifying his body, later in life Luther turned fiercely critical of monastic asceticism, which he saw as exhibiting a twofold error. Monks avoided suffering of the body when it was necessary and deliberately chose it when it was unnecessary.

First, monks rejected the necessary suffering of the body by avoiding ordinary pains and challenges, which Luther called daily martyrdom. As Heiko Oberman pointed out, for Luther, the concept of "the church of the martyrs" did not merely denote a long past phase in the history of the early church but referred to the church's ongoing existential condition.[14] Luther described various forms of externally imposed suffering and persecution of faithful Christians on account of the gospel as martyrdoms that had predictably characterized and will continue to mark the true church of all ages. Moreover, in addition to martyrdom resulting from religious persecution, true Christians also offered themselves in daily forms of martyrdoms, by faithfully and self-sacrificially fulfilling their roles as spouses, parents, and good citizens. Luther emphasized the significant burdens carried daily through engagements in the estates of family, church, and state. In his 1522 treatise *The Estate of Marriage*, Luther thus described the murmurs of a discontent husband and father:

> *Alas, must I rock the baby, wash its diapers, make its bed, smell its stench, stay up nights with it, take care of it when it cries, heal its rashes and sores, and on top of that care for my wife, provide for her, labor at my trade, take care of this and take care of that, do*

> *this and do that, endure this and endure that, and whatever else of bitterness and drudgery married life involves? What, should I make such a prisoner of myself? Oh, you poor, wretched fellow, have you taken a wife? Fie, fie upon such wretchedness and bitterness! It is better to remain free and lead a peaceful, carefree life; I will become a priest or a nun and compel my children to do likewise.*[15]

Luther's last sentence stressed the irony of monastic life. While monks claimed to embrace additional deprivations through their celibacy and withdrawal from society, they actually fled the everyday sufferings, routine deprivations, and hard work inherent in the roles of spouses, parents, and citizens. Moreover, Luther emphasized that abandoning earthly roles and institutions for the sake of seemingly higher spiritual purposes was not supported by Scripture. In fact, the Bible said nothing of monks in monasteries. Conversely, Scripture elevated as examples of God-pleasing individuals the patriarchs of Genesis. Luther observed that "in the histories of these patriarchs, we do not see that they fasted on certain days, abstained from domestic and civil responsibilities, and tortured the flesh."[16] These patriarchs walked with God, while also attending to their own and their family's physical needs, farming, raising cattle, managing households, getting married, and having children. This contrasted sharply with monks' approaches to the pursuit of a holy life, to the significance of the body and the response to its needs, which diverged significantly from biblical examples.

However, the monastic error did not end there. Having spared their bodies the pains of marriage, parenthood, and other divinely established ordinary estates and affairs, monks embraced the second error. They subjected their bodies to self-imposed pain through mortifications, depriving themselves of food, sleep, comfort, and inflicting physical harm. Since the 1520s, Luther's writings regularly included sharp critiques of what he saw as monastic practices oppressing the body, including misuses of medicine. For instance, his 1520 *Discussion on How Confession Should Be Made,* attacked those who condemned taking medicine during a season of fasting.[17] In his 1522 *Fourth Sermon at Wittenberg*, Luther taught that one should not abstain from meat during church fasts, if it negatively affected health.[18]

For Luther, medieval monastic rules exhibited a profound theological confusion regarding the religious significance and application of the law. Luther saw the scope of God's law as going beyond divine commandments of the Old Testament. Theologically, Luther understood law as comprising all God's rules and commandments in the Bible, including also those given in the New Testament to the church, such as in the writings of Paul, other epistles, and the words of Christ himself. Luther contrasted this broader understanding of law with the gospel, or the promises of God, also found throughout the whole Scripture. In sum, for Luther, the entire Bible contained both the Gospel and the law, not limited to a particular book or a Testament.

As previously discussed, Luther emphasized that observing the law (or biblical commandments) availed nothing in matters of salvation. However, while not soteriologically efficacious, biblical commandments still played two important functions. In this regard, Luther closely followed Paul's letter to the Romans. First, because sinful people could not fully observe God's commandments, knowledge of God's law produced awareness of one's sin. According to the Sermon on the Mount, a lustful look at a woman was equivalent to committing adultery, and an angry outburst against one's brother invited divine judgment. How could anyone fully avoid falling into these or similar sins? The first use of the law was to (intentionally) produce a guilty conscience and despair over one's inability to meet God's requirements. Fortunately, having recognized the depth of their sin, sinners could turn to Christ and cling in faith to God's promises to justify them not based on their acquired righteousness but on account of their faith alone.

The second function of the law (understood broadly as biblical commandments) was to restrain evil in civil society. In this way, Luther's view of the law was deeply steeped in his context of late Christendom, where secular laws largely reflected what were believed to be biblical principles. By curbing immorality, protecting the innocent, and restraining evil and oppression, righteous civil law rooted in God's law would become a means of actively loving one's neighbor. According to Luther, the ultimate purpose of divine law was love, to be manifested in earthly laws as the attainment of peace and harmony.

Luther taught that the divine law, the gospel, and the sacraments were eternally established and not subject to modification, being founded and, in case of the promises and sacraments, ultimately fulfilled by God. In contrast, human laws and rules should be applied with flexibility, in order to serve their proper purpose of love. According to Luther, if human laws and rules were not exercised with a degree of flexibility in accordance with specific circumstances, they could lead to injustice in the pursuit of justice.

Luther found an illustration of this flexible application of human laws and rules serving a greater purpose of peace and harmony in the story of Abram (before he was renamed Abraham) and Lot dividing the lands in Genesis 13.[19] While sharing the same stretch of land, due to their large possessions and numerous tents and livestock, Abram and Lot faced a lack of sufficient resources to properly sustain cattle and their caregivers, which had led to infighting between their herdsmen. Recognizing the need for a solution, Abram suggested that he and Lot separate and settle in different areas. Luther highlighted that, being the older brother and the original recipient of the divine promise of the land, Abram could lawfully unilaterally decide how to divide the land. However, instead of claiming first what could lawfully be his own, Abram offered Lot to choose his preferred part of the land on which to settle. By humbling himself and relinquishing his due rights, Abram manifested brotherly affection, preserved peace and harmony, and ultimately demonstrated love in action.

Luther contrasted the moral of this story with monastic theological confusion regarding the purpose and application of the law, leading to their abuses of health. For Luther, in matters of the body, monks disregarded biblical teachings on the contextually sensitive exercise of rules and instead applied the same rigid ascetic requirements to all members of their communities. In his lectures on the Old Testament, Luther repeatedly invoked the practices of the monastic order of Carthusians, as exemplifying such theological errors. He encountered Carthusians while living as a student and friar in Erfurt, which was also home to a Carthusian monastery. Luther witnessed young Carthusians, supposed to be in the prime of health, limping with canes along the streets, looking pale and exhausted. When asked, they attributed their deteriorated health to prolonged vigils depriving them of sleep. For Luther, Carthusians' broken bodies visibly embodied consequences of the theological misinterpretation of the law.

Luther recalled the ways in which Carthusians rigorously adhered to strict dietary rules, which they practiced regardless of their physical strength. For instance, all the members of their order were expected to permanently abstain from consuming meat. According to Luther, even if a Carthusian fell seriously ill and would benefit from a bit of meat to gain strength, his brothers would still never allow him the tiniest bite. In fact, Luther's Carthusians "even if they could save this wretched fellow's life with one morsel of meat, they would not do it."[20] As exemplified by Carthusinas, medieval monastic practices contradicted the biblical example of applying human laws with flexibility stemming from love. In contrast, by rigidly applying the laws of their own design in pursuit of their spiritual goals, they lost sight of love as the true purpose of religious law.

Luther further critiqued Carthusians in his commentary on Genesis 29:28 and, later, on Genesis 48:17–18, for exemplifying the medieval monastic confusion between what he described as the "arithmetic" and "geometric" application of the law.[21] Luther defined the "arithmetic" application as ensuring the same numeric equality regardless of the recipient. As an example, a loaf of bread had a fixed price on a marketplace, regardless of the buyer's age or gender. In contrast, the "geometric" application was proportionate and adapted to individual circumstances. Thus, while a man, a woman, or a child would pay the same price for the same amount of bread on the marketplace, they actually required varying qualities of bread for sustenance. Luther noted that well-run households and wisely governed nations applied rules "geometrically," considering individual limitations and circumstances.

Moreover, Luther observed that the human body required a "geometric" application of laws and rules. This must be reflected in the principles of good medical practice, which, while following particular rules, should tailor and adjust them based on a patient's constitution and specific condition. Luther invoked a widely accepted belief of early modern medicine that, depending on a person's constitution, one person's potent drug would be another person's poison. Without consideration of a particular patient's unique needs, a physician would act more as a killer than a healer.

This, too, was an error of monastics. They imagined their asceticism to be spiritual medicine, but instead they misused ascetic practices to destroy their bodies. Rather than applying their spiritual rules "geometrically," Luther's Carthusians, like other monks, applied them "arithmetically," by commanding a rigid adherence to strict regulations of eating, bathing, and sleeping, irrespective of individual needs. Luther dramatically contrasted good physicians saving bodies with their material medicine with zealous monks torturing, crippling, or even destroying bodies with their spiritual "medicines." He vividly painted a picture where a concerned physician was trying to save a sick monk by persuading his monastic brothers to allow modifications to their strict ascetic rules. But Luther's cruel Carthusians remained unbendable, thereby "with their harsh abstinence they killed many whom they could have saved with one dish of chicken broth, a piece of meat, or cleaner clothing."[22]

In essence, the tragic irony of monastic asceticism was that, while zealously striving to please God, monks' deliberate infliction of suffering on their bodies ultimately produced results contrary to the commandments of Scripture. By rigidly applying their rules for spiritual purposes in an "arithmetic" manner, the monks impaired their own and their brothers' health, directly violating Paul's mandate in Colossians 2:23 to "spare the body" and perhaps even the divine commandment against killing. Moreover, by depriving their bodies of their natural needs and subjecting them to extreme exhaustion, monks became less capable of fulfilling their own duties and especially the duties owed to their neighbors. In the pursuit of divine reward, monastic bodily asceticism ultimately embodied disobedience to God.

At the same time, Luther's attacks on monastic bodily mortifications did not amount to his dismissal of ascetic practices as altogether useless or spiritually harmful. In 1537–1538, around the same period when he first developed his critique against Carthusians in his lectures on Genesis, Luther also delivered a series of sermons on the Gospel of John. While refraining from praising monks, these sermons presented a more nuanced view of ascetic practices, particularly fasting. They reveal that Luther's main concern was not with ascetic practices per se but with what he perceived as their extreme abuse and, especially, the misinterpretation of their theological significance within medieval monastic contexts.

Luther addressed fasting in his commentary on John 3:13–14, discussing the unique significance of the Incarnation for salvation.[23] Christ descended to earth, was born of the Virgin Mary, and then ascended back to heaven, where he was now seated at the right hand of the Father. Luther emphasized that Christ did not intend to ascend back to heaven alone. While on Earth, Christ as the bridegroom united himself with the church as his bride through what Luther described as the engagement ring of faith. In Christ, the church will also be carried to heaven. According to Luther, since Christ alone had been able to accomplish both spiritual descension and ascension, he literally created through himself the only way back to the Father.

In contrast, Luther identified his usual religious antagonists—the Jews, the Muslims (whom Luther referred to as the Turks), and the Catholics led by the Pope—as devising alternative ways of getting to heaven. They sought justification by adhering to their own codes of piety, which they believed drew them closer to salvation and which they diligently strived to observe. Luther conceded that these soteriologically oriented moral systems included and mandated some behaviors that indeed were outwardly pious and commendable, such as aiding the poor, establishing charitable institutions, and promoting religious practice. The real issue, however, lay not in the ethical deficiencies within these salvation-seeking moral systems but in their foundational basis upon human works, which, by themselves, could never pave the way to heaven. For Luther, these human-devised, human-dependent systems contrasted starkly with Christ, who, by his own descent and ascent, created the way to salvation through himself. For instance, according to Luther, without Christ, the elaborate piety of the "Turks" remained external, creating an appearance of holiness without internal transformation.

After critiquing the reportedly superficial piety of the Turks, Luther turned his scrutiny to what he saw as yet another fraudulent way to heaven, this time aided by ascetic practices, designed by theologically erring monks. Among the followers of this fraudulent way Luther counted St. Bernard, who purportedly had abstained from food and drink for such prolonged periods, that his lungs began to rot. As a result, in Luther's version of the events, St. Bernard's extraordinary devotion made his breath unbearably foul. The pious but stinky St. Bernard was expelled from the monastery's choir by his brothers and forbidden from approaching other monks.

Up to this point, Luther's mocking depiction of St. Bernard's trials proceeded like another one of his biting attacks on the foolishness and cruelty of the monastic abuse of the body. However, Luther's sermon suddenly took a surprising turn:

> *Let me say here that fasting is not an evil; it is a good work. Nevertheless, it is not the resurrection and the life. Fasting may be a good work incumbent on me, but it is not something that is in heaven or something that descended from heaven; much less will it lead and take us to heaven. These works may be good; but they did not come down from heaven, nor have they ever been in heaven.*[24]

This unexpected endorsement of (moderate) fasting as a good work reveals that, for Luther, at least limited fasting in itself was not theologically problematic. Indeed, it would have been difficult for him to completely dismiss the practice of religious fasting, as it seemed to have been implicitly affirmed by Christ. Luther's real concern was the misinterpretation of theological significance of fasting and other ascetic practices, which mistakenly ascribed to them soteriological significance. Fasting could not achieve what Christ did, by bringing the earth and heaven together through his descension, incarnation, and the subsequent ascension to provide a path to salvation through himself. Fasting was merely a human work, and as such, while commendable under certain circumstances, could not contribute to salvation.

This illuminates a crucial theological stake behind Luther's critique of monastic self-infliction of bodily suffering. For Luther, self-imposed suffering was motivated by a fundamental soteriological confusion. Together with the medieval Catholic church, monks believed and taught that God justified individuals on account of their Christian faith and meritorious works. Monks considered their ascetic practices spiritually meritorious, aiding in earning their justification. For Luther, this medieval belief underscored the true reason why monastic communities tended to be so stringent in adhering to their laws and rules, even at the expense of their health. They assumed that observance of their rules would create a pathway to salvation, by making them holy, as required by God for justification. However, Luther repeatedly emphasized that such practices, being merely human works, could not be salvific. While ascetic practices were not inherently wrong, they became wrongful if used indiscriminately to the detriment of one's health and, crucially, when motivated by the desire to merit salvation.

Luther's reflections on ascetic practices were influenced by his own experiences as an Augustinian friar. He recalled mortifying his flesh out of concern for his own salvation as well as to aid the spiritual condition of others. As a good medieval Christian, Luther believed that through his spiritual merit he could assist those undergoing a painful cleansing from their sin in purgatory. For example, during a visit to Rome on business for his Augustinian order, with the goal of aiding his deceased grandfather's soul, Luther climbed the twenty-eight marble steps of the Scala Santa on his knees, reciting the Lord's Prayer on each step.[25]

While Luther's fervor was significant and would not be shared by all medieval monks, his zealous, theologically driven embrace of bodily mortifications would not be uncommon for an observant monastic. In 1518, while still a friar, Luther wrote to his spiritual mentor Johann von Staupitz, confessing that due to the severe austerity of his fasting, clothing, and work, he became weakened and exhausted to the point of feeling near death.[26] As a reformer, he leveled severe criticisms at his past mistreatment and even abuse inflicted on his body. In the lectures on Genesis, Luther condemned his former lifestyle as that of "a murderer and the worst persecutor of [his] own body," recalling how he "used to fast, pray, watch, and fatigue [himself] beyond [his] strength."[27]

The few surviving written descriptions of Luther's appearance and his visual portraits of that period of his life confirm this reminiscence.[28] In 1519, Luther participated in the Leipzig disputation against the renowned debater Johann Eck, a professor of theology at the University of Ingolstadt and a passionate defender of Catholic faith. This disputation was pivotal in Luther's journey toward the Reformation, since the presentation of his views during the debate ultimately led to his censure and excommunication by the Pope a year later. The Leipzig disputation also provided us with the earliest available description of Luther's physical appearance. Petrus Mosellanus, a humanist well regarded by Luther, was among the considerable audience drawn to the debate. Mossellanus provided a description of Luther as a person of medium height, so emaciated that "one can almost count his bones through the skin."[29] This description aligned with Luther's own later recollection of his monastic body as malnourished, exhausted, and abused by his physical austerities.

A year after the Leipzig disputation, we encounter a similar, but now a visual representation of a thin, weary Luther, depicted on an engraving by his supporter and friend, Lucas Cranach the Elder.[30] During that period, Luther remained an Augustinian friar for another year, albeit deeply involved in religious controversy and publishing some of his most renowned polemical writings. Later, Lucas Cranach the Elder (followed by his son Lucas Cranach the Younger) produced some of the most celebrated images of Luther, praised for their ability to capture both Luther's spirit as well as his physical appearance. In this 1520 engraving, Luther appeared worn out, with sunken cheeks, a bony face, and a contemplative yet exhausted, almost stoic expression. The next surviving portrait of Luther by Cranach the Elder came in the following year of 1521, after Luther's excommunication, during his period of hiding in Wartburg castle under the alias of Junker Jörg, a country squire. In this painting, Luther was portrayed in a black high-collared robe, with a trimmed beard, the familiar slender physique and drawn, weary face.

Luther's nine-month seclusion in Wartburg led to changes in his bodily appearance. His correspondence during that time indicated that his confinement within the castle grounds and his forced sedentary lifestyle resulted in his overeating and suffering from constipation. Luther emerged from his Warburg seclusion a physically transformed man. Now a leader of the new Protestant movement, he left behind for good both his Catholicism and his haggard monastic physique. For the remainder of his life, Luther was never again described as thin. Contemporaries remembered him as stout, and not long before his passing, Luther casually referred to himself as "a fat doctor."[31] Surviving images from this post-Wartburg period certainly depicted him as overweight. This transformation of Luther's physical appearance had been explained by lifestyle changes, his diet, his love for beer, and his multiple health issues, including kidney stones, which likely contributed to bloating.

However, Luther's newly enlarged body—and its artistic representations—also conveyed theological statements.

Even in his lifetime, Luther already became a symbol of the Reformation. His visual depictions served not merely to capture his likeness but also to communicate specific messages about his ideas and beliefs, often represented as inseparably tied to his physical appearance, even in purposefully unrealistic or grotesque ways. A notable example was the famous engraving of the seven-headed Luther, commissioned by Johannes Cochlaeus, a theological opponent from the Diet of Worms. Each of Luther's seven heads represented different personas he embodied to corrupt Christendom, including doctor, fanatic, fool, church visitor, churchman, criminal, and Barabbas.[32] Likewise, multiple images of Luther were produced by his supporters to capture the man for posterity as well as to promote a particular version of Luther's (and the Reformation's movement) unfolding legend. Luther's portraits were even described as "iconic," not only for their prominence but also, metaphorically, for their almost religious significance for the early reform movement.[33]

According to Lyndal Roper, the visibly massive Luther depicted in portraits from the 1530s displayed a remarkable departure from traditional medieval representations of religious leaders.[34] Roper argued that this difference was deliberate, aimed to visually convey two important messages about Luther's role and significance for the Protestant church. First, the representations of Luther's large body intended to evoke the traditional powerful presence of a large, commanding man, whose monumental stature conveyed a sense of authority.[35] In many of the Cranachs' paintings, Luther was depicted alongside the Saxon Electors—two monumental, towering male figures of spiritual and secular command, both with visible bodily presence. This contrasted with portrayals of Luther by his opponents, where his stature was literally diminished and appeared normal-sized, despite his real-life massive proportions.

Second, Roper suggested that Luther's appearance evoked a traditional archetype of the father of the family. During his lifetime, Luther's marriage to Katharina von Bora was closely watched and even idealized. Luther's "fatherly" figure represented a new view of a Christian leader: not a celibate monk, but a husband and a father, leading his family, as he led the church.

This also conveyed what Roper described as the "earthliness" of Luther's spirituality, embracing food, drink, family, and hearty conversation about religious matters around the table at home surrounded by followers and friends.[36] Luther's new appearance without words communicated a rejection of the medical Catholic religious ideal. An ascetic monk was obliterated from Luther's own image just as he was from his writings.

Roper's analysis of the visual representations of the "stout" Luther as conveying a traditional sense of authority and fatherhood provides important insights. However, one must not overlook its ultimate connection to the center of Luther's theological agenda—his renewed vision of Christian soteriology. Luther's own embodiment as a reformer communicated a statement about salvation. A monk's exhausted body symbolized a lifestyle of mortifying the flesh, humbly laboring for one's own and others' salvation. By contrast, the "fat doctor's" body communicated an alternative statement of confidence in salvation by God's grace alone, without the need for bodily mortifications. Salvation was no longer earned through merits, including those obtained through ascetic practices. Luther's own body proclaimed without words that his own life, most literally, embodied this fundamental conviction.

Physical Suffering as a Sign of Righteousness and a Mark of the Church

Luther was acutely aware that not all physical suffering was self-chosen. Many troubles and dangers to the body were undesirable and appeared to be unwarranted by those who suffered from them. Luther's lectures on Joseph's afflictions in Genesis 39–40 vividly expounded his theological wrestling with the question of seemingly undeserved physical suffering, situated within broader themes of his thought. Joseph had been sold by his jealous brothers to passing slave traders and subsequently purchased in Egypt by a captain of Pharaoh's bodyguard.

In Genesis 39, Joseph had found favor with his Egyptian master, who elevated him to oversee his entire household.[37] However, he faced a dire predicament when his master's wife began persistent sexual advances, but Joseph was unmoved in remaining faithful to God and to his master. One day, when they were alone, the mistress grabbed Joseph's clothes, demanding compliance. Joseph, however, managed to free himself and flee, leaving his garment behind. Furious at being rejected, the master's wife accused Joseph of attempted assault, alleging that he fled and abandoned his clothes when she screamed. Outraged, Joseph's powerful master had him thrown into the dungeon for Pharaoh's prisoners.

Genesis 39 does not provide many details about Joseph's initial experiences in confinement. Verse twenty states only that "Joseph's master took him and put him into the prison, the place where the king's prisoners were confined; he remained there in prison," while the following verse twenty-one claims that "the Lord was with Joseph and showed him steadfast love; he gave him favor in the sight of the chief jailer." While the biblical text leaves out what might have happened to Joseph during the time that passed between these two events, Luther's imagination filled in the space between these two verses with a captivating story of Joseph's angst and God's deliverance.

Luther dramatically portrayed newly imprisoned Joseph's intense physical suffering. He was thrown into the dungeon to be tortured with bonds and punishments in preparation for the execution for a shameful crime he did not commit. There, in an Egyptian dungeon, cut off from his family and betrayed by his brothers, having lost his previously somewhat secure position and his honorable reputation, Luther's disgraced Joseph was unseen by all. And it was in that moment of what appeared to be complete abandonment and hopeless isolation when, to Joseph, "Christ comes and lights up hell with gracious eyes."[38]

At this juncture, the somber story of Joseph's unearned and overwhelming suffering became an uplifting narrative of his radical consolation. While everyone rejected the despised Hebrew slave, Christ saw him in the dark depths of his confinement and proclaimed "Behold, I am present, Joseph; let it be enough for you that I am mindful of you."[39] The repetition of the phrase "the Lord was with Joseph" in verses twenty-one and twenty-three served for Luther as a triumphant acknowledgement that, despite appearances to the contrary, Joseph had never been truly alone. At this point, a sense of intense joy radiated through the tone of Luther's lectures. Although Joseph's suffering was severe and brought him to the brink of death, God never abandoned Joseph and always intended to redeem him. Yet for Christ's help to begin, Joseph must have first fully despaired of all earthly means of help.

While Genesis 39 was silent on the circumstances of exactly how Joseph managed to win the chief jailer's favor, Luther continued to employ his vivid imagination to fill in the details of the story. After experiencing the comforting presence of Christ with him, Joseph's whole disposition began to change. While externally his body still suffered in the Egyptian prison, his conscience was becoming joyful, peaceful, and healed. Luther insisted that Joseph's consolation was not brought about by the change in his tortuous conditions of imprisonment. On the contrary, realizing God's comforting presence while still confined in darkness—literally and spiritually–started Joseph's liberation. It was necessary for the restoration of Joseph's well-being to begin internally before it was manifested outwardly.

Unlike other prisoners "groaning, wailing, and raging" in the dungeon, Luther's Joseph, newly consoled by the Holy Spirit, displayed remarkable peace, steadfastness, and compassion for the troubled state of others.[40] He began teaching and comforting other prisoners, which caught the attention of the chief jailer, who marveled at such inexplicable behavior. The jailer inquired about the reason for Joseph's imprisonment, and upon hearing his story, the jailer became convinced of Joseph's innocence. And then the unexpected happened: the jailer, now converted to Joseph's cause, freed the criminal slave from his bonds, and elevated him to oversee other prisoners. Thus, initially chained in confinement, Joseph's bodily torments came to an end.

Luther's Joseph now enjoyed a new degree of freedom. He could move freely within the prison grounds, overseeing other prisoners, distributing food, settling disputes, punishing transgressors, and defending the innocent. He even wore a sword! The alleviation of Joseph's physical suffering was his second divinely provided consolation, following the first spiritual comfort he received while still in bonds. According to Luther, this sequence of spiritual consolation preceding a physical one illustrated a general pattern of God's work of comforting and delivering Christian souls and bodies.

Luther pondered the reasons behind Joseph's repeated misfortunes. Joseph had suffered a great injustice from the hands of his brothers, who, motivated by jealousy, secretly sold him into slavery. After a while, God granted the enslaved Joseph favor with his master, thus providing some relief to his circumstances. Yet, a new, worse disaster awaited. Despite significant personal risk in his highly vulnerable position, Joseph resisted sin and chose virtue by rejecting his mistress's advances. However, instead of being rewarded, Joseph's integrity led to his dramatic downfall. Why did God allow Joseph to experience such undeserved tribulations? For Luther, a major reason for Joseph's afflictions was pedagogical, teaching important spiritual truths about suffering to future generations of Christians who will learn Joseph's story. In other words, Joseph did not merely endure his physical suffering for the sake of his own spiritual formation, but ultimately for the sake of the spiritual formation of the church.

In particular, Joseph's suffering reminded the church of the inevitable grave afflictions awaiting believers and provided an example of enduring such trials faithfully as witnesses of the gospel to the world. While lecturing on Genesis 39, Luther repeatedly referred to Joseph as a "martyr."[41] Like Christian martyrs of the early church, Joseph did not deserve his suffering but bore it because of his righteous behavior. Furthermore, the ancient meaning of martyr was "witness," as martyrs produced converts to Christianity through public suffering for the truth. Similarly, Luther's depiction of Joseph's extraordinary endurance of afflictions served as a testament to the integrity of his cause and his faith.

By drawing from early Christian martyrdom literature, Luther described Joseph's initial torments in confinement as his "passion," which nearly ended in his death. He extended this parallel by calling Joseph's deliverance at the end of Genesis 39 a form of resurrection, followed by his ascension to the position of ruler of Egypt. Luther emphasized that, like Joseph, Christians would inevitably face similar or even more intense challenges and troubles as those around them, but true believers must bear their passion differently, showing hope and love. While the eventual deliverance of all Christian bodies from pain was not guaranteed, spiritual benefits were certain for those who had faith. The inexplicable Christian peace and manifestation of love for others amid tribulations would stand in stark contrast to the anguish of the suffering world, bearing witness to the power of Christian faith.

As Luther painted the picture of the tormented and bonded Joseph lying in a dungeon on the brink of death, it was easy to imagine that he was struck by God's wrath. Yet, throughout Joseph's ordeal, divine love and favor never departed from him, though they were obscured by his outwardly grim circumstances. The example of Joseph illustrated the uncomfortable truth of God often subjecting his beloved ones to divinely imposed afflictions, including physical suffering.[42] Teaching the church the mystery of what Luther termed God's "alien work" was another significant pedagogical goal of Joseph's story.

This term "alien work" (*opus alienum Dei*) appeared as early as in Luther's 1513–1515 Pre-Reformation lectures on the Psalms. The concept was embedded in his subsequently developed theology of the cross, of which it became an important part, appearing in the *Ninety-Five Theses* and later in the fourth thesis of the Heidelberg Disputation. Luther drew inspiration for his theology of God's "alien work" from late medieval mystical tradition. He borrowed the term from Isaiah 28:21, stating "the Lord will rise up as on Mount Perazim, he will rage as in the valley of Gibeon to do his deed—strange is his deed!—and to work his work—alien is his work!"

God's "alien work" imposed afflictions and tribulations for the sake of spiritual goals. It seemed terrifying and even evil, and certainly non-divine. Luther frequently likened the external appearance of God's alien work to that of the devil's work. Hence, Luther used the term "alien work" in order to emphasize that while God's actions indeed manifested wrath and punishment, these were ultimately "alien" to God's nature. This expression of divine activity contrasted with God's "proper work" (*opus proprium Dei*), which saved, healed, and restored. At the same time, God's "alien work" and "proper work" operated in sequence, as essential aspects of the full scope of the divine economy of salvation. God's "alien work" of inflicting pain and despair led to awareness of one's vulnerability, need, and sin. It moved the soul to respond to God's "proper work" of salvation and deliverance. A perception of God's "alien work" as purely negative and painful exposed a problem of human comprehension, to be ultimately corrected by the lenses of faith. Just as by faith Christians came to see the hidden God in the suffering of the crucified and rejected man Jesus, they ultimately learned to see God hidden behind and working through their own suffering.

The concept of "alien work" remained a crucial theological-exegetical key for Luther's understanding of many hermeneutically challenging biblical stories. For example, Luther used it to exegete the story of the Canaanite woman repeatedly rejected by Jesus in Matthew 15, which Luther saw as also providing a biblical illustration of the proper human response to God's "alien work."[43] After the Canaanite woman asked Christ to exorcise a demon from her sick daughter, Jesus initially ignored her, and ultimately refused, stating that he had been sent to Israelites. When the woman persisted in begging for his help, Jesus retorted that it would not be appropriate to throw the children's food to the dogs. Despite this harsh reply, the woman did not give up. Instead, she pointed out that even dogs ate the crumbs that fell from their master's table. Surprisingly, Jesus responded by praising the woman's great faith and granting her wish. For Luther, this story summarized the essence of God's alien work—a hard-spoken divine "no" concealing deep within a divine "yes," revealed through faith.

God also used his "alien work" for Christians' spiritual formation. For Luther, such formation was intricately linked to the strong relationship between suffering and faith, which Luther elaborated upon in his theology of the cross. While Luther's theology of the cross primarily focused on the connection between faith and divine suffering, Luther extended this connection to also include human afflictions.[44] The theology of the cross underscored the revelation of God hidden in the suffering of the man Jesus, which the fallen human reason perceived as showing foolishness, vulnerability, and impending death. Luther posited that God, concealed in the suffering on the cross, was only revealed through faith. Just as human reason apart from faith could not comprehend God hidden in suffering, so it was quick to interpret human afflictions as a sign of God's anger or abandonment. However, for Luther, Christians would be able to find and experience the consoling and loving presence of God concealed within their pain and tribulations, if they strived to maintain faith in God's promises against the temptation to fall into a perfectly rational despair based on their unfavorable external circumstances.[45] Here Luther relied on 1 Corinthians 10:13 promising that "God is faithful, and he will not let you be tested beyond your strength, but with the testing he will also provide the way out so that you may be able to endure it." For Luther, suffering frequently served as a test of faith, ultimately aimed at deepening and strengthening it.

Furthermore, suffering worked to cultivate humility, by stripping an afflicted Christian from self-confidence. In this respect, Luther's thought was influenced by medieval mystical tradition's teaching about reducing or even annihilating the self through suffering in order to produce union with

Christ.[46] Unable to alleviate afflictions with their own limited means, Christians were driven to call upon God, clinging to him alone for deliverance. This posture of relinquishing self-reliance and embracing humble reliance on God embodied the foundational expression of lived Christian faith, in which the fostering of suffering played a key role.

This process of spiritual formation or re-formation through suffering was closely linked to the experience of *Anfechtungen*, translated as "assault" or "temptation." [47] A crucial concept for Luther's theology of suffering, *Anfechtung* was an experience of inner spiritual turmoil, characterized by spiritually oppressive feelings of profound despair, defeat, depression, and doubt. Additionally, *Anfechtung* could include outer struggles or suffering of the body, although Luther considered the latter to be less severe than internal spiritual afflictions.[48] Alister McGrath has shown that, for Luther, *Anfechtung*, it was not merely a perception or subjective experience but a result of the genuine assault by the forces of the devil, death, and the world.[49] Nonetheless, God remained the ultimate providential author of *Anfechtung*, utilizing it for spiritually formative purposes through God's "alien work."

Drawing from Exodus 33, Luther employed vivid graphic imagery to metaphorically capture the perception of *Anfechtung*-producing "alien" divine activity. Moses asked God to reveal God's glory, but the Lord refused to show Moses his face. Instead, as God passed by, he allowed Moses to catch a glimpse of the divine back. Luther utilized this image of the divine backside (*posteriora*) as symbolizing God's "alien work." God turned away from the faithful, hiding God's face and, instead, showing his "backside." According to Luther, through the story of Joseph, the church needed to hear the following divinely pronounced words:

> *When God works, He turns His face away at first and seems to be the devil, not God. Thus in the present account His face was turned toward the harlot and the tyrant; He disregards Joseph and cherishes these alone. Thus Jeremiah also complains: "Thou art near in their mouth" (12:2). Therefore they boast that God is at their side, is well-disposed toward them, and cherishes them. "God dwells here!" they cry out. But Joseph, Jacob, and Abraham do not have this face turned toward them. This means that the devil is dwelling here.*

> *"You cannot see My face" (Ex. 33:20). For God is accustomed to lead and govern His own as is described in the song of Habakkuk: "Thy paths are in many waters, and Thy footprints are not known." Likewise in Is. 30:20–21: "Your eyes shall see your Teacher, and your ears shall hear the word of One giving admonition behind you." And Christ says to Peter: "What I am doing you do not know now, but afterward you will understand" (John 13:7)."*[50]

Joseph's story served as a dramatic example of enduring *Anfechtung* when confronted with God's hiddenness. While consistently remaining faithful, Joseph endured slavery, imprisonment, and intense suffering. Crucially, even when repeatedly faced with the divine "backside," Joseph did not abandon his faith. He relied on the insight that God's "alien work" was alien to God's true view of him as God's child. Through his unwavering faith, Joseph was eventually spiritually consoled and physically delivered. His life served as an example for the church, struggling with *Anfechtungen* and doubting divine goodness amid suffering. The account of Joseph's misfortunes and triumphs consoled the church by testifying to the unwavering power of God's benevolence toward faithful sufferers, despite appearances to the contrary. It confirmed and lucidly illustrated the proclamation of Romans 8:28 that ultimately all things, even pain, "work together for good for those who love God, who are called according to his purpose." It reminded Christians to resist feeling discouraged and overwhelmed by dark and frightening circumstances, instead remaining firmly focused on God's promises. Luther's parting advice to the afflicted church hearing Joseph's story was to "close your eyes and sustain yourself with the Word."[51] This principle was vital for living a Christian life, especially in light of the inevitable suffering awaiting Christians through God's "alien work."

Physical Suffering as Painful Divine Discipline and Bitter Spiritual Medicine

In his seminal study, Ronald Rittgers described Luther's and the early Lutheran project of reform as "a reformation of suffering," intending to reshape the medieval Catholic attribution to suffering of a soteriological function.[52] Rittgers encapsulated this connection as follows:

> *In pre-Reformation Christianity, justification entailed a fundamental and gradual change of a person's nature—sinfulness had to give way to righteousness if the person was to enter heaven. Suffering played a necessary and indispensable role in this righteous-making process; suffering was, quite literally, salvific. Despite the well-known and well-studied late medieval debates about the respective roles of divine agency and human agency in salvation, every theologian agreed on this basic point: one had to become righteous to enter heaven. Grace was essential to this process, and so was some measure of human contribution, no matter how minimal. Suffering was an important part of this human contribution.*[53]

In medieval theology, suffering was perceived as positively contributing to Christian spiritual development in several ways, all of which maintained unambiguous connections to the individual's advancement toward salvation. In particular, patient endurance of suffering was perceived as rendering satisfaction for the penalty of sin. As previously discussed, penance was a crucial element of the medieval Catholic soteriological system. The sacrament of penance offered a path to forgiveness of sin and restoration to a state of grace through heartfelt contrition, full confession, absolution, and the performance of works of satisfaction for sin. This view of suffering as a work of satisfaction for sin presented suffering as meritorious for salvation.

Luther took issue with this medieval perspective on suffering on two levels. First, he raised soteriological objections. Luther emphasized that Christ offered complete satisfaction for human sin, rendering unnecessary any additional human works of satisfaction. Furthermore, for Luther, the idea of human suffering (or any other human works of satisfaction) being able to make amends for sin drastically underestimated the awful enormity of human transgression. If anyone doubted the immensity of sin, they should recall that the price paid for their redemption was the sacrifice of God's only begotten Son.

Second, as Rittgers demonstrated, Luther saw the medieval theology of suffering as presenting a pastoral problem.[54] The interpretation of suffering as an expression of divine anger and a form of punishment for sin instilled in medieval Christians the fear of God's wrath and uncertainty about their spiritual standing with God. For medieval Christians, such lack of presumption about God's attitude toward an individual sinner aligned with normative sensibilities of experiencing "pious doubts" regarding one's own salvation. However, for Luther, such fear and uncertainty ultimately robbed medieval Christians from an ability to suffer faithfully, patiently, and with hope, stemming from the reliance on God's goodness toward each individual sinner, justified by faith. Therefore, Luther's "reformation of suffering" became a deeply pastoral project aimed at reshaping religious perceptions of suffering in order to enable Christians to endure it well.

In contrast to viewing suffering as a work of satisfaction for sin, Luther sought to propose an alternative theological understanding of suffering, which he developed in his 1518 *Sermon on Indulgences and Grace*.[55] Luther composed the sermon several months after penning his famous *Ninety-Five Theses*, popularly regarded as a starting point of the Protestant Reformation. However, the *Ninety-Five Theses* were written in Latin and, therefore, originally only accessible to educated male elites. In contrast, the *Sermon on Indulgences and Grace* was written in German and subsequently printed as a pamphlet. It quickly became the first early modern religious bestseller, widely and frequently reprinted and disseminated across the Holy Roman Empire, popularizing Luther's ideas. This short sermon of only about fifteen hundred words in length became instrumental in elevating Luther to the status of religious celebrity.

While the main aim of the *Sermon on Indulgences and Grace* was the critique of indulgences, its theses six through nine also outlined Luther's new approach to suffering. In thesis six, Luther refuted the medieval belief that sinners needed to offer punishment or satisfaction, including as meted out by the medieval Church, to pay the penalty for their sin. Drawing on Ezekiel 18:21–22 and biblical narratives, such as Christ's forgiveness of Mary Magdalene in Luke 7:36–50, the paralyzed man in Mark 2:1–12, and the woman caught in adultery in John 8:1–11, Luther asserted that the only divinely required satisfaction for sin was sincere, heartfelt repentance. This repentance did not guarantee sinners freedom from suffering, which would still occur as an inherent aspect of their walks with Christ, but not as a penalty they owed to God for their sin.[56]

Nevertheless, in the following theses seven and eight, by citing Psalm 88, Luther admitted that occasionally God did impose suffering as punishment for sin. However, Luther stressed that the imposition of such punishment belonged to God alone. It should not have been appropriated by the medieval Church in the form of works of satisfaction imposed as a requirement for the full absolution from sin. Furthermore, in thesis nine, Luther criticized the theological distinction made by some medieval preachers between satisfactory (*satisfactorias*) and curative (*medicatiuas*) suffering. The former rendered satisfaction for sin, while the latter promoted spiritual improvement.[57] For Luther, the theological concept of satisfactory suffering was erroneous. The purpose of all divine punishment was ultimately Christian betterment and benefit.

This general framework for approaching retributive suffering as curative, not satisfactory, persisted through Luther's later writings, including his mature lectures on Genesis.[58] While Luther's lectures on the first part of the story of Joseph in Genesis 39–40 expounded his theology of undeserved physical suffering, his lectures on the continuing adventures of Joseph in Genesis 42–45 outlined a theological interpretation of suffering as a deserved consequence of one's actions.

Genesis 42–45 described the encounters between Joseph and his treacherous brothers who had previously sold him into foreign slavery. In Genesis 41, following his release from prison, Joseph was eventually elevated by Pharaoh to a position of power in Egypt. At that point, famine had spread throughout the land of Egypt. However, owing to Joseph's prophetic dreams and his administrative foresight, in preparation for lean years, Egypt had stockpiled abundant reserves of grain from the years of former prosperity. Meanwhile, in the land of Canaan, also struck by famine, Joseph's father Jacob decided to send his sons to Egypt in order to purchase grain for his household. There Jacob's sons met Joseph—now a high-ranking official wearing Egyptian attire—but failed to recognize him.

However, Joseph immediately recognized his family, but instead of disclosing his identity, he acted as a complete stranger. Joseph accused his brothers of being spies and had them imprisoned for three days. He subsequently ordered them released but kept Simeon, one of his brothers, in custody. As a condition of Simeon's release, Joseph demanded that the brothers bring to Egypt their youngest sibling Benjamin. Benjamin, Rachel's other son, remained at home with their father Jacob, to whom he was particularly dear. Despite his seemingly cruel treatment, Joseph still showed care for his family by having their sacks fully loaded with grain, giving them travel provisions, and even secretly returning their payment.

Back home, the brothers had to overcome Jacob's grave reluctance to let go of Benjamin, but eventually they returned to Joseph—their youngest sibling among them. During dinner, Joseph had his silver cup secretly placed in Benjamin's sack. The brothers were detained and searched and, upon discovering the cup, Joseph told them to leave, except for Benjamin, who, as a punishment, would remain as his slave.

Luther vividly portrayed to his audience the dramatic effects that Joseph's decision to keep Benjamin had on his brothers, who fell into an utmost agony and despair. They rightfully recognized their troubles as a punishment for the injustice they had long ago done to Joseph. They knew that their leaving Benjamin behind would strike their elderly father with inconsolable grief and bring him to his grave. Luther enhanced the biblical description of the brothers' appeals to Joseph with moving visual details. While pleading for mercy, they were weeping and wringing their hands, tearing their clothes in great distress. Shaken and brokenhearted about their unfulfilled promise to bring Benjamin back and their father's impending devastation, Luther's Judah begged for Benjamin's release, instead offering himself as a slave, sobbing and stretching out his hands to Joseph. Judah's plea exemplified the power of a prayer arising out of utter desperation. It was certainly impossible for Joseph to remain unmoved by this display of his family's sincere anguish. With hidden tears, Joseph revealed his identity to his brothers and assured them they had nothing further to fear from him. He reassured them against feeling guilty or apprehensive over their past betrayal, since the misfortune once imposed upon him and intended for evil, God had used to produce good.

Just as the story of suffering originally imposed on Joseph by his brothers conveyed important insights about the spiritual functions of unearned afflictions, for Luther, the story of suffering inflicted by Joseph on his brothers communicated additional important truths about the divine use of well-deserved pain. In particular, Joseph's treatment of his brothers modeled

God's use of suffering as divine discipline for God's people. In Luther's words, "in trials God conducts himself toward His saints just as Joseph conducts himself toward his brothers."[59] Luther even referred to such use of suffering as a divine "game." While God's actions might appear as intending to break or destroy sinners, God's true motivation was to restore and bless them.[60] This divine "game" was part of God's "alien work." However, the main difference in the divine "game" applied to Joseph's original suffering and the suffering of his brothers was that Joseph's tortuous imprisonment came as a consequence of his virtue, while Joseph's brothers earned their suffering through their wickedness.

Luther emphasized that Joseph's actions toward his brothers were not motivated by vengeance. He did not make them suffer out of hatred or with the goal to destroy them in retribution for their past crimes. On the contrary, the text of Genesis described Joseph as emotionally agitated and even weeping, while he was subjecting his brothers to a well-deserved turmoil. The final scene of the reunion showed the deep love Joseph sustained toward his family and his desire for the restoration of their relationship despite his siblings' original betrayal. Unlike medieval Catholic theologians, Luther's Joseph maintained the correct theological outlook of not viewing suffering as providing satisfaction for sin.[61] His goal in subjecting his brothers to afflictions was to bring to their minds the awareness of their transgression, make them face the perspective of severe punishment, and thus produce repentance and an ultimate realization of God's mercy. This story of Joseph punishing his brothers taught the church the dynamics of God's application of suffering on his disobedient children.

In order to illustrate this use of afflictions, Luther offered theological metaphors describing suffering, especially diseases and other instances of physical pain, as forms of divine corporal punishment.[62] For example, by commenting on Joseph's treatment of his brothers, Luther concluded, "Therefore you see in what spirit Christ punishes those who are his and what a fiery furnace of love, not only spiritual but also physical, there is."[63] Luther found the theme of suffering as sometimes serving as divine corporal discipline in the Bible, including in Psalm 94:12, Psalm 118:18, Proverbs 3:11–12, and Hebrews 12:3–11. Luther specifically identified various tribulations affecting the body, including sicknesses, plagues, and famines, as occasionally acting as divine "rods," inflicted to bring awareness of one's sin and God's displeasure in it, for the purpose of producing a sinner's repentance and reform. He compared divinely imposed suffering with teachers and fathers "whipping" and "chastising" with a "rod" sons whom they loved.[64]

In his sixteenth-century context, Luther did not seek to make an argument in support of physically punishing children. Rather, his references to corporal punishment reflected a vision of discipline assumed in his cultural context to be a natural way of bringing up offspring. Luther noted that caring parents or teachers did not enjoy whipping children but had to strictly discipline them for the sake of imparting right and wrong. Similarly, without delighting in it, God might choose to impose a form of physical suffering with the goal of repentance and edification, while still maintaining his love for the disobedient.

At the same time, Luther's theological interpretation of suffering as serving, at least occasionally, as a form of divine corporal punishment for sin revealed internal tension. As discussed earlier, in light of his insistence on justification by faith alone, Luther fully rejected the medieval view of suffering as having a salvific dimension, by serving as a work of satisfaction and rendering the penalty for sin. For Luther, God did not require retribution in order to remit transgression, but fully absolved sin based on sincere, heartfelt repentance and faith in divine forgiveness. God stood as a loving father eager to forgive and restore, not as a stern judge inflicting punishment for the committed crime, regardless of the guilty party's sincere regret. As Rittgers observed, Luther believed that the medieval perspective on suffering as a work of satisfaction resulted in unwarranted spiritual anxiety over one's experiences of suffering that ultimately impeded one's ability to bear afflictions well.[65]

At the same time, as noted earlier, Luther felt bound by Scripture to allow, at least in some cases, the interpretation of suffering as God's punishment for sin. However, this approach to the experiences of physical suffering as a means of divine corporal discipline could similarly produce a fear of divine anger directed at the erring sinner, which Luther so desperately wanted to avoid. This tension in Luther's thought between his reluctance to interpret suffering as God's punishment and his compulsion to do it, at least occasionally, in light of Scripture, was manifested in the conclusion of his lectures on the story of Joseph:

> *Thus God afflicts us with various disasters, not to punish us, although this really is a punishment. But He takes no pleasure in it.*[66]

While Luther grappled with the idea of physical suffering serving as divine corporal punishment, in his lectures on Genesis, he also employed an alternative metaphor for physical suffering as divine "remedies" (*remediis*) or "medicine" (*medicina*) for sin.[67] This echoed the medieval designation of certain forms of suffering as "curative," which, in his earlier works, Luther extended to describe the function of all forms of suffering. While exegeting Genesis, Luther further developed this metaphor specifically linking suffering to medicine, healing a sinner. For example, Joseph's treatment of his brothers was due to his desire "to heal and preserve them in soul and body," as he intended to "arouse grief and contrition and to induce them to seek health and cleansing for themselves."[68]

According to Luther, God likewise "uses powerful and bitter remedies to make it [sin] manifest and to cleanse it."[69] This statement reflects the reality of early modern medical practices, which, centuries away from anesthesia and elaborate pharmaceutical production, were indeed painful and bitter, at times more excruciating than an injury or disease itself. Consistent with the harsh medical treatments of his times, Luther described God scrubbing people until blood was let out, performing a sort of agonizing but medically necessary divine phlebotomy.[70] Elsewhere Luther spoke of divine burning, cutting, and bloodletting, all of which were common medical interventions of his day.[71] While these divine remedies were painful, they were always performed for the sinners' benefit, in order to purge their sin and spiritually heal them.

Luther's lectures on the story of Joseph reveal a hermeneutically spacious theology of physical suffering, intentionally holding together its several distinct interpretations, all of which Luther saw as supported by the Bible. As illustrated by Joseph's torments in prison, faithful Christians may endure seemingly undeserved suffering despite—or even because of—seeking to live faithful and righteous lives. Like Jesus, they suffered under the attacks of the devil and the persecution of the unbelieving world. Similarly, as illustrated by the story of Joseph's brothers, suffering could also affect Christians as a deserved consequence of their sins. Suffering would afflict their bodies as divine corporal punishment for transgression and heal them as bitter spiritual medicine. Regardless of its immediate source or underlying cause, all suffering ultimately reflected God's "alien work," serving as an essential means of spiritual formation for God's church.

Resisting the Suffering of the Body

The importance of the experiences of suffering for the spiritual life of the church in Luther's thought has not escaped both historical and more recent scholarly attention. In the last fifteen years, a number of significant studies have highlighted how Luther's pastoral and polemical teachings instructed Christians to properly recognize, endure, and embrace suffering as a gift from God that was essential for faith formation, moral transformation, theological discernment, and pious living. However, these important insights into Luther's "positive" theology of suffering have inadvertently obscured Luther's views on the possibilities of actively combatting suffering. I will show that, at least when it came to bodily suffering, Luther's mature theology did not imply outward passivity in the face of affliction. On the contrary, while upholding the beneficial functions of suffering, in his lectures on Genesis, Luther also pastorally mandated its intentional prevention and counseled active resistance to actual suffering.

While this approach came to characterize Luther's mature thought, it took years to develop, and his earlier writings on suffering revealed a more ambiguous stance. For example, Luther's important 1527 treatise, *Whether One May Flee from a Deadly Plague*, exhibited tensions in its exploration of its stated question.[72] Following an outbreak of the Black Death in Wittenberg, despite the Saxon elector's order to the Wittenberg University faculty—of which Luther was part—to leave the city, Luther chose to stay to help the city pastor with providing pastoral care to the distressed residents. Shortly following the outbreak, the questions were raised among clergy about the moral permissibility for Christians to abandon their pestilence-stricken communities. Pastors from an affected region of Silesia wrote to Luther twice seeking his advice on this matter. In response, Luther composed *Whether One May Flee from a Deadly Plague*, a fourteen-page pamphlet in the form of an open letter, which enjoyed a wide circulation.

Whether One May Flee from a Deadly Plague is sometimes cited as Luther's religious affirmation of medicine and preventative measures. Indeed, in this pamphlet, Luther compared the use of medicine to eating when hungry or putting on clothes when cold—a point echoing his debate with Karlstadt over the use of means, which will be discussed in the next chapter. He also criticized those who refused any precautions against the plague and deliberately put themselves in danger. Luther accused such individuals of recklessness, tempting God, and bearing guilt for potentially infecting their neighbors.

However, when read in its entirety, the treatise's primary agenda was not to mandate the use of medicine. First, Luther argued that those who were under communal or familial obligations to care for others had a moral and spiritual duty to remain with their plague-infected communities. Recognizing the real threats posed by the decision to stay during a plague outbreak, Luther offered his readers spiritual consolations to help them cope with fear, while performing their duties. Luther also urged the government to maintain and staff hospitals in order to provide care for the needy and alleviate families' burdens of attending to their sick.[73]

Second, Luther contended that individuals without explicit obligations to care for others were morally permitted to flee. Drawing from biblical examples of avoiding dangers, Luther generally considered escaping the plague under such circumstances to be a prudent option. However, he also introduced this choice as available to those with weaker faith. Luther affirmed that those who felt strong enough to stay and potentially face death, while still taking reasonable precautions, did not err in their decision to remain; rather, they exhibited commendable, strong faith. In essence, under specific conditions, fleeing the plague was merely an option for those with weaker faith, not a mandate. This distinction highlighted an apparent tension in Luther's instructions about whether refusing to escape bodily dangers was a sign of spiritual recklessness or a demonstration of strong faith.

This mid-career tension was resolved in Luther's mature works, particularly his lectures on Genesis. Luther observed that, when confronted with severe famine, Abram and his wife Sarai did not remain starving in their land but chose to move to Egypt. In Egypt, Abram exercised caution by presenting Sarai as his sister, in order to protect himself against her potential suitors. Likewise, their son Isaac repeatedly exercised precautions and guarded his life by fleeing precarious situations and using favors to ensure the safety of himself and his family. Similarly, Isaac's son Jacob, facing Esau's threat, fled and later sought to reconcile by offering gifts. When famine threatened his household, despite his internal reluctance, Jacob repeatedly sent his sons to Egypt to procure food. While in his treatise on the plague Luther cited many of the same Old Testament stories as providing positive biblical examples of safeguarding life and mitigating dangerous situations, in his lectures on Genesis, these biblical examples were elevated to mandates.

According to Luther, if Christians were forced to choose between their physical well-being and remaining faithful to Christ or loving their neighbors as themselves, the latter two took precedence. However, under regular circumstances, Christians were compelled to diligently seek and employ available faithful and prudent methods of protecting their bodies. In Luther's Genesis lectures, resisting bodily dangers or suffering through spiritually acceptable means became a spiritual obligation. Christians who indiscriminately exposed themselves to danger or refused to avail themselves of reasonably accessible means to ward off bodily threats, including disease, "sin[ned] gravely."[74]

For Luther, the story of Joseph in Genesis 40:12–15 again pedagogically illustrated this important principle regarding suffering.[75] From the onset of his grave misfortunes, Luther's Joseph understood the importance of resisting suffering, which he attempted to the best of his abilities, while maintaining ultimate faithfulness to God. When first captured by his brothers, he tearfully pleaded with them not to sell him away. However, after his efforts to elicit his brothers' mercy had failed, Joseph subsequently endured the suffering of his enslavement and later imprisonment in the dungeon with patience, hope in God, and internal preparedness to meet death or even greater afflictions. As noted earlier, Luther's Joseph made commendable use of his painful circumstances to actively care for other prisoners, comfort them, and teach them about the hope they had in the true God. While bearing his afflictions faithfully and using them for the service of his neighbors, he recognized a newly presented opportunity to escape his dire and dangerous circumstances, presented by the cupbearer. At that moment, Luther's Joseph did not hesitate but "seized this opportunity with singular zeal."[76]

Luther's Joseph lived out the principle given to the early church by Paul in 1 Corinthians 7:21. According to Paul, if someone became a Christian as a slave, their enslavement should not be a cause of concern; however, if an opportunity arose to gain freedom, they should avail themselves of it. Similarly, Joseph used his God-given ability to interpret dreams to plead with the cupbearer to petition to Pharaoh for his release. Luther's Joseph considered the chance to advise the cupbearer on the meaning of his dream as a potentially divinely provided way of rescuing him from imprisonment. Importantly, for Luther, if Joseph were to refuse pursuing this opportunity to be relieved of his painful and precarious circumstances, it would amount to negligence and testing God's goodwill.

At the same time, while diligently pursuing his chance to end his suffering, Luther's Joseph did not become emotionally attached to this opportunity. Rather, he remained spiritually open and internally prepared for the possibility of his pursuits ending in failure and him remaining in prison, if this was God's will. According to Luther, Joseph modeled for the church the following principle:

> *Paul hands down in 1 Cor. 7:21: "Were you a slave when called? Never mind. But if you can gain your freedom, avail yourself of the opportunity." We should not bring evils and dangers upon ourselves. But when we are afflicted either by chance or by God's will, then whatever misfortune there is must be borne steadfastly and with great courage, yet not in such a way that we neglect the plans and assistance by which we can be liberated. For it is tempting God to despise the remedies for evils—the remedies offered and shown by God.*[77]

This passage illustrated a dialectic characterizing Luther's theology of suffering, evident through his multiple engagements with the subject in the lectures of Genesis. Internally, Christians must accept and bear their suffering with patience and peace, but externally they ought to resist it. In order to elucidate this important principle, I will situate it within the broader context of another famous dialectic in Luther's thought—his theology of the "inner" versus "outer" person.

Luther outlined his theological distinction between an inner and an outer person in his programmatic 1520 treatise, *The Freedom of a Christian*.[78] According to Luther, the inner and outer persons were not two distinct individuals but two dimensions of the same personhood, possessed by every individual. The inner person embodied the immaterial, spiritual dimensions of human existence—such as the soul, spirit, and conscience—and was expressed through an individual's beliefs, thoughts, and emotions. The only true need of every inner person was the Word of God or the Gospel, to which the inner persons had to respond in faith, which justified them before God. The justification by faith brought liberation to the inner persons. They became free from fearing God's ultimate condemnation and from the burden of earning salvation. They also became free to call upon God as their Father and fully love God with their hearts, souls, minds, and strength as well as love their neighbors as themselves. Luther insisted that this freedom of the inner persons was absolute and could not be hindered by anyone; it was predicated only upon the inner persons' firm attachment to God's promises and clinging to the gospel in faith with all of their beings. Paradoxically, Luther described this attachment as the inner person's bondage to the Word of God. The gospel exercised complete dominion over a Christian's inner person, and, through this dominion, made this inner person completely free.

However, this amazing liberty was confined to the domain and experiences of the inner person. It did not extend to the outward actions of Christians, which fell within the domain of their outer persons. In contrast to the inner person, the outer person constituted the external dimension of personhood, encompassing actions and behaviors. The foundational orientation of the outer person of a Christian was showing love toward one's neighbor, relentlessly seeking first not one's own but the neighbor's good and benefit. For Luther, the manifestations of active love and service to the neighbor properly belonged to the outer person, not only because they were expressed outwardly but also because they ultimately had no bearing on the spiritual standing of the inner person. Christians did not perform good works in order to merit justification. However, while virtuous works were not a prerequisite, they were an essential consequence of and testimony to one's salvation. Therefore, the freedom of the inner person, received with salvation, ought to drive and compel the outer person to live out the love of Christ for the neighbor. Luther summarized the implications of his theology of the inner and outer person in his famous formula: "A Christian is a perfectly free Lord of all, subject to none. A Christian is a perfectly dutiful servant of all subject to all."[79]

Luther initially developed his dialectic of the inner and outer person as a theological trope for explaining the role of faith and works in Christian life. He later extended it to expound other aspects of his thought, particularly his theology of the two kingdoms.[80] According to Luther, Christians simultaneously lived under the authority of two domains or kingdoms—the spiritual kingdom (or the kingdom of God) and the secular or temporal one (or the kingdom of the world). While all Christians must be subject to the authority of both kingdoms, this authority encompassed strictly separate spheres, extending to distinct dimensions of Christian life. In matters of faith, the kingdom of God ruled over a Christian's inner person through the Word of God, while the kingdom of the world had legitimate authority over a Christian's outer person through secular rules and laws. Luther stressed that, while citizenship in the kingdom of God was eternal and spiritually preeminent, the outer person's citizenship in the temporal kingdom also held significant importance. Righteous civil authority restrained evil and oppression, curbed immorality, and protected the innocent; therefore, for Luther, the outer persons' participation in the affairs of the state could become a praiseworthy expression of Christian service to the neighbor.

While Luther's theology of the inner and outer person has not typically been extended to his theology of physical suffering, I propose that this dialectic can help elucidate the tensions inherent in Luther's teachings on the internal forbearance and external resistance of afflictions. In their inner persons, Christians must accept their suffering and endure it well by maintaining internal attitudes of patience, peace, hope, and above all, faith in God's benevolence toward them, despite their painful circumstances. According to Luther, although human reason, tainted by sin, would incline Christians to succumb to fear and despair, they must firmly cling to God's Word that suffering was not intended for their destruction but would ultimately somehow work for their good and their spiritual benefit. Christians should deliberately attend to the positive, spiritually formative role of bodily suffering for their inner persons, which can manifest in various ways, from serving as bitter medicine for the disease of sin to conforming them to Christ through the pains of persecution.

Nevertheless, while internally recognizing and welcoming the spiritual benefits of suffering and enduring it well, in their outer persons, Christians must not deliberately seek it out or impose it upon their bodies. Moreover, Luther taught that, when afflicted by physical suffering, Christians should purposefully and diligently utilize available means to resist it. To act otherwise would not only be imprudent but would also contradict the examples set in the Bible and potentially neglect divinely supplied means for deliverance from pain, destruction, and death. The use of medicine provided a way of fulfilling the spiritual obligation to outwardly resisting physical suffering.

3

EARLY MODERN REFORMATIONS OF MEDICINE

DURING THE SUMMER of 1530, while remaining at the halls of Coburg Castle under the protection of the Elector of Saxony, Luther embarked on the task of crafting a sermon urging Christian parents to ensure the education of their (male) children by keeping them at schools.[1] Just a few months earlier upon his arrival at Coburg, Luther had delivered there his renowned "Sermon on Cross and Suffering." Now, with the Diet of Augsburg in session and Luther previously declared an outlaw in the Holy Roman Empire, he was compelled to refrain from participating in the Diet's meetings, providing theological guidance from the safety of the Castle through his prolific writings. The issue of educating children held longstanding significance for Luther. The early stages of the Reformation initially had an adverse effect on schooling in German lands. The closure of Catholic churches and monasteries, along with their established schools, initially disrupted the educational opportunities previously available to children. This disruption was exacerbated by the slow pace of opening new Protestant schools, coupled with a rising wave of popular suspicion regarding traditional education and a growing sentiment that it was inconsequential compared to the more financially lucrative pursuits of trade or commerce.

Luther had already publicly stated his opinion about the rising anti-education sentiment in the previous year, by penning a preface for a book by his friend Justus Menius. In this preface, Luther described families who neglected to provide education for their children as "shameful, despicable, damnable parents who are no parents at all but despicable hogs and venomous beasts, devouring their own young," and vowed to deal with them more thoroughly in another book.[2] During his sojourn at Coburg Castle in the summer months of the following year, Luther fulfilled his promise by composing *A Sermon on Keeping Children in School*, which Luther intended

An earlier version of this chapter was published as an article in *Archive for Reformation History* 114, no. 1 (2023): 51–78.

to be immediately printed and widely distributed. It served as a sequel to Luther's 1524 treatise *To the Councilmen of All Cities in Germany* wherein he urged city magistrates to establish and maintain schools.[3] Luther's Coburg sermon went on to exhort parents to take advantage of these new schools for their offspring.

In addition to its praise of education, the *Sermon on Keeping Children in School* contained Luther's most explicit and extensive acclaim of the practice of medicine.[4] Luther expressed concern over who would fill the ranks of the next generation of physicians if boys were kept away from schools. He referred to physicians as "lords," in acknowledgment of the honorable and necessary nature of their work, validated by both experience and Scripture. In this regard, Luther cited the book of Ecclesiasticus, which, though considered deuterocanonical, he considered valuable for religious instruction. Luther emphasized that while human bodies were free gifts from God, the proper maintenance of these gifts required the training and expertise of doctors. He pondered whether pestilence, flu, and syphilis might be expressions of God's displeasure toward Germans' lack of gratitude for his gifts of healthy bodies, manifested in the popular neglect of schooling children so they would eventually be trained to properly steward these blessings as physicians.

Luther's praise of physicians was more modest in his private remarks, made in informal settings to his household and circle of friends, who recorded and later published them as Luther's "Table Talk."[5] As Luther aged and his health deteriorated, he was attended by some of the best German physicians of his era, who nevertheless struggled to cure him of his numerous maladies. "To live medically is to live wretchedly," Luther reportedly scoffed at a strict diet prescribed by his contemporary doctors, which reportedly led patients exhausted to the point of death but failed to heal their ailments.[6] However, despite his complaints about physicians' failures, Luther refrained from making broader claims about the futility of medicine in general.[7] Earlier, in his programmatic treatise *To the Christian Nobility of the German Nation Concerning the Reform of the Christian Estate,* Luther outlined his comprehensive proposed reform of university curricula in theology and law, while briefly mentioning that he left the task of reforming medical departments to physicians themselves.[8] In Luther scholarship, this stance once had led to a conclusion that Luther regarded the practice of medicine as ultimately irrelevant for theology.[9] While this conclusion was later refuted, scholarly investigations into Luther's theology of medicine have been notably scarce.[10]

This chapter will address this previously overlooked topic and investigate Luther's theological perspectives on medicine, with particular attention to his instructions regarding its proper use. While a number of Luther's works provide glimpses into his theology on medicine, I will focus on Luther's lectures on the Old Testament, where his theologizing about bodily healing and medicine was most developed. I will contend that Luther's instructions regarding the proper use of medicine should be understood in the context of his theology of means and, especially, of his original theology of idolatry, conceptualized as the misplaced trust in created entities rather than in their divine creator. Luther found in Old Testament narratives surprising examples that modeled the necessity of using medicine, while simultaneously maintaining emotional detachment from it and instead relying on God for healing. In addition to being theologically necessary to avoid idolatry, this emotional detachment was also rational, since, for Luther, medicine's healing abilities were spiritually supplied by God's Word.

Furthermore, I will contrast Luther's teachings on medicine with an alternative early modern Protestant view developed by a key figure in the Radical Reformation, Andreas Bodenstein von Karlstadt. I will argue that Karlstadt's Radical Protestant approach to medicine shared with Luther a foundational concern with misplaced trust but fundamentally differed in its understanding of how proper Christian trust ought to be expressed. The chapter will subsequently explore Luther's theology of other, nonmedical forms of healing, which he also approached through the lens of idolatry. I will show that Luther perceived supernatural, miraculous healing and natural medical healing as exhibiting a parallel causal structure. Both medical and miraculous healing derived their source from the same divine agency which was subsequently channeled through different kinds of created means. In conclusion, I will discuss Luther's vision of the cosmic spiritual warfare for human health, which has been raging between demonic and angelic forces since the dawn of human history.

Medicine and Healing in the Early Modern Era

In order to comprehend early modern religious teachings regarding medicine and healing, it is crucial to first understand the cultural milieu in which these teachings were produced. The onset of the sixteenth-century Protestant Reformations unfolded amid a transition from medieval naturalistic medicine to scientific medical knowledge. This transition commenced in the fifteenth century, witnessing the rise of "Renaissance anatomy," marked by advances in anatomical knowledge and a growing acceptance of dissection practices. A significant milestone in this transition was Andreas Vesalius's seminal work, *De Humani Corporis Fabrica*, published in 1543, three years before Luther's passing. Traditionally, this period of change has been seen as concluding with William Harvey's groundbreaking discovery of blood circulation, made public in 1628. However, it is worth noting that contemporary historical scholarship is reevaluating conventional narratives of "Renaissance anatomy" and the "scientific revolution." Instead of viewing the history of science and medicine as marked by distinct eras, modern research presents the history of medicine as a dynamic continuum, characterized by coexisting, competing, and often merging traditions. This more nuanced perspective challenges the notion of paradigm shifts in medical knowledge. With this in mind, we can understand medicine during Luther's time as influenced by new developments in anatomical knowledge while still deeply entrenched in medieval medical epistemology.

In the sixteenth century, the study of medicine comprised diverse ideas and methodologies drawn from various disciplines and intellectual pursuits. During Luther's lifetime, medicine had not yet embraced the scientific method, entailing the rigorous testing of hypotheses through experimentation. Instead, medical knowledge was informed by the theoretical precepts of natural philosophy, complemented by discoveries gained from observations, including based on increasingly more common dissections. In the Middle Ages, the synthesis of ancient Greek and medieval Arab medical texts translated into Latin formed the foundation of medical education at universities. During the Renaissance, the humanist curricular reform significantly influenced training of physicians. By emphasizing the study of ancient sources in their original languages, humanists rediscovered and expanded the previously known corpus of ancient medical sources written in

Greek. By reviving classical pedagogies, humanist curricula emphasized the importance of liberal arts, particularly rhetoric, for medical education. By the sixteenth-century, rhetorical eloquence was considered an essential skill for physicians' professional training.

Furthermore, astrology, which studied the impact of celestial bodies on human activities, was frequently connected to medicine. While Luther himself remained skeptical of astrology, it was perceived by many learned physicians as a respectable field of knowledge.[11] Alchemy, on the other hand, was generally disregarded by medical faculties at universities but was practiced in other contexts in relation to healing. Medical practice in Luther's time frequently intertwined religious and magical elements.[12] Naturalistic and religious healing methods were often employed concurrently, both by individuals and communities. For instance, as discussed earlier, during outbreaks of pestilence, people would engage in religious rituals such as penitential processions, alongside naturalistic attempts to halt its spread.

The Protestant Reformations also witnessed a transformation in medical charity. In the Middle Ages, works of medical charity were primarily carried out by monasteries. However, with the advent of Protestantism, this responsibility was increasingly shifting to the government. Starting from the sixteenth century, city magistrates began hiring city physicians. Their duties included providing medical care to the poor who could not otherwise afford their services, in addition to supervising sanitary conditions in the city and offering health advice to the authorities. Although the term *public health* did not appear until the early seventeenth century, the concept itself was already developing in the sixteenth. The nascent concern with the promotion of public health was linked to the Protestant Reformation's ideas about the Christian commonwealths' civic duty of poor relief.[13]

At the core of medical and other naturalist healing practices during Luther's era was a particular sixteenth-century perception of the human body. During the early Reformation and before Vesalius's groundbreaking discoveries made public in the 1540s, this perception was still firmly based on select works by second-century Greek physician and philosopher Galen.[14] It must be noted that the medieval Galenic system did not fully represent the writings of Galen himself. Until the mid-fifteenth century, physicians had access only to parts of Galen's prolific works, which had been transmitted into Latin through Arabic translations, often with additional Arabic influences. The medieval Galenic anatomical knowledge was established based on these sources. According to medieval Galenic anatomy, the body was composed of four fluid humors (phlegm, blood, black bile, and yellow bile), which respectively reflected the four elements of the natural world (water, air, earth, and fire). These humors were subsequently associated with specific pairs of natural qualities (cold and wet, hot and wet, cold and dry, hot and dry).

The Galenic system posited that harmony between the four humors, elements, and qualities resulted in good health. In contrast, an imbalance of humors was responsible for susceptibility to particular diseases and other health detriments. In addition, humoral balance was believed to influence personality and temperament, which also meant that the undue dominance of some humors or their combinations in the human body could impact behavior and emotional disposition. For instance, the insufficient presence of yellow bile, regarded as hot and dry, would negatively affect mental sharpness and intelligence, whereas the prevalence of blood, considered hot and wet, was linked to simplicity and a naive attitude.

In addition to the four fluid humors, the body was imagined as containing groups of organs governed by three "principal members." These principal members were the heart, the liver, and the brain, each possessing distinct operations and functions. The body also contained *spiritus* (pneuma), connecting the work of the soul with the work of the body. Vital pneuma was a source of life produced in the heart, transmitted through the body by arteries along with blood. Galen's model lacked the concept of a unified circulatory system. Instead, it proposed two separate vascular systems: veins carrying venous blood produced in the liver and arteries carrying blood mixed with pneuma produced in the heart. These systems generally remained separate. Blood was not moved by the heart but was "attracted" by organs needing it to receive nourishment. Additionally, nerves constituted a third system of vessels running through the body. They originated in the brain and produced psychic (or animal) pneuma.

The organs and four humors were responsible for the body's proper functions, termed "virtues" and classified into animal and natural. Natural virtues, such as growth, nutrition, and reproduction, were merely the products of nature and characterized both plants and animals. Animal virtues, such as sensation, thought, and voluntary motion, were governed by the brain, and, therefore, only peculiar to animals. Galen's understanding of virtues, their classification, and their assumed roles in bodily operations relied heavily on the highly theoretical framework posed by Plato. Notably, Galen saw himself as a physician-philosopher and argued for the synthesis of knowledge of the human body and a love for philosophy in the making of a good physician, a notion resonating with medieval medical education.

While Galen's approach to functional anatomy was based on Plato's speculative writings on the human soul, his study of gross anatomy was informed by the practice of dissection. In his book, *On Anatomical Procedures*, Galen advocated for dissections' crucial role for medical knowledge, outlining specific steps in conducting them, while emphasizing the guiding principle of "seeing for oneself."[15] Contrary to a common myth that the medieval Church prohibited dissections, Galen's insistence on "seeing for yourself" was not rejected by late medieval anatomy. The dissections of animal and—since 1315—of human cadavers were occasionally performed and officially recorded in late medieval Europe; during the Renaissance, their importance for the study of anatomy was increasingly emphasized.[16] Nevertheless, it was not until the mid-sixteenth century that dissections became a regular part of medical curricula at universities. This was partly due to practical difficulties in obtaining corpses that could be used for this purpose and due to challenges of preserving them for a sufficient time to allow for the procedure to be publicly performed. Additionally, in the late Middle Ages, dissection was perceived as a repulsive practice, commonly performed by assistants, while the medical training of physicians remained largely theoretical and lecture-based.

In 1453, following the fall of Constantinople, the Latin West received an influx of ancient Greek writings imported from the East, including the full surviving collection of Galen's works. Owing to the efforts of Renaissance humanists, the entire corpus of Galen's works was translated into Latin, compared with previously available Arabic translations, and widely disseminated. This newfound access to Galen's complete works, along with the Renaissance's artistic focus on accurate visual representation of human bodies, played a crucial role in the development of what historians now term

"Renaissance anatomy." The pinnacle of "Renaissance anatomy" was the 1543 publication of *De humani corporis fabrica libri septem* (*On the Fabric of the Human Body in Seven Books*) by Andreas Vesalius. Appearing three years before Luther's death, this work presented a detailed description of human anatomy with intricate illustrations based on Vesalius's extensive dissections of human bodies.[17] While Vesalius has been hailed as the pioneer of modern anatomy, he himself viewed his work as a reform of the Galenic tradition, not a break away from it.[18] Indeed, rather than presenting a radical departure from medieval Galenic knowledge, "Renaissance anatomy" was understood by its proponents as a stage of "new Galenism," seeking to rectify the mistakes of medieval anatomy and further develop it in line with Galen's own principles.

While generally only learned physicians possessed a detailed understanding of medieval anatomy, a basic Galenic view of the human body was common cultural knowledge in Luther's era. Luther's contemporaries believed that their bodies contained four types of fluid humors in perpetual motion. They also shared the assumption that disease or other health detriments were caused by an imbalance of these humors. Consequently, the approach to physical healing, whether practiced by a learned practitioner or a family member, was to recover the proper balance between humors, by restoring the proper circulation of fluids within the body.

The circulation of bodily fluids was commonly assessed through paying attention to urine, sweat, stool, or menstrual blood. Their obstructions or surpluses were deemed perilous and required attention. Therefore, practices such as bloodletting, expectorating, purging, and inducing sweating formed the cornerstone of sixteenth-century treatments. Herbs were also utilized extensively, both internally and externally. In addition, various environmental factors, including weather, air, climate, or the season of the year were considered potential influencers on humoral balance. Healing practices aimed to rebalance bodily fluids by adjusting one's exposure to certain environments. Excessive and inordinate passions were viewed as culprits for humoral harmony, while moderation was esteemed and promoted as beneficial for health. In early modern medicine, the distinction between preventative and therapeutic approaches was often blurred. Since external and environmental factors were seen as affecting humoral balance, alterations in diet, habits, daily routines, and exercise were considered therapeutic and used to treat illnesses. Finally, diseases were treated by "transferring" them to objects or substances possessing similar or opposite properties. For example, a red rash or bloody discharges could be treated by proximity with or application of red-colored plants, food, or wine.[19]

Since early modern Europeans viewed disease as a unique imbalance within each affected body, this individual nature of disease necessitated an individualized nature of treatment. Taking into account a sick person's "constitution" was crucial for appropriately modifying cures. Constitution was one's physical makeup, reflecting the assumed composition of their body, humors, and temperament, popularly understood and described in terms such as "strong," "delicate," or "feeble."[20] Although primarily determined at birth, constitution was also influenced by habits, life events, and experiences. Differences in constitution between individuals explained why some were more prone to contracting diseases while others remained unaffected despite exposure. Depending on the constitution, a treatment beneficial for one person could be harmful to another.

In the Reformation era, most illnesses were treated within the household. Medical advice was typically sought and circulated within the immediate and extended family, including seeking the opinions and experiences of neighbors and friends. Medical knowledge was transmitted within families from one generation to the next. A notable influence on home-based medical knowledge and practice during Luther's time stemmed from the growing adoption of printing press technology, which enabled the dissemination of medical guidance literature aimed at the general public. These popular medical works offered counsel on hygiene, health preservation, and household treatments. By the mid-sixteenth century, they were widely printed and found in many homes.

While women were not formally trained in medicine, they took on the primary responsibility for domestic cures, thus playing a central role in early modern healing and health promotion.[21] Basic family treatments were typically plant-based, and most women knew how to use local herbs to relieve fever and alleviate common medical conditions. At home, women dressed wounds and made salves for cuts and burns. Additionally, outside of their immediate households, they served as midwives, assisting with labor preparation, childbirth, and some postnatal care. Unlike other types of early modern healing practitioners, sixteenth-century midwives were neither formally trained nor part of a guild. They learned their craft through informal apprenticeships with an older and more experienced midwife from their community.

Sixteenth-century naturalistic healing was often intertwined with the supernatural, including religious and magical practices. This included prayer, and, especially in Catholic areas, supplication to saints, pilgrimages, and the use of sacramental and other elements as healing objects. As previously discussed, different saints were believed to possess the power to address various illnesses. Magical healing frequently involved the use of charms, amulets, and incantations. A variety of folk healers without formal training practiced in their communities, relying on experience. They blended knowledge of herbal medicine and the ability to treat simple wounds with forms of magic. Curiously, executioners also provided some basic folk medicine. Often doubling as torturers, executioners knew how to both inflict wounds and how to treat them. Additionally, albeit illegally, they sold certain parts of executed individuals' bodies, such as hair, which were believed to possess medicinal powers.

In contrast to the "unlearned" folk healers, trained practitioners of early modern medicine included various structured groups, such as apothecaries, surgeons, barber-surgeons, and university-educated physicians.[22] With the exception of physicians, these groups operated by organizing themselves into guilds. Early modern guilds served as more than just trade associations. Their members were expected to share a particular way of life, both professionally and socially. As previously discussed, in the absence of formal licensure, guilds maintained professional standards, ensuring that only those who achieved an acceptable level of training and knowledge were allowed to practice. This concern for the integrity of practice also served to bar outsiders and suppress competition. Relatedly, guilds functioned as the custodians of medical knowledge, with medical recipes kept secret and transmitted only within particular families or the guild. By Luther's lifetime, it became virtually impossible for a woman to join a professional guild, and they were excluded from healing professions other than midwifery.

A number of early modern medical practitioners were itinerant, except for apothecaries, who were always settled in a particular place and ran their practices out of their apothecary shops. In many communities, apothecaries were not merely pharmacists but also fulfilled the role of medical providers. Apothecaries made syrups, oral drugs, poultices, and plasters using a variety of ingredients. Their recipes were elaborate and could include dozens of elements. They utilized herbs, roots, and other natural substances, including, from a modern perspective, seemingly odd ones, like animal excrements or mouse tails. Starting from the sixteenth century, apothecaries increasingly used chemical ingredients such as mercury. It was occasionally possible for an apothecary's widow to run a shop she inherited from her husband, though only with the help of male partners, belonging to a guild.

While apothecaries provided medicines and administered simple treatments, for more complex bodily manipulations, early modern people typically sought the help of surgeons. Like apothecaries, surgeons learned their skills through apprenticeships within their guilds, providing training, ensuring the quality of practice, and protecting surgical knowledge from outsiders. Specific surgical techniques were considered secrets, meticulously guarded by families and guilds, and passed down to the next generations with great care. Surgery was frequently a family business, with sons following in their fathers' footsteps. The scope of sixteenth-century surgery was limited and primarily focused on limbs; many surgeries were amputations. Like many other medical procedures, in the absence of anesthesia and painkillers, surgery was excruciatingly painful and dangerous, often leaving patients at risk of infections.

Surgeons and barber-surgeons belonged to separate guilds, with the latter considered a less trained group. As the name suggests, they were barbers who were also taught to conduct simple surgical interventions. Barber-surgeons pulled teeth and performed the common early modern procedure of bloodletting. Military and navy employed their own surgeons, and early modern warfare, with its acute need for treating battlefield wounds, significantly contributed to the development of surgical techniques.

In Luther's era, compared to other medical practitioners, common people were the least likely to consult university-educated physicians. Physicians' services were expensive, and there was a cultural chasm between learned doctors and the predominantly illiterate general populace. University education for physicians in Luther's era typically lasted four years and was primarily theoretical and lecture-based. All university students were male, and most of those studying medicine came from the middle class, as the cost of higher education was prohibitive for the poor and few wealthy nobles chose to pursue a medical career. The curriculum relied heavily on memorization and repetition, with each year building upon and expanding the material from the previous year. Students were required to memorize definitions and, at the end of their studies, defend a master's thesis, demonstrating their rhetorical skills. Students also attended public dissections, albeit infrequently. While physicians in training were encouraged to seek practical apprenticeships, and many did, practical learning was not a required component of university education. Consequently, compared to other healers, physicians were often recognized more for their "learnedness" in medical matters rather than for superior practical skills.

Physicians were typically called upon to treat painful or dangerous maladies that sufferers and their families, based on experience, did not expect to simply run their course and for which they could not get help elsewhere. Early modern physicians would typically travel to visit the sick in their homes. The diagnostic processes varied drastically from contemporary ones, concerned with identifying signs and symptoms shared among affected individuals. In contrast, as previously mentioned, early modern disease was considered unique to each patient. With little insight available into the internal workings of the body, medicine emphasized making a diagnosis based on external signs, typically through observation and examination of the patient's body or excrements by hand. Furthermore, as Mary Lindemann showed, early modern doctors employed qualitative descriptions rather than quantitative assessment techniques. For example, instead of measuring the pulse in beats per minute, they would define it as rapid, fluttering, feeble, or pounding. Finally, listening to the patient's narrative was crucial for determining the problem and the individualized course of treatment.

Martin Luther's Theology of Medicine

Against this cultural background, Luther developed his religious teachings on medicine, which were primarily based on his interpretation of biblical stories of healing. For Luther, scriptural engagements with the subject were not just responses to their own contexts but written to provide valuable lessons to future generations of the church. Particularly important for Luther's medical biblical theology were the accounts of King Hezekiah's illness and recovery as narrated in Isaiah 38 and 2 Kings 20, with a brief mention in 2 Chronicles 32:24. Despite some differences in the narrative structures of these accounts, Luther read them as telling the same story, which he exegeted in his 1527–1530 lectures on Isaiah.[23]

Luther's retelling of Isaiah 38 began with a serious illness afflicting King Hezekiah. Urging the king to arrange his affairs, the prophet Isaiah warned him of his imminent death. In deep distress, the weeping Hezekiah fervently prayed to God. In response to the king's desperate supplication, Isaiah received a divine promise that God would heal him, prolong his life by an additional fifteen years, and even defend his city against its enemies. Isaiah ordered a lump of figs to be applied to Hezekiah's boil, resulting in his recovery. The grateful king offered God a song of praise, recounting his sorrow in illness and his appeal for divine healing.

Luther interpreted Isaiah 38 as explaining the appropriate understanding and use of medicine to past and future audiences of the Bible. In his song of praise, Hezekiah recalled his despair after the initial failure of human means of healing. But then God spoke, to which Hezekiah credited his recovery. Therefore, Luther read the passage as comparing the life-giving power of human things with the life-giving power of the Word of God. Luther interpreted Hezekiah's own acknowledgment in Isaiah 38:16, "Lord, by these things people live," as crediting life to the earlier mentioned divine speech.[24] Luther's Hezekiah communicated a theological insight that, rather than being created, sustained, and restored through the power of material processes, human life depended on the power of the divine Word. Therefore, Luther drew the following conclusion for his audience:

> *So here the king knows by experience that there is no power to heal in the medicine, but there is power in the Word, just as nourishment is not a matter of bread and food, but of the Word. The Word accomplishes marvelous things in the human body. Not medicines and food, but only the Word changes the body [. . .].*

> *Though we should swallow all kinds of medicine, it accomplishes nothing without the Word.*[25]

In order to understand Luther's argument linking the sustenance and restoration of physical life to the divine Word, we must consider the multivalent meanings of the "Word" in Luther's theology, particularly in its relation to his understanding of causality and created means. For Luther, first and foremost, Jesus Christ was God's uncreated, enfleshed, and self-revelatory Word, the logos of John 1. Christ the divine Logos both communicated and effectuated the gospel or God's promises, which Luther also referred to as God's Word. Furthermore, Luther contrasted the fundamental functions of human words and the divine Word.[26] As David Steinmetz explained, human words were discursive "call-words" (Heissel-Wörter), utterances whose role was limited to naming already-existing things. In contrast, God's Word was the active and generative "deed-word" (*Thettel-Wort*).[27] A key biblical text for Luther's theology of *Thettel-Wort* was Genesis 1, according to which God created by speaking. Using Genesis 1 together with John 5:17, Luther developed a robust theology of the Word as both creative and perpetually active in, within, and through creation.

Luther resisted a possible inference that, once God launched into motion natural processes in Genesis 1, he subsequently allowed creation to function on its own, according to divinely set patterns. On the contrary, the uncreated Word was always working as the first cause immanent within the created means. While created means obscured to human sight the Word's presence and work in and through these means, this invisible activity was nevertheless real and perceivable by a believer through faith.[28] Luther's theological vision of medicine outlined in his lectures on Isaiah 38 reflected his overarching understanding of causality. The efficacy of medicine was perpetually conditioned upon the fundamental power of the healing divine Word working through it.

While ascribing the power to heal to the Word, Luther nevertheless insisted that medicine had to be employed as created means for enacting divine healing. Having promised Hezekiah recovery, God did not produce it in a direct and unmediated way. Rather, Isaiah was able to successfully treat the king's inflammation through an application of figs, which Luther perceived as a natural medicine for poulticing the king's boil. For Luther, Isaiah's use of medicine served to preemptively respond to future skeptics who, while correctly acknowledging that the primary healing power resided with the Word, would otherwise wrongly hesitate to use medicine. It is for that reason that Isaiah engaged in medical work. He was the biblical archetype of a physician. Luther used Isaiah's medical practice to outline (somewhat erratically) his instructions regarding medicine:

> *Here Isaiah was made a physician. Here the physicians have their patron saint. For you heard in the song above [Isa. 38:10–20] that all things are kept and cared for by the Word. Then the ungodly cry: "If the Word does everything and provides nourishment for everything, we do not want to eat or take medicine." For them he takes up this example. As for you, make use of means. Do not rely on them but use them, since God has created them. If they do not help, commit the matter to God. Do not say: "Doctor, if this will not help this time, I refuse to take it anymore." Yes, you want to have your own way! So we all go beyond the proper use of means by clinging to them, as our papists altogether cling to works. Others despise works altogether, so does this song ascribe the power to the Word and not to the medicine. Yet it does not forbid that we use them, but the prophet's example supports their use, since he poultices the wound with a cake of figs.*

In this commentary, Luther formulated his own medical-theological principle, which became the hermeneutical center of his commentary on Isaiah 38: "Use medicines, but do not rely on them; rely on God."[29] Luther outlined this in response to what he saw as two prevalent errors. The first error was using medicine with an improper affective disposition, which Luther described as "clinging" or, elsewhere in Isaiah, as "trusting" or "relying" on medicine for healing.[30] Luther acknowledged that such misuse of medicine could be committed by anyone, but he specifically cited it as illustrative of medieval Catholicism. According to Luther, this misdirected reliance paralleled what he viewed as the mistaken Catholic reliance on human works to achieve what was solely accomplished by God. The critique of such misuse of medicine was an expression of Luther's broader attack on the medieval tradition that he saw as promoting trust in human works instead of God's grace and power alone.

The second error was "despising" or rejecting medicine on spiritual grounds by the so-called ungodly.[31] They were likely members of the Radical Reformation, with whom Luther had been engaged in an extensive public argument about the role of created means in the life of a Christian. While correctly ascribing all healing power to the Word, "the ungodly" consequently erroneously rejected the importance of created means and purportedly concluded that medicine was unnecessary. Luther's mocking portrayal of this group's alleged refusal to take medicine or even eat suggests a reference to his reported dispute with Andreas Karlstadt, revealing competing religious approaches to the role and use of medicine among early Protestants.[32]

Andreas Karlstadt's Radical Alternative

Andreas Bodenstein von Karlstadt (1486–1541) was once Luther's colleague on the theological faculty at the University of Wittenberg.[33] Initially opposed to Luther's emerging reform ideas, Karlstadt eventually became an ally during the controversy over indulgences in 1517 and later an ardent supporter of Luther's teachings on justification by faith. Karlstadt led the early Reformation in Wittenberg while Luther was hiding in Wartburg Castle in 1520–21 after being excommunicated at the Diet of Worms. However, their close alliance began to fracture when Karlstadt, in Luther's absence, implemented a series of what Luther considered dangerously radical reforms. Within two years of his removal by Luther from the Reformation leadership, Karlstadt abandoned his professorship at the University of Wittenberg and moved to the countryside, becoming a pastor at a local parish in Orlamünde. During this time, Karlstadt published his programmatic treatise *The Meaning of the Term Gelassen and Where in Holy Scripture It is Found* under the pseudonym "the new layman."[34]

This treatise was deeply influenced by the medieval German mystical tradition from which Karlstadt had derived the theological concept of *Gelassenheit* ("abandonment" or "yieldedness").[35] According to medieval German mystical writings, the way of Christian faith required the intellectual and emotional abandonment of every desire and attachment to anything other than God.[36] The Christian soul needed to be emptied or cleansed of all worldly attachments in order to make room for God's direct work on the soul, so that such a "yielded" soul could achieve complete unity with the divine. Karlstadt's work focused on the meaning and pursuit of such Christian "yieldedness."

Luther shared Karlstadt's theological appreciation of German mystical tradition. Luther's theology was particularly indebted to the teachings inspired by the early fourteenth-century German mystic Meister Eckhart, such as the work of Eckhart's student Johannes Tauler, whom Luther highly praised.[37] Luther also popularized an anonymous fourteenth- or fifteenth-century German mystical treatise in the post-Eckhartian tradition, which he initially erroneously attributed to Tauler and which he published in two editions, accompanied by his own prefaces, under the title *Theologia Germanica*.[38] Luther ranked this mystical treatise, also exploring the concept of Christian "abandonment," as third in influence on his thinking, following the Bible and Augustine. However, although both Luther and Karlstadt shared a significant theological interest in the medieval mystical idea of Christian "yieldedness," unlike Luther, Karlstadt developed a radical approach to applying the idea of "yieldedness" to the daily life of a Christian.

For example, in the *Meaning of the Term Gelassen and Where in Holy Scripture It is Found*, Karlstadt taught that the pursuit of Christian abandonment also required a detachment from valuing and actively seeking external means. As a recurrent illustration, Karlstadt utilized a common sixteenth-century concern over not having sufficient food.[39] While Karlstadt acknowledged the practical necessity of food for survival, he condemned the worry about meeting this need as "unyielded" and therefore sinful. He frequently summarized, paraphrased, and directly quoted Jesus's admonitions against anxiety about food and clothing, emphasizing God's fatherly care for his followers. Karlstadt interpreted this as a Scriptural mandate for Christians to detach from concerns over sufficiently meeting their physical needs.

Moreover, Karlstadt taught that true surrender of all created things should ultimately result in a yielded person no longer taking pleasure in eating. By losing its enjoyable quality, eating would be appropriately reduced to merely addressing a basic and low physical necessity. Finally, in one's progress toward a greater yieldedness, the tasks of material provisions would also eventually lose their urgency, as unrelated to the all-consuming spiritual orientation of a yielded life. He pointed to the example of horses and mules, who, according to Karlstadt, did not concern themselves with food but knew that God or their masters would feed them. Karlstadt emphasized that God would take care of supplying physical nourishment for God's children, although possibly a meager one, as was often the case. For Karlstadt, such attitudes of "abandonment" were essential practical expressions and indicators of maintaining faith and trust in God's fatherly benevolence. According to Karlstadt, any "unyieldedness" regarding the deficiency of food could only stem from the deficiency of faith.[40]

Furthermore, Karlstadt called for what he termed the "yieldedness" of intellect. In *The Meaning of the Term Gelassen*, he summarized the problems arising from the lack of mental surrender as follows:

> *Human beings have intellect which enables them to be wise and to plan ahead. It allows them to build cities and houses, to make weapons and all kinds of protection. This leads people to become rather unyielded when they ought to leave shelter and protection to God and not to seek more. I could demonstrate this by reference to several prophets, but I won't for the sake of brevity, and merely refer to what God says, "You put your trust in your own defenses which you made for yourselves," (Jeremiah 48:7; Isa 2:11, 17; 9:5; 16:8; 31:3). Therefore God will forsake you and surrender you to your enemies. Thus many princes and warriors were destroyed who might otherwise have survived and recovered before God.*[41]

This brief deliberation also highlighted Karlstadt's teachings regarding the avoidance of harm and response to threats. Actively attempting to prevent or stop potential dangers, including by planning ahead, building shelter, or making weapons, was a natural inclination of the human mind. Nevertheless, it could be a spiritually suspicious or even downright harmful activity. For Karlstadt, a yielded mind "leave[s] shelter and protection to God."[42]

Immediately following his discussion on the "yieldedness" of intellect, Karlstadt explicitly invoked medicine. He referenced the Old Testament story in 1 Samuel 17 of David killing Goliath with a simple slingshot, as opposed to using a regular weapon, such as a sword or a bow. "That is a simple matter and not worth writing about," wrote Karlstadt regarding David's choice of arms. "But the sick should take notice who put a deceptive trust in doctors and herbal medicine (2 Chronicles 16:12)." Karlstadt cut off this discussion with a warning: "Hence, all external things are to be clearly avoided and yielded, so that they might not deceive us as the Jews were deceived who said, 'The temple of the Lord, the temple of the Lord'—*templum domini, templum domini*, Jer 7:4 or who fled to the ark, Jer 3:16."[43]

What did Karlstadt attempt to communicate about medicine through this collection of Scriptural references, found in a crucial part of his treatise addressing the "yieldedness" of the intellect? The Biblical account implied that the young David's choice of this seemingly inadequate weapon was due to his familiarity with it as a traditional shepherd's tool, as opposed to his likely inexperience with a sword and heavy armor. However, Karlstadt interpreted the story as signifying David's deliberate abandonment of conventional weapons in favor of something ill-suited for a battle, while trusting in God's help. Karlstadt used this as a paradigmatic model to discourage the sick from relying on medicine and physicians. In support, he also referenced a passage from 2 Chronicles 16:12. This passage implicitly condemned Judah's King Asa, who, after developing a severe foot ailment, "even in his disease he did not seek the Lord, but sought help from physicians." Unlike David, who trusted God's supernatural assistance over the power of a man-made weapon, Asa looked for help from physicians rather than appealing to God.

Karlstadt believed that proper Christian trust must be directed at God and away from external means. Moreover, for him, a Christian posture of not trusting external means involved more than emotional detachment; it called for their practical abandonment. The more one emotionally detached from and practically set aside the use of created things, the greater one's trust became in the availability of divine intervention, unmediated by anything external and material. Such trust would lead to an emotionally and practically "yielded" reliance on God's action. Conversely, active, practical employment of external means ultimately indicated a lack of proper Christian trust and "yieldedness." Therefore, Karlstadt was deeply suspicious and, at times, outright discouraging of intentionally planning and seeking ways to provide for one's physical needs, taking precautions against health hazards and using medicine in times of sickness.

Karlstadt's strong suspicion of external means had to be reconciled with the reality that employing at least some created means was necessary for maintaining physical life, compelling him to affirm their limited use. However, such use had to occur without attachment or enjoyment, with the fear of God, and, crucially, out of sheer necessity. For instance, Karlstadt stated that, when eating, one must do it as a sick person who took his food fearfully, without joy or want, and purely as medicine for survival.[44] While this passage addressed the use of food, it also implied that Karlstadt did not explicitly condemn the use of medicine altogether. Moreover, in his 1524 treatise *Regarding the Sabbath and Statutory Holy Days*, he listed gathering herbs to prepare medicine for the sick among acceptable Christian activities.[45] However, as his treatise on the *Meaning of the Term Gelassen* suggested, one had to exercise spiritual caution in using medicine, as it had the potential to mislead its users.

Like other "external" means, medicine posed a potential spiritual threat of deception. To illustrate this, Karlstadt briefly referenced two Old Testament passages without actually quoting them. Jeremiah 7:4 critiqued the misguided reliance on the physical building of the temple by the people of Judah, who interpreted it as proof of God's continuing presence with their nation. Jeremiah 3:16 claimed that in the days of restoration and glorification of the embattled city of Jerusalem, the ark of the Covenant, once believed to house the God of Israel, would lose its sacred importance. Both passages spoke of the already occurred or impending desacralization of key material objects associated with ancient Jewish worship. Karlstadt believed this indicated that divine presence had no longer been associated with or bound by human-made creations, even with a presumed religious significance.

For Karlstadt, these passages delivered a crushing biblical blow to an assumed connection between the material world and divine action. Material objects and practices associated with them still suggested the reality of such a connection, thus deceiving Christians as they once deceived Old Testament Jews. Karlstadt consistently denied the significance of the material world for spiritual purposes, reluctantly allowing exception only for Scripture. However, in his *Meaning of the Term Gelassen*, Karlstadt demanded that even the Bible ultimately must be yielded in favor of the Spirit's direct teaching to the soul, unmediated by this material book. Karlstadt emphasized that John

6:63 taught that flesh profited nothing with regard to matters of the Spirit. In line with this, medicine and its practice were ultimately the work of the flesh and for the flesh. While it could be used in some circumstances, medicine was a created means, posing a threat of possible spiritual deception, and therefore should ultimately be yielded and avoided. Karlstadt's theological suspicion of medicine was profoundly grounded in his broader theology of means.

Medicine, Means, and Idolatry

Like Karlstadt, Luther's theology of medicine was also deeply rooted in his theology of means. However, Luther's approach to means differed dramatically from the one developed by Karlstadt and led him to different conclusions. Per the earlier discussion of causality, for Luther, while God's Word remained the first cause of all things, the Word typically accomplished divine goals in creation by working in and through created means.[46] For example, the words of the Bible, the flesh of Christ, and the material elements of the sacraments were all divinely used to render saving grace. Similarly, the ever-active Word utilized external means in order to govern and preserve creation. Luther saw this as both acknowledged in the Bible and confirmed by experience. From the beginning of time until the present day, the Word continued to use food to satisfy people's hunger, the sun and fire to keep them warm, and medicine to heal them.[47]

For Luther, God's original intent for humankind was likewise to employ means in order to produce, restore, and sustain creation.[48] In Genesis 2:15, God charged Adam with tilling and keeping the garden of Eden. Luther vividly imagined Adam sowing seeds, digging the ground, and even "planting little plots of aromatic herbs" throughout the garden in order to eventually reap abundant crops. For Luther, the Bible testified that, with the progression of history, God had increasingly involved his creatures (both people and angels) as co-laborers in divine work, as stated by Paul in 1 Corinthians 3:9.[49]

Luther repeatedly stressed that God's employment of people and material means for his purposes was a matter of divine preference, not compulsion. In this respect, Luther drew upon and constructively developed a well-established distinction in medieval theology between God's absolute and ordained power.[50] This classical medieval distinction, notably outlined by Thomas Aquinas and utilized by a number of high medieval theologians, understood God's "ordained" power as the power God chose to exercise in the created world.[51] In contrast, God's absolute power encompassed a range of alternative possibilities for the manifestation of divine power, which God had not pursued.

Aquinas affirmed that God could have chosen—and still has the ability to do—what God has opted not to do, thus making God's absolute power literally absolute. However, God's choice of manifestations of his ordained power was not determined solely by the unrestricted freedom of divine will. In addition to affirming the principle of noncontradiction as bearing upon divine action, Aquinas also spoke of divine goodness, justice, and particularly wisdom as factors influencing why God chose to and continues to act as God does. For Aquinas, although God's goodness, justice, and particularly wisdom did not necessitate God creating and redeeming the world in a specific way, the creation and redemption as established by God were not merely contingent. Instead, God's ordained power manifested through them expressed divine character.

This classical distinction between God's ordained and absolute powers had been subsequently developed in the Scotist, and especially the late medieval Nominalist, schools of thought. In particular, the pioneer of Nominalism, William of Ockham, made this dialectic a core principle in his theology. In reaction to earlier condemnations of radical Aristotelian thought in Christian theology, which stressed determinism, while still adhering to the principle of noncontradiction of divine action, Ockham emphasized God's supreme freedom. God's ordained power was radically contingent in the sense that God could have freely chosen, and could still choose, any other way of manifesting it. Unlike Aquinas, Ockham rejected the possibility of God's ordained power being influenced by God's goodness, justice, and wisdom. For him, the expressions of divine ordained power were grounded in the supreme freedom of divine will, which alone determined what was good, just, or wise.

These philosophical explorations of divine will and action ultimately probed the question of the contingency of human salvation and whether God had been limited in his options for how to redeem humanity. In a series of claims, which provoked their share of his contemporaries' outrage, Ockham claimed that God could have chosen to become incarnate not in a man, but in a stone, or could have required individuals to hate, rather than love, him as a condition of salvation.[52] A century after Ockham's death, his famed intellectual admirer, Gabriel Biel, developed, systematized, and further popularized his intellectual mentor's thought, including teachings on the contingency of divine power. However, for Biel, God's absolute power did not merely encompass a wide array of noncontradictory possibilities, some of which God might still choose to pursue according to the absolute freedom of divine will. Rather than remaining hypothetical, manifestations of God's absolute power occasionally broke into the created world, which otherwise functioned according to God's ordained power. Biel cited the examples of the immaculate conception of Mary and of Paul receiving the blessed vision of Christ while still a sinner on the road to Damascus as instances where God's absolute power circumvented the order established by his ordained power.

Having been schooled in nominalism and Biel's teachings earlier in his life, Luther the reformer became vigorously critical of their many aspects. However, he preserved the nominalist distinction between God's absolute and ordained power, although he constructively modified it. Affirming the medieval understanding of God's ordained power as God's chosen mode of power manifested in creation, redemption, and other divine activities in this world, Luther further characterized God's ordained power as typically operating through the mediation of created means and beings, including human works and activities. God's choice to use the mediation of his creation for channeling his ordained power was not a matter of compulsion but of divine preference. Furthermore, God's ordained power was manifested through the regular causal effects of created means. For instance, the warming—or burning—effects of the sun, fire, and even candles were expressions of God's ordained power, which established these means to provide his creatures with light and warmth.

Like Biel, Luther thought that God might, albeit uncommonly, choose to exercise his absolute power, extending or even circumventing the regular causal effects of created means and human efforts. Common sense understood such manifestations of divine absolute power as miracles. Luther recognized that Scripture recorded stories of miraculous deliverances when rescue through ordinary means was simply unfeasible, such as supplying manna to the Israelites in the desert or preserving Jonah inside the whale. However, for Luther, God's provision for people's needs through miraculous interventions of his absolute power were primarily (though not exclusively) a matter of the distant past. Over time, God's preferred method of exercising his power had been through ordinary means. For example, while God initially created man from the Earth and a woman from his rib, he subsequently desired to have new people formed by means of the unions of men and women. Luther saw this current divine preference also recognized by Augustine who taught that God governed the world by allowing his creatures to function through the exercise of their distinctive activities.[53] In addition to the authority of Augustine, Luther believed that his teachings on God's ordained power being primarily expressed through means were also confirmed experientially. It was basic knowledge that one had to get near fire if feeling cold, or eat food if feeling hungry, rather than waiting for God's supernatural intervention to meet these needs.

In light of his emphasis on God's preference to exercise divine ordained power through ordinary means, Luther concluded that expectations of miracles through appeals to God's absolute power should become the recourse for Christians only after ordinary means designated by God's ordained power had been unsuccessfully tried and exhausted.[54] Luther also applied this principle to medicine. He was concerned that a correct acknowledgment of God's absolute power over everything might lead to an erroneously passive attitude, based on the assumption that "If God wants to preserve me, I will survive in a time of famine and plague even without food and medicine; but if I am to perish, all those things will not help at all."[55] For Luther, this was a misdirected and presumptuous expression of faith, focusing on God's absolute power manifested in miracles. In contrast, proper faith had to utilize God's ordained power manifested through ordinary means, including the use of medicine. Luther insisted that people "must keep the ordered [ordained] power in mind and form our opinion on the basis of it" and that God "does not command us to act in accordance with this absolute power, for He wants us to act in accordance with the ordered [ordained] power."[56] If medical means failed to produce recovery (a common occurrence in sixteenth-century Europe), then the sick ought to pray earnestly and with endurance for a possible miraculous healing while also not abandoning too quickly their efforts to be healed medically.[57]

For Luther, the Bible, particularly the stories of the patriarchs in Genesis, endorsed this vision for the use of means. The Old Testament patriarchs had to work the ground, tend cattle, grow and buy food, and otherwise ensure their own and their households' physical survival and sustenance using regular means. When faced with severe famine in the land of Canaan, patriarch Jacob sent his sons to Egypt twice to procure grain, the second time accompanied by his favorite youngest offspring Benjamin, despite feeling significant emotional reluctance. As the recipient of God's special promises and a descendant of Abraham and Isaac, Jacob could have been especially assured in his family's divinely warranted survival and prone to trust in God's miraculous deliverance of his family from famine, without pursuing the regular opportunities of obtaining food, which were practically and emotionally challenging. Although Luther's Jacob prayed in faith and clung to God's promises, he nevertheless had to use common, established means for preserving and feeding his household, just like his heathen neighbors. Similarly, God could have saved Noah, Noah's family, and all the animals from the impending flood by supernaturally keeping them alive without an ark. Nevertheless, God tasked Noah with working for his and others' preservation, by building a giant boat, using particular materials and measurements well suited for the purpose. God also did not wish for Luther's Noah to sit around in the floating ark waiting for a miraculous supply of food. On the contrary, God tasked him with an important responsibility to collect and store sufficient and appropriate provisions for all inhabitants of the ark.

In sum, from the Bible, tradition, and experience, Luther concluded that commonly "God makes use of definite means and tones down His miracles in such a manner that He makes use of the service of nature and of natural means."[58] Consequently, Christians were to do likewise, by not expecting miraculous interventions of God's absolute power but instead utilizing created means with gratitude to their creator, as illustrated by the stories of the patriarchs and later confirmed by 1 Timothy 4:4–5. This overarching principle also extended to the use of medicine, as Luther specified in his commentary on the story of Noah. According to Luther, like all other means, "the use of medicine is permitted, yes even necessary; for it is the means created for the preservation of health."[59]

While Luther's theology of means supplied the first context informing his theology of medicine, the second context was provided by his theology of idolatry.[60] As discussed earlier, Luther rejected the late medieval typology of different forms of faith. For Luther, Christian faith was trust in God's promises, including the incredible promises to forgive and justify sinners on account of their faith alone. True faith relied on God as the only source of salvation, goodness, and benevolence "for us." Human reliance on anything other than God was the affective disposition contrary to faith. Luther conceptualized such misplaced trust in created means rather than in their divine creator as idolatry.

A concern with idolatry was crucial for Luther's theological thought. While this concern was expressed throughout his writings over the years, Luther's 1530 *Large Catechism* remains a good reference point for a summary of his theology of idolatry.[61] In his exposition of the first commandment ("You shall have no other gods before me"), Luther thus outlined his vision of faith, trust, and idolatry:

> *A "god" is the term for that to which we are to look for all good and in which we are to find refuge in all need. Therefore, to have a god is nothing else than to trust and believe in that one with your whole heart. As I have often said, it is the trust and faith of the heart alone that make both God and an idol. If your faith and trust are right, then your God is the true one. Conversely, where your trust is false and wrong, there you do not have the true God. For these two belong together, faith and God. Anything on which your heart relies and depends, I say, that is really your God. [. . .] Idolatry does not consist merely of erecting an image and praying to it, but it is primarily a matter of the heart, which fixes its gaze upon other things and seeks help and consolation from creatures, saints, or devils. It neither cares for God nor expects good things from him sufficiently to trust that he wants to help, nor does it believe that whatever good it encounters comes from God.*[62]

In sum, while traditional critiques of idolatry largely focused on the worship of actual human-made statues and images, Luther redefined idolatry as a turn of one's trust away from God. Remarkably, idolatry also served as the chief hermeneutical lens for Luther's exegesis of the book of Isaiah, which he read as a disputation against the idolatry of the Jewish nation. For Luther, the Israelites' worship of human-made idols, criticized by Isaiah, was merely a manifestation of the shift of the Israelites' trust to their own ideas and works, and away from the work of God.[63] For Luther, such progression of idolatry was paradigmatic. Before affecting external practices, idolatry always originated internally, as a weakening of trust in God and increasing trust in other spiritual and material sources of provision, comfort, and healing.

With this in mind, we are now equipped to discern the theological stakes behind Luther's repeated calls in his lectures on Isaiah to use medicine, without relying on it. Certainly, following Luther's logic, putting one's trust in medicine would be misguided, since, as he previously claimed, it was the divine Word working through medicine as opposed to the medicine's intrinsic qualities that ultimately enacted healing. However, even more importantly, one's reliance on medicine would be idolatrous, since it would constitute an erroneous placement of trust in created means rather than in their divine creator. For Luther, such misdirected trust would corrupt one's proper expression of Christian faith, which was both solely sufficient and essential for salvation. In other words, Luther's affirmation of the use of medicine as a divinely created means was conditional. Lest the use of medicine become idolatrous, its use should be accompanied by a proper affective disposition and orientation of trust.

Supernatural Healing in Martin Luther's Thought

Luther's exegesis of the narrative of the bronze serpent in Numbers 21 offers another significant engagement with the question of bodily healing.[64] Luther preached on this story as part of his 1539 sermon on John 3:14, where, in an apparent reference to the book of Numbers, Jesus refers to Moses lifting up a serpent in the wilderness, as analogous to the Son of Man having to be lifted up. While Luther's primary goal in interpreting the story of the serpent was to explain the meaning of Jesus's words about the Son of Man, in doing so, Luther also produced a remarkable theological discussion of bodily healing based on Numbers 21:4–9, a passage that relates the story of how the Israelites, on their way to the promised land, became weary of a prolonged detour in the wilderness and began gripping against Yahweh and Moses's leadership. In response, Yahweh sent snakes with poisonous bites, causing many to die. Terrified, the Israelites repented and pleaded with Moses to seek divine intervention against the snakes. In response to Moses's prayer, Yahweh commanded Moses to create out of bronze and set on a pole a statue of one such poisonous serpent. Anyone bitten by an actual snake would live if they looked upon this serpent of bronze.

Other than the brief summary above, these six verses in the book of Numbers provide no additional details about the deadly snakes or the precise effects of their poisonous bites. Nevertheless, Luther painted his audience a detailed and horrifying picture of the consequences of the snakes' attack with an artistic liberty generally characteristic of his reconstruction of biblical scenes.[65] In the hot climate of the desert, Luther elaborated, their bite caused immediate bodily swelling and redness, followed by fever. These symptoms were certain to become lethal unless the body part affected was immediately amputated. Otherwise, victims' bodies became inflamed to the point of causing their death from dehydration. Luther explained that this must have been the origin of these reptiles being designated "fiery snakes," since their bites produced feverish inflammation and their angry breath nearly set the air on fire. In addition, while Luther acknowledged that such snakes were historically unknown in Germany, he concluded with a dire warning that some had been allegedly spotted in a grove near Wittenberg.

Back to the biblical narrative, Luther's theological imagination continued to produce a picture of what must have been the Israelites' astonishment and skepticism in response to Moses's seemingly absurd claim that in order to recover from a snake's poisonous attack, one needed only look at a bronze statue of a serpent upon a pole. Many of Luther's Israelites suffering from the snakes' bites must have deemed this to be a ridiculous medicine.[66] They wanted Moses to give them real medicine: "a drink, a cooling plaster, a cooling drink, to take away the venom and the fever."[67] The Israelites reasonably suggested to Moses that they should remove the attacking serpents with a pair of tongs and immerse victims' bitten body parts in cold water to combat fever. In addition, it must have been emotionally hardly bearable for Israelites who had recently been assaulted by actual fiery snakes to face a statue molded in the image of their deadly attackers. For these reasons, despite their desperate circumstances, many of Luther's Israelites simply lacked faith to follow Moses's frightening and irrational instructions. They refused to look up at the bronze serpent and, as a result, died in their unbelief from the poisonous bites.

A key move in Luther's exegesis of this story of healing came next. How did a simple gaze at the serpent statue make Israelites well? Luther stressed that neither the bronze statue nor the ritual of facing it contained within themselves any healing power. It was God's Word or divine promise attached to this simple ritual that healed those who believed it. For Luther, simply casting a gaze at the serpent would not be sufficient. One had to look at the serpent clinging in faith to the Word that they would indeed be healed, as promised by God through Moses. According to Luther, "Just looking at the serpent did not affect the cure; it was faith in the Word that did it."[68] Luther further stated,

> *It was the Word that healed the Israelites, the Word spoken by God (Num. 21:8): "Whoever looks at this bronze serpent shall suffer no harm from the bite or sting of any fiery serpent." It was the Word "Whoever looks at the serpent" that was effective. There God was speaking and promising aid, not the serpent. Whoever believed in this Word and promise of God and looked at the serpent was obedient to God.*[69]

Reading Luther's exegesis of Numbers 21 alongside that of Isaiah 38, we encounter a strikingly similar theological hermeneutic of healing. While commenting on the story of Hezekiah's sickness, Luther stressed that the king's healing was accomplished by God's Word acting in creation through the mediums of a medicinal fruit and the work of Isaiah, the physician. Similarly, discussing Numbers 21, Luther stressed that the Israelites' miraculous healing was likewise accomplished by the Word of God through the mediums of a bronze snake and a ritual of gazing at it. The main distinction between these two types of healing lay in the foundational distinction between the kinds of means employed by the Word. In Isaiah 38, they were ordinary natural healing means that were established and perpetually designated as such by the Word. In Numbers 21, they were supernatural, miraculous healing means which the Word designated as such only temporarily. The Word typically preferred using the former, medicinal sort of means while deploying the latter, miraculous ones occasionally or only once.[70] At the same time, ultimately, both medical and miraculous healings alike were animated by the same divine first cause and achieved due to the fundamental power of the divine Word, working in and through a diverse set of created means. Furthermore, a faithful pursuit of either miraculous or ordinary medical modes of healing required vigilance against idolatry, through maintaining a proper orientation of trust.

Luther explicitly introduced the concept of idolatry in his interpretation of the story of the bronze serpent in his discussion of the serpent's religious "afterlife." In insisting that it was not the snake statue by itself that had cured Israelites in the desert centuries before his era, Luther mustered an argument for a controversy about religious practices of healing of his own day. Along with other early Protestant Reformers, Luther attacked traditional medieval folk attempts to attain healing through the intercession of saints, including through acts of devotions, votive gifts, relics, and pilgrimages.

Appeals to saints for the restoration of health was a major dimension of medieval religious healing practices. As discussed earlier, the two fundamental religious assumptions behind appeals for miracles in the Middle Ages were the usefulness of saintly mediation in order to solicit divine intervention and a belief that such mediation happened through an exchange. In Philip Soergel's words, "invoking the saint created a contractual obligation" for a petitioner who vowed to render certain acts of devotion, which could include votive gifts or a pilgrimage to the shrine of the cooperating saint, if the latter came through.[71] At the same time, as Vauchez noted, that while interactions between a saint and a petitioner continued to be based on a "fair exchange" model throughout the Middle Ages, starting in the early fourteenth century, these interactions were becoming less automatic and increasingly manifested as a relational expression of devotion that was more personal and affective in nature.[72]

Both the bartering and affective dimensions in medieval searches for supernatural healing were deeply concerning for Luther. Luther saw these transactional and relational modes of seeking saintly mediation as stemming from a misguided trust in the power of a deceased saint as well as in the supplicant's own efforts to negotiate recovery from a saint. By contrast, as discussed earlier, for Luther, one had to rely for healing on God alone. Luther's equation of misdirected trust with idolatry shed light on idolatry as the main theological stake in Luther's polemics against seeking saintly assistance.[73]

In particular, Numbers 21 provided Luther with a biblical warning against what he saw as idolatry of relying on saints for healing. For Luther, the bronze serpent was a proto-saint. Luther recalled how in 2 Kings 18:4, Hezekiah destroyed Moses's bronze serpent which had by then become an object of worship for Israelites. Again, Luther employed his vivid imagination, recreating a history of the Israelites' evolving devotion to the serpent.[74] Initially, amazed by what they assumed to be divine power dwelling within the serpent, Israelites began offering sheep and oxen as sacrifices to the statue. In difficult seasons, Israelites would carry the serpent out into the wilderness where they would flock to it and worship. Later, Luther speculated, the godly king David must have had the serpent hidden away from such inordinate popular adoration, while still preserving it as a historical artifact of the Israelites' glorious delivery from Egypt. By the time of Isaiah, however, devotion to the serpent was flourishing. In Luther's telling, the Israelites undertook pilgrimages to the serpent, burned incense to and worshipped it in great numbers. Unfortunately, for Luther's Israelites, since the Word of God was manifested in the serpent in a particular historical moment and had since departed, the serpent could no longer provide healing or deliverance. Instead, the statue became an "object of idolatry" or a destination for the misplaced hope of a people who lost the true orientation of their faith.[75] Luther's contemporary Germans were unfortunate imitators of such a misplaced search for healing, as, in their pursuits of recovery, they offered their devotion (and their money) to long-deceased saints and religious institutions supporting such devotional practices.

The Medical Devil

Luther's battles for health were fought against a powerful, albeit covert, adversary. As Heiko Oberman masterfully demonstrated, while Luther's concern with the devil retained certain medieval undertones, it was more than an inherited folk superstition. Rather, Luther's view of the devil was a distinct and original development of his theology, permeating the entirety of his thought.[76] Luther portrayed the entire history of humanity as being caught between the competing actions of God and the devil. Luther's devil was the humankind's powerful and formidable enemy, attacking every dimension of human existence. The devil especially never tired or rested from plotting against the gospel and its true believers. Spiritually, the devil tempted Christians to doubt God's promises, in order to weaken their reliance on God as a benevolent Father and undermine their confidence in being justified by faith.

Additionally, Luther's devil harassed people physically, through disease, famine, persecution, and other conditions that deprived the body of its needs. As Bernhard Lohse noted, Luther perceived disease and other bodily ailments as belonging to a special domain of Satan's malicious power. This was due to their connection to death, the power of which Hebrews 2:14 ascribed to the devil, although Luther taught that ultimately even death was subject to God.[77] For Luther, the story of Job served as a confirmation of God's ultimate sovereignty over human life but also of the devil's ability to infect human bodies. Just as God's Word invisibly worked through the material world, the devil similarly acted secretly through ordinary means, harming the proper functioning of the body. Moreover, the devil meddled with the efficacy of medicine, the work of physicians, and healing practices.[78] In a private conversation, Luther once responded to an accusation of a physician being responsible for his patient's death. Luther purportedly remarked that while physicians bore responsibility for incorrect diagnoses or inappropriate treatments, the ultimate accountability lay with the devil, who used physicians' mistakes to murder their patients.[79]

However, the main way in which Luther's devil chose to operate in this world was not through direct interference with medicine but through deception. Paul's assertion in 2 Corinthians 11:14 that Satan masqueraded as an angel of light was foundational for Luther's demonology.[57] As Susan

Schreiner pointed out, for Luther, it was not just God who remained hidden and acted in ways seemingly alien to his character. The devil also kept himself concealed, appearing under a guise and behaving in ways opposite to his true nature.[80] Luther's hidden devil was the counterpart of his hidden God. While God appeared hidden in suffering, foolishness, and weakness, the devil concealed himself by promoting seemingly righteous living and good works, perceived as holy, zealous, and intensely religious, yet fundamentally contrary to God's Word.

This represented a historical innovation of Luther's demonology and marked a significant departure from medieval views of the devil.[81] In the Middle Ages, the devil was firmly associated with sin, both being attracted to it and encouraging it. In contrast, Luther's devil was drawn to righteousness, attacking it by forging a false holiness and encouraging the deceived to ambush the truly righteous. While the devil was always intent on attacking the truth, Luther believed these assaults intensified over time. After Christ's resurrection opened the way to heaven for Gentiles, the devil's fury only grew stronger until the Reformation's rediscovery of the gospel incited the devil's ultimate rage.

Remarkably, the devil's deceiving nature was manifested in his work as a counterfeit or even real healer, as Luther vividly depicted in his lectures on the book of Deuteronomy. In particular, Luther read Deuteronomy 13:1–3 and 18:21–22 together to offer warnings against what he saw as false miracles of healing, instigated by the devil.[82] In their original contexts, these passages were concerned with identifying false prophecies. Deuteronomy 13:1–3 declared that even if religious prophecies were supported by real supernatural signs and miracles, they nevertheless ought to be distrusted, if they directed the community toward following other gods. Deuteronomy 18:21–22 provided reassurance that if a prophecy made in the name of the Lord failed, it had never been divinely issued in the first place.

For Luther, these two Deuteronomy passages were entirely applicable to his own time. Luther was concerned by reports he had heard of what he believed to be false or counterfeit miraculous healings that allegedly occurred due to pilgrimages, relics, or other forms of saintly intercession. Luther was troubled that such false miracles directed people away from the Word of God, just as described in Deuteronomy 13:1–3. He suspected that such healings or even the sicknesses that prompted these healing pursuits might have been intentionally staged by the devil.

In his lecture on Deuteronomy 18:21–22, Luther warned his audience that the devil knew how to manipulate human bodies in surprising ways, which the devil applied to manufacturing counterfeit physical healings.[83] The devil was able to produce a false appearance of a person having a blind eye, injuring a body part, or generally falling sick. The devil could even produce an impression of death, such as by suspending a drowned person's breathing for hours, while actually keeping him alive. However, after the desperate victims of the devil's deception had been driven to appeal to saints or other devotional objects and vow their devotion and spiritual remuneration in exchange for healing, the devil would promptly remove the appearance of sickness. Thus, his deceived victims would fall into a spiritual trap of spreading the glory of a healing object or a saint. While the devil exercised most of such false healings in relation to false diseases that existed only in appearance, sometimes the devil could provide (or withhold) real healings to advance his evil mission. Luther's devil was remarkably knowledgeable about the functioning of the human body, herbs, and medicine.

Luther's insistence on the devil's remarkable medical knowledge posed a practical problem. How could one discern whether a healing came from God or the devil? Luther's solution was paying attention to its spiritual implications. A genuine healing miracle would point people to faith and God's Word. But if a miracle ultimately highlighted the power of other spiritual works or objects, it was likely the devil's doing. In sum, by using both staged and real illnesses and healings, the devil's goal was to seduce Christians into redirecting their devotion and trust for healing to saints and other presumed sources of spiritual power. Thus, for Luther, a quest for bodily recovery became an idolatry, a deposit of trust in something other than God. Christians had to exercise spiritual vigilance, lest by gaining bodily wellness, they might hurt their spiritual well-being. A suffering human body was a battlefield on which the devil raged warfare for the human soul.

Fortunately, for humans, they could count on the support of angels. In many ways, Luther's teachings on angels laid the foundation for their subsequent elevation in the German Reformation.[84] Luther frequently mentioned angels, starting from his early pre-Reformation lectures on the Psalms and until his late lectures on Genesis. Philip Soergel argued that, while Luther's perspective on angels retained many medieval sensibilities, overall, it reflected Luther's central Protestant concerns, especially with faith.[85] In particular, Soergel identified three main themes in Luther's angelology, namely, the continuing importance of angelic activity for the fulfillment of God's purposes, lively but invisible angelic presences permeating the human realm, and angels providing spiritual examples of faith and humility. In addition, from his mid-career to late writings, Luther also characterized angels as preservers of humanity against diabolic destruction.

This latter perspective became important for Luther's teachings on medicine, which portrayed angels as the adversaries of the devil in the battle for human wellness. In his commentary on the story of Lot escaping Sodom in Genesis 19, Luther elaborated on the significance of angelic medical intervention. According to Luther, "the fact that new remedies become known when new diseases make their appearance—this is not a matter of the diligence of human beings; it is a service of the angels, who direct and urge on the hearts of physicians just as Satan directs and urges on his own."[86] While Satan and his evil spiritual aides tirelessly assaulted people with illnesses and other calamities, angels were busy guarding the effectiveness of medicine against the devil's ploys, thus protecting humanity from destruction. Invisible to humans, angels and the devil were locked in cosmic medical combat. This spiritual struggle for humanity's life and health began with the earliest days of history, as described in Genesis.

4

THE GENESIS OF MEDICINE AND GENDERED PAIN

MARTIN LUTHER SPENT his early years in reasonably good health. Raised in a moderately affluent household, he was unlikely to suffer from malnutrition and poor living conditions that commonly affected lower-class children, making them more susceptible to crippling household injuries and infectious diseases.[1] The first and only surviving description of a physical malady from Luther's early years was an injury he sustained at the age of nineteen.[2] While returning on horseback from Erfurt to his parents' house in Mansfeld, he accidentally cut his leg on a short sword hanging on his side. The pierce opened an artery, resulting in profuse bleeding. A local surgeon fetched by Luther's traveling companion to attend to him in a nearby village was unable to close the wound, so Luther had to be carried back to Erfurt. Overnight, the wound reopened and he nearly died from severe blood loss. Insignificant as this episode might seem, it sheds light on the proximity of the dangers abounding in mundane sixteenth-century activities, the high risks of injury, and the speed with which even a minor accident could become life-threatening. Luther recalled his recovery from that wound as a period during which he learned to play the flute, which later comforted him on the way to his anticipated death sentence at the Diet of Worms.

Luther's health began to face challenges during his early years as a reformer. As previously discussed, he blamed his ascetic lifestyle as a friar for ruining his health and nearly bringing him to the brink of death, and the surviving descriptions of Luther from that period attest to his extreme exhaustion. In addition, the intense stress of his deepening confrontation with Rome contributed to a slow deterioration of his health. In 1518, Luther undertook a long journey to Augsburg on foot in order to appear before Cardinal Cajetan at the Imperial Diet, which could have ended in his arrest. Toward the end of his trip, he felt so unwell that he had to hire a wagon for the remaining three miles. Similarly, on his way to the 1521 Diet of Worms, he developed a high fever and became very ill. The overwhelming tension of this early period as a reformer eased but never fully disappeared later in Luther's life, as he remained entangled in perpetual religious controversies, bitter polemics with his opponents, and political uncertainties and threats to the future of the Protestant movement. In addition to chronic stress, Luther's constant overexertion in his multiple roles as a university professor, city pastor, biblical expositor, and the leader of the German magisterial Reformation movement exacerbated his increasing health issues.

Luther's more serious medical problems began in his late thirties while he was confined to the grounds of Wartburg Castle. In addition to significant weight gain, Luther's diet and sedentary lifestyle led to severe constipation. In every letter sent to his friends monthly from May to October 1521, Luther vividly lamented his constipation, which he claimed became to him *molestia vexatus* (a vexatious handicap).[3] He also referred to his constipation as "his relic of the cross." In his letter to Spalatin, he complained that after five days of trying to gain relief, his eventual stool left him "bathed in blood" and "what took four days to heal immediately tears open again."[4]

In addition to recurrent constipation, uric acid stones became another malady that plagued Luther for the rest of his life. Between 1526 and 1545, he experienced seven recorded attacks and nearly died after an episode during the Schmalkaldic League meeting in February of 1537. Four days after his arrival, Luther passed a small stone, after which he endured eight days of agonizing pain accompanied by urine retention. The unprecedented efforts to save Luther's life underscored the incredible political significance of his living body for the German reform movement. The best stars of German medicine of that time were ushered to Luther's bedside. Each one of the eight German princes present at the league called on their personal physician to attend to Luther's condition. In addition, a surgeon from a nearby town was summoned, and Luther's friend delivered additional medicines from Erfurt.

The list of treatments performed on Luther vividly illustrates the eclectic nature of the best sixteenth-century learned medicine: he was given plenty of water, hot compresses, massaged, and fed almond broth. Later, recalling his illness in Schmalkald, Luther complained that physicians gave him so much to drink as if he were a big ox and manipulated his body until even his private parts became lifeless.[5] Doctors attempted to remove a stone by inserting into his urethra a golden suppository provided by the elector's physician. In addition, Luther took medicine prepared by his wife from fresh garlic cloves boiled together with fresh horse droppings.

Yet none of these extraordinary measures succeeded in getting Luther to pass urine, and he was likely approaching acute kidney failure. Still in excruciating pain, Luther demanded to be taken back to Wittenberg to pass away next to his family. He was transported back in the Elector's private carriage, the jolting of which on the bumpy road caused him such agony that two people walked beside the carriage, trying to stabilize it. However, although the journey was torturous, the rough road did the trick—and Luther was finally able to pass what he estimated in a letter to his wife to be three to four liters of urine in two hours, followed by passing six stones the next day. Nevertheless, he remained in pain, so he made his confession preparing to die. However, the following morning he woke up alive, reportedly exclaiming in astonishment, "I lay down last night expecting to be a corpse today!"[6] It took Luther at least another five months to sufficiently recover before he could resume preaching and lecturing. Although never as severe, he continued to experience kidney stone attacks for the rest of his life, which were agonizing enough to often prevent him from traveling on horseback.

In addition to kidney stones, Luther might have suffered from gouty arthritis, which likely contributed to the stone attack. He complained of acute pain in his feet, and plaster casts of his hands made upon his death showed evidence of arthritic deformities. Additionally, he was plagued by a chronic ulcer on his left calf which, according to common practice of his day, was treated by keeping the wound artificially open to allow for chronic bloodletting. Luther also experienced recurrent headaches, vertigo, and a persistent ringing in his ears. He reportedly compared his head with a "cathedral chapter" overwhelmed by noise.[7] These conditions affected his vision, and it appears that toward the end of his life he lost the sight in his left eye.

From a historical distance, attempts have been made to retrospectively diagnose Luther's numerous maladies and identify their probable causes. Luther's obesity, his (by early modern standards) sedentary lifestyle, perpetual overexertion, and chronic stress were named as factors that contributed to the development of many of his conditions. Medical inadequacies of his era sometimes exacerbated his illnesses instead of relieving them. As his medical issues remained insufficiently addressed, they became more pronounced with age. Additionally, Luther consistently maintained an unhealthy diet and poor hydration habits. He abstained from water, which he believed to be contaminated, and drank beer instead.

While Luther might have agreed with some of these explanations for his ailments, for him, the underlying cause of his body's suffering and aging was theological. He viewed both physical suffering and medicine as having spiritual histories. Their histories, traced to the primordial times, were told in the book of Genesis. This chapter will discuss how, based on his reading of Genesis, Luther constructed an origin story of physical suffering and medicine. I will show that, for Luther, medicine was divinely established, beginning with the tree of life in the garden of Eden, which Luther viewed as yielding medicinal fruits that enabled perpetual health. Moreover, in a departure from the medieval line of thought linking the origin of disease to Adam and Eve's disobedience, Luther taught that the historical emergence of most human illnesses was the flood of Genesis 6–9, not the fall of Genesis 3. In addition to describing the origins of suffering and medicine, Luther read Genesis as also recounting those of idolatry, from its inception intertwined with the story of human aging and disease. Finally, I will discuss Luther's theological vision of women's reproductive suffering based on his interpretation of Genesis 3:16, highlighting how he used this interpretation to depart from some aspects of the tradition of patriarchy in Christian thought, while ultimately reaffirming it.

The Genesis of Medicine

In early June of 1535 at the University of Wittenberg, Luther began a lecture series on Genesis. The previous month, he had declared his intention to dedicate the rest of his life to expounding Moses's books, of which he considered Genesis to be the first. Over years he adhered to this objective by offering a new Genesis lecture every Monday and Tuesday, with a few intermittent interruptions. Luther concluded this series in November 1545, ten years after beginning this project and three months before his death.[8]

Despite his extraordinary prolific creative output, Luther was not a systematic theologian and never wrote a treatise that provided a comprehensive and ordered account of major doctrines, themes, and emphases of the new Protestant thought. This first systematic exposition of emerging Lutheran theology was Philip Melanchthon's 1521 *Loci Communes*, which Luther highly regarded and saw no need to supersede with another Protestant *summa*. Nevertheless, while not formally intended as an exercise in systematic theology, Luther's lectures on Genesis came closest to providing a summary of his thought by espousing its main themes in connection with his biblical exegesis. Heiko Oberman described these lectures as "an introduction to Luther's world of faith."[9]

While Luther's expositions of Genesis maintained some continuity with the preceding tradition, they also represented a significant departure, particularly from the interpretive principles of patristic and medieval exegeses. As discussed earlier, starting from Augustine, Christian theologians in the West interpreted the Bible following an overarching hermeneutical principle that distinguished between the four levels of meaning or "senses" of Scripture: literal, allegorical, moral, and anagogical. The allegorical sense was used to elucidate the meaning of difficult passages and establish connections between the events of the Old and New Testaments; the moral (or tropological) sense conveyed the ethical import of the text, and the anagogical sense focused on prophecies of future events, the return of Christ and the Last Judgment.

A hallmark of Luther's evangelical reading of Genesis was his repeated criticism of the allegorical reading of Scripture, which often served as the preferred medieval hermeneutical approach to the Old Testament. Luther insisted that Genesis should be read primarily as a book of history narrating actual events. He criticized his theological predecessors, including even his typically favored Augustine, for abandoning its literal reading in favor of allegory. As Jaroslav Pelikan has shown, Luther's critique of the preceding exegetical tradition encompassed several major points.[10] He charged patristic writers with misinterpreting the ethical applications of Scripture, privileging teachings on asceticism and celibacy, and downplaying the reality of human emotions and weaknesses. As a result, according to Luther, Scriptural emphases on grace had become subsumed under the promotion of legalistic moralism. He also blamed medieval scholastics for conceding undue theological influence to pagan philosophers, particularly Aristotle, whose conclusions they sought to harmonize with Scripture. Nevertheless, while frequently critical of the preceding tradition of interpreting Genesis, Luther's lectures consistently engaged it and occasionally acknowledged its insights. As mentioned earlier, for Luther, the insistence on the primacy of Scripture did not mean juxtaposing the Bible against tradition but rather ensuring that the tradition of interpretation did not distort what he saw as the literal meaning of the Word of God.

However, what Luther understood to be the literal, plain, or historical meaning of Genesis was not its "literal" meaning in the contemporary sense of the word. His method differed from modern scholarly explorations of the possible "original" meanings of texts assigned to them in their initial contexts. In contrast, for Luther, the true plain historical meaning of Genesis was only available through its "Christianized" readings.[11] Unlike medieval exegetes who generally perceived Christ and the Holy Spirit as anticipated and indicated through allegorical and anagogical senses of Scripture, Luther's lectures depicted them as real, literal actors in the events of Genesis. In addition, Luther believed that the moral meaning of Genesis was plainly communicated through the history and narratives of the lives of its patriarchs and matriarchs, serving as examples of faith. This is the paradox of Luther's early Reformation approach to Genesis, positioned between medieval and modern exegesis. By insisting on a literal reading of the text against the medieval allegorical approach, he nevertheless practiced such a literal reading through a thoroughly Christianized and evangelical hermeneutical framework, which might have further obscured what a contemporary reader of the Bible would see as its "literal" meaning.

Luther did not shy away from acknowledging challenges in understanding the meaning of Genesis texts, their moral import, or the seeming repetitions or omissions in their narratives. While attempting to resolve some of these difficulties, with regard to others, he acknowledged different hermeneutical possibilities and their shortcomings without necessarily firmly advocating for a particular solution. Luther ascribed the ultimate authorship of Genesis to the Holy Spirit, who spoke through Moses. When faced with interpretive difficulties, Luther advocated a posture of humility in accepting the words of the Holy Spirit even when their meaning was not entirely clear. For Luther, Genesis recorded historical events just as God desired to communicate this history to subsequent generations of humanity. One of such historical occurrences described in Genesis was the divine establishment of medicine.

In the twenty-first century, the idea of reading the Bible as a history of medicine would seem rather strange. However, as David Steinmetz observed, the Bible was the ultimate "sixteenth-century book," used to explain and provide guidance on all kinds of human endeavors, from policies of taxation to theories of child-rearing and education. Therefore, it was also consulted for explanations of such intrinsic human experiences as suffering and healing, with the accounts of Genesis 2 and 3 seen as especially important.

In Genesis 2, after creating the first people, God placed them in the bountiful garden of Eden, with the tree of life and the tree of the knowledge of good and evil planted in its midst. God allowed Adam and Eve to freely eat fruit from any tree except the tree of the knowledge of good and evil, warning them that the consequence for disobedience would be death. However, in Genesis 3, prompted by the serpent, Eve and Adam ate the forbidden fruit, leading to their expulsion from the garden. In the history of Christian thought, the first people's first disobedience to a divine commandment was termed *the fall*, signifying Adam and Eve's fall into sin. Since Augustine, the Western tradition taught that Adam and Eve's original sin had since been transmitted to their descendants, affecting all generations of humanity, now separated from the presence of God.

For Luther, the second and third chapters of Genesis also narrated the origin story of medicine. He taught that while Adam and Eve's bodies, like those of other creatures, were naturally subject to decay and death, they remained unaffected by physiological decline before their sin.[12] In Luther's garden of Eden, this decline and death were prevented by the first people's access to the fruit from the tree of life. For Luther, the fruit of the tree of life functioned as the first "medicine" or a "remedy."[13] It sustained their bodies in a state of perpetual health and youthful vigor, defying age-related biological decline. After their exile from the garden, Eve and Adam lost access to the fruit of the tree of life, returning to their natural progression toward senesce, the biological inconveniences of which were further exacerbated by their sin.

Moreover, with the available medicine of the fruit of the tree of life, Luther's first people possessed physical abilities far surpassing those ultimately inherited by their posterity. Luther's Adam enjoyed an unimpeded procreative prowess. His keen eyesight allowed him to see for a hundred miles as easily as his descendants could see for half. Even the production of Adam's bowel movements was more pleasant. Luther's Eve would get pregnant more often, with more children, and had considerably easier pregnancies.[14] She would also have never gotten any wrinkles! The first people's children would wean sooner and perhaps begin walking right away, foraging for food on their own, just like baby chicks.

Luther was careful to clarify that the amazing medicinal power of the fruit of the tree of life did not stem from inherent qualities of the fruit itself. Instead, it originated "through the potency of the Word" with God having supplied the fruit with its age-defying healing power.[15] This shows an already familiar interpretive strategy consistent with Luther's earlier theological engagements with medicine in his Old Testament commentaries. Whether discussing the fruit of the tree of life, the bronze serpent, or the "natural" remedy of a fig poultice, Luther believed that the healing power of any medicine was originally divinely supplied. Thus, the fruit of the tree of life stood as simultaneously a natural and a supernatural remedy, an archetype of all future medicines to be discovered.

Luther observed vestiges of the former medical order in the world around him. Uncommon occurrences of women bearing twins, triplets, or even quadruplets served as echoes of the woman's uninhibited procreative power, which would have been the norm had Eve not sinned.[16] Just as God initially chose to channel divine healing power through a fruit of a tree, so plants, fruit, and seeds continued to possess medicinal qualities.[17] Furthermore, Luther emphasized that both the fruits from the tree of life and the tree of the knowledge of good and evil were kinds of food. When eaten, the former maintained the first people's youthfulness and health, while the latter brought to their bodies decay and eventual death. Luther observed that, as in the garden of Eden, throughout centuries different types of food had served for people as sources of either bodily strength or bodily destruction.

For Luther, in paradise, Adam and Eve must have enjoyed a variety of delicious agricultural and animal produce. After all, God explicitly permitted them to eat fruit from all but one tree and put them to work watching over animals and tending a bountiful garden that presumably yielded a diverse variety of produce. However, after the fall, in Genesis 3:18, God confined Adam to eating the plants (or the herbs) of the field. For Luther, this divine command had a dual significance. On the one hand, it was a punitive reduction of Adam's diet in response to his disobedience. Luther understood herbs or plants of the field to mean grains and beans, such as peas, fennel seeds, millet, and rice. No longer could poor Adam enjoy butter, milk, eggs, cheese, or a variety of fruit. Luther imagined the meager feast Adam would serve his guests at his children's weddings, consisting only of herbs of the field and plain water!

However, as seen in the earlier discussion of Luther's hermeneutical approach to scriptural narratives of physical suffering, he held in tension divine discipline and divine grace. While restricting Adam's dietary choices to a simple plant-based diet as a form of punishment, God also ensured his healthy eating to keep his body strong and resilient. No wonder that on this healthy food regimen, Adam and his descendants enjoyed extremely long lives, as recorded in Genesis! Moreover, Luther interpreted Genesis 9:3 to mean that following the flood, God permitted Noah and his family to expand their diet. Noah and his descendants were now allowed to consume meat and a variety of other foods. They could even drink wine! However, as the story of Noah showed, this new dietary addition was soon abused. Wine led to drunkenness, while the numerous newly available food choices resulted in overeating and gluttony. These sins were only exacerbated with time. Luther criticized what he saw as the novel gastronomical indulgences of his own time, including drinking wine on an empty stomach and using foreign spices to increase appetites and deliberately alter the natural tastes of food.

For Luther, such misguided dietary choices reflected the original sin, manifested in a transgressive eating choice. Just as Adam and Eve's eating of the forbidden fruit first brought about death, so the sins of gluttony and the immoderate abandonment of plain foods in favor of a wide variety of "unnatural" ones continued to cause their descendants' bodily destruction. At the same time, while Adam and Eve's first sin was expressed through tasting the forbidden fruit, the nature of this original sin was not gastronomical. Their transgressive eating was an external manifestation of the first idolatry.

The Genesis of Idolatry

In addition to reading Genesis as an origin story of medicine, Luther also read it as an origin story of the church and its paramount struggle with idolatry.[18] In the Middle Ages, theologians created a powerful narrative of the Catholic Church as the one true church founded by Jesus Christ. Jesus promised to establish his unconquerable church upon the rock of Simon Peter, whom the Catholic tradition eventually came to regard as the first pope. Jesus gave Peter the keys of the kingdom of heaven (Matt 16:19) the power of which was interpreted as the spiritual authority uniquely held by the Roman church. Jesus could not have possibly abandoned his church, as he promised his disciples to always be with them even to the end of the age (Matt 28:20). Against persecution, pagan assault, and heretics, the Catholic Church was visible in her dogmas, councils, sacraments, and church hierarchies, claiming descent through apostolic succession. Against this history of one true, holy, Catholic, and apostolic church, Protestants stood as yet another heretical movement, one of many successfully survived and defeated by the true church in Rome. The question of the Eastern Orthodox Church was typically avoided in this narrative, with the full polemical force of sixteenth-century Catholic apologists thrown at Protestants.

In response to this Catholic narrative, early Protestants felt compelled to produce a counternarrative telling an alternative history of the true church. Additionally, Luther was pressed to offer his ecclesiology in response to alternative Protestant ones, including those developed by Anabaptists and Sacramentalists, who used many of the same arguments as Lutheran reformers but arrived at different conclusions. John Maxfield contextualized Luther's interest in critically engaging the inherited view of church history as part of a broader interest in the study of history during the Renaissance, pursued by humanists critical of medieval tradition.[19] Early modern Christian humanists championed a return to original sources for a better understanding of history and, ultimately, the promotion of educational reform. Maxfield argued that within this intellectual context, Luther also sought to return "to the sources" of the history of the church for the sake of its reform.

For Luther, the original source of the history of the church was the book of Genesis. According to Luther, by forming Adam out of the earth, God founded in him the first church, to which God soon added Eve. This first church of Adam and Eve was created for the same purposes as the church in all future ages: to worship and rejoice in the Lord while trusting and obeying his Word. Paradoxically, Luther described the tree of the knowledge of good and evil as the first altar to practice such reverence and obedience. However, the first congregation was confronted by the devil, who attacked God's Word with his own and led the newly established church "away from the Word of God to idolatry."[20]

In the history of premodern Christian thought there were various interpretations of what exactly happened in the fall that corrupted souls with original sin and caused human separation from God. One interpretation associated the fall with the act of eating the forbidden fruit as the first manifestation of willful disobedience to God's Word. Augustine's understanding of the fall as the original expression of human pride was another influential medieval approach. In contrast, Luther offered a new hermeneutic of the fall, influenced by his Protestant vision of faith.

Luther rejected a popular scholastic view portraying Eve's temptation as her growing desire to eat the forbidden fruit, which she saw in the garden day after day until finally the Serpent's words became for her the last straw. For Luther, Eve's real temptation was believing a word that contradicted the one spoken to her by God. God warned Adam and Eve not to eat fruit from the tree of the knowledge of good and evil, or they would surely die. Adam and Eve should have firmly trusted that what God told them was beneficial and true. When the Serpent came to Eve, it used words to attack God's Word, thereby enticing the first people to trust a lie and fall into idolatry.[21]

Luther's Serpent (who was really Satan in disguise) executed a clever, multiple-step operation. The first stage was to make Eve doubt if God really meant what God had clearly stated. Luther stressed that the snake did not approach Eve by explicitly criticizing God or initially implying that God's Word was untrue, malevolent, or harmful. Nor did the Serpent challenge the fact that God spoke to people and gave them his authoritative commandment. Instead, the serpent cast doubt on Eve's understanding of God's Word by asking, "Did God really say?" Luther explained that,

> *It is as if Satan were saying: "Surely you are very silly if you think that God did not want you to eat from this tree, you whom He*

> *appointed lords over all the trees of Paradise. In fact, He created the trees on your account. How can He, who favored you with all these things, be so envious as to withhold from you the fruits of this one single tree, which are so delightful and lovely?" Satan is seeking to deprive them of the Word and knowledge of God that they may reach the conclusion: "This is not the will of God; God does not command this."*[22]

To Eve's initial credit, in her response to Satan, she accurately confirmed God's prohibition to eat the forbidden fruit. However, the disaster occurred as she continued her response, adding (in Luther's translation) that the consequences of eating the fruit would be that "lest perchance we shall die."[23] Luther's Eve now doubted the certainty of the outcome of her disobedience! Her trust in God's Word had weakened. Seizing on this new uncertainty, Satan advanced his attack. At this point, he explicitly denied the truthfulness of God's warning, while presenting Eve with enticing and desirable outcomes of trusting his word over God's. According to Satan, eating the fruit would make humans like God. Thus, Satan lured Eve into another "lapse" of unbelief, pulling her further away from God's Word. Indeed, Eve moved from doubting God's Word to its outright rejection. Even before she touched the fruit, when Eve rejected the truthfulness and goodness of God's Word and believed another word instead, her fall had already occurred.

Luther interpreted the fall as the first occurrence of idolatry. As discussed earlier, for Luther, idolatry first happened internally as trust placed in something over God, which then manifested in misguided actions. In light of this, Luther perceived Eve's act of eating the fruit as merely an external expression of her internal fall into idolatry. The sequence of events in Genesis 3 presented a paradigm of the progression of idolatry, applicable throughout human history. Idolatry started with weakening trust in God's Word, followed by acts of disobedience, excusing and defending sin, and yet ultimately facing God's punishment.

Moreover, Genesis 3 revealed Satan's general strategy for tempting Christians to abandon God's true instructions. When Luther's devil began his original temptation, he did not directly deny that God spoke to people, question God's authority in giving commandments, or attack God's goodness or character for prohibiting certain things. Instead, the devil used deception, appearing to clarify something important that God said under the guise of reverence and better understanding of God's Word. Luther saw Satan's initial strategy as being imitated by future heretics in the history of the church. Just as the devil invoked God's Word, so did all heretics appeal to Scripture, by quoting it selectively and shrewdly.

Luther's Satan presented himself as a profoundly spiritual and venerable being. Luther depicted the Serpent's persuasive tactics in the garden as somehow employing religious language, under the pretense of diligently seeking to obey God more fully. According to Luther, if the devil were to promote something unambiguously outrageous and immoral, "it would be easy to be on one's guard against him. But here, when he propounds another word, when he discourses about the will of God, when he uses the names, 'God,' 'the church,' and 'the people of God,' as a pretext, then people cannot so readily be on guard against him."[24] For Luther, Satan's strategy of employing spiritualized reasoning and discourse, invoking the Word of God, has proven remarkably effective over the centuries, leading people into idolatry.

Moreover, the Serpent enticed Eve by highlighting for her the significant advantages of eating the fruit—its delicious appearance, beauty, and especially promised wisdom. Eve's temptation was furthered by her realization of the considerable personal gain she could achieve by abandoning her belief in God's Word. For Luther, it was crucial that Satan tempted Eve to desire wisdom that went beyond and ultimately contradicted the wisdom already offered to her by God's Word. This was a classic expression of idolatry, when people "give up the Word and worship their own thoughts."[25]

Although Adam and Eve fell into idolatry and suffered its consequences, Satan did not succeed in destroying the original church. In Genesis 3, alongside his rightful condemnation, God offered Adam and Eve a comforting promise of redemption in Jesus Christ. Following the fall, Luther's history of the church continued with Cain and Abel. Since Augustine, Cain's building of his own city had been understood as the founding of a godless society, "a city of man" and of the world, perpetually opposed to the spiritual "city of God." Luther's interpretation significantly diverged from this established paradigm.[26] Rather than founding a pagan society, Luther's Cain established a false church, characterized by sin, pride, deception, violence, and determination to worship God on its own terms. From then on, the history of the church of the gospel became inseparable from the history of the false church, which was intensely religious and tried to masquerade itself as the true one.

Luther identified the early true church with the Old Testament patriarchs and observed that its defining traits continued to mark the evangelical churches of his own time.[27] For example, the true church could be extremely small, just as when it consisted only of the righteous Noah and his family. Like Noah and Abraham, who believed God and were counted as righteous, the church of the gospel believed God's Word and his seemingly impossible promises, thereby receiving salvation. Finally, just as the faithful church in the Old Testament faced persecution and suffering at the hands of the unrighteous, so did true Christians in Luther's own time.

Luther's overarching perspective on history was shaped by his strongly apocalyptic outlook. Rather than viewing it through the lens of human progress, Luther saw it as a trajectory marked by deepening moral, physiological, and environmental degradation influenced by the expanding reach of sin and idolatry, until this historic decline would be gloriously reversed at the eschaton. Throughout the ages, the true church remained small, surrounded by the world where false church(es) flourished, obscuring the church of the faithful and propagating various false teachings in the name of the true religion. Nevertheless, through the true church, the gospel continued to persevere and advance: first, with God's Word and promises revealed in the Old Testament; then with the incarnation, crucifixion, and the resurrection of Jesus; and, finally, for Luther, through the rediscovery of the gospel by evangelical reformers. During this history of salvation, the devil's rage deepened and his attacks intensified, contributing to an ever-expanding array of causes and instances of physical suffering.

The Genesis of Physical Suffering

Premodern Western theologians believed that, as a consequence of the fall, humanity became subject to physical corruption, suffering, and disease, ultimately leading to death. This belief was rooted in the connection between sin and death, such as in Romans 5:12 stating that "just as sin came into the world through one man, and death came through sin, and so death spread to all because all have sinned." Paul further elaborated on the relationship between sin and death, asserting that "because of the one man's trespass, death reigned through that one" (Rom 12:17) and that "many died through the one man's trespass" (Rom 12:15). In addition to Romans, the divine proclamations in Genesis 3 regarding Eve's increased pain during childbirth and Adam's hard labor and eventual return to dust also led premodern theologians to link Genesis 3 to the rise of human physical suffering.

Medieval scholastics probed the question of whether human suffering existed when Adam remained in the state of innocence or original righteousness before the fall. By drawing on the medieval philosophy of potentiality, they generally agreed that while Adam's body in the state of innocence could not suffer in actuality, it could suffer and become corrupt in potentiality.[28] Adam's potential for suffering and corruption became actualized after the fall. A similar dialectic of actuality and potentiality was also applied to the question of the origin of death. The medieval scholastic tradition generally regarded death as a natural state for creatures but taught that for humans it only existed in potentiality before the fall, due to the access to the tree of life. After original sin occurred and Adam and Eve became expelled from paradise, their death became actual and necessary. This new actuality of death was also associated with the arrival of diseases, following the fall.

Along with medieval thinkers, Luther maintained that death was a natural stage in the existence of all created beings. Animals had died in the garden even before the first humans' disobedience. As Luther explained in his commentary on Genesis 2:9, even Adam and Eve would have eventually been transferred from physical to spiritual existence. However, unlike medieval doctors who saw the fall as the onset of the actuality of bodily pain, corruption, and disease upon humanity newly plagued by sin, Luther did not read Genesis 3 as the main turning point from health to widespread physical ailments.[29] According to Luther, a multitude of diseases struck humanity later. Rather than being an origin story of disease, for Luther, the fall of Genesis 3 was an origin story of aging. Newly separated from the medicine of the tree of life, the first man and woman for the first time experienced the natural deterioration of their bodies.

Luther put forth two reasons to support his assertion that the widespread emergence of diseases occurred later in human history. First, God's punishments in Genesis 3 were specific and limited in nature. In particular, they focused on hard work for the man, childbearing troubles for the woman, and, eventually, death for both of them. As Luther observed, God did not threaten Adam with stroke, leprosy, or epilepsy! Second, Luther took notice of unusually long lifespans attributed to people in the first chapters of Genesis. It appeared that drastic reduction in people's longevity only came after the flood described in Genesis 6–9.

John Headley argued that Luther interpreted the period between the fall and the flood as a "golden age."[30] He considered this time to be the youth of humankind, characterized by greater holiness, simplicity, austerity, and moderation than the subsequent eras. For Luther, a fuller access to God's revelation in later ages had weakened the church's faith. In contrast, despite receiving a more opaque knowledge of spiritual things, Luther's first patriarchs maintained a remarkable faith in the promised offspring of Eve. In addition to their spiritual superiority to the future church, the patriarchs of that era were also superior morally and physically. According to Luther, the pre-flood "church" honored familial and marital bonds. The extended lifespans of that period allowed generations to remain closely connected. Luther's first patriarchs adhered to a vegan diet of plants, seeds, and herbs, as commanded by God to Adam. Their only drink was water, and wine was unknown. Luther depicted the daily lives of these early faithful as simple and unadorned. They were unfamiliar with luxuries like silk, gold, and silver, practiced straightforward economic exchanges, and wore simple clothes made from plant materials. For Luther, this primitive lifestyle's intimate connection with the natural world explained the pre-flood patriarchs' superior health, physical vigor, and unusually long life spans.

Luther speculated that human lifespans were dramatically reduced after the flood, presumably due to the emergence of previously unknown diseases.[31] He thought that the appearance of those new diseases was caused by the dramatic worsening of ecological conditions. For Luther, the flood described in Genesis was an actual historical event that triggered the first ancient environmental crisis with far-reaching consequences. The salt water that covered the earth damaged the good soil. It destroyed trees, piled up sands, and multiplied the number of harmful plants and animals. The resulting damage to the earth affected agricultural production, thus negatively impacting the quality of people's food and, consequently, their health.

In the aftermath of this first environmental crisis, new, ever-threatening diseases continued to emerge and proliferate due to humanity's ever-increasing sin. For Luther, this dynamic had persisted until his own time. Luther noted that in his childhood, syphilis was unknown in Germany. However, it first appeared in Europe around his adolescence and spread so rapidly that, according to Luther, it affected even newborn infants. He observed a similar trajectory in the transmission of what he referred to as the sweating sickness, a previously unknown malady causing a severe outbreak in Wittenberg. Luther recalled circulating accounts of people with snakes nesting in their bellies and worms dwelling in their brains as evidence of the expanding health crises in German lands. With his apocalyptic sensibility, Luther suspected that the rapid propagation of new diseases likely heralded the approaching Judgment Day. While new diseases multiplied, older forms of suffering persisted, including the recurrent and ancient experience of women's reproductive pain, rooted in the fall.[32]

The Genesis of Gendered Pain

Donald Mowbray has demonstrated that medieval questions about the origin of pain and suffering were deeply gendered.[33] With the exception of the collaborative early Franciscan systematic theology, *Summa Halensis* (1236–45), other major scholastic approaches discussed the issue of potential suffering and corruptibility of the human body before the fall with reference to Adam's body. In contrast, the condition of Eve's body in the state of original righteousness invited from medieval scholastics two other questions, both traced to Augustine. The first one wondered whether Eve's virginity would have been physically preserved after sexual intercourse before the fall. This question was based on complex distinctions between different meanings of "corruption." A medieval consensus maintained that while Eve's hymen would have been open (or "corrupted") during sex in the state of innocence, intercourse would have occurred without what was seen as the corruption by sexual desire, pleasure, or other passions. Although Adam would have also lost his virginity if he had sex in Paradise, in the Middle Ages, the question of the corruptibility of the body during intercourse was primarily interrogated about Eve. Scholastic theologians also wondered whether Eve would have experienced suffering during pregnancy and childbirth in the state of innocence. They speculated that Eve would have been likely to experience some burdens of pregnancy but not the intense suffering that came as a punishment after the fall.

In medieval Christianity, Genesis 3:16 had few rivals among biblical passages in its importance for establishing a religious approach to women's reproductive experience and their roles in the family and society. In this passage, God tells Eve that, as a consequence for her disobedience, he "will make your pangs in childbirth exceedingly great; in pain you shall bring forth children, yet your desire shall be for your husband, and he shall rule over you." Premodern theologians read Genesis 3:16 as meting out punishments not only for Eve but for all women, seen as Eve's descendants. They agreed that Eve was subjected to both physical and spiritual chastisements, though they differed in distinguishing which ones were imposed upon her body and which affected her soul. For example, *Summa Halensis*, providing a synthesis of the Franciscan intellectual tradition, described the hardships of pregnancy and pains of childbirth as bodily punishments. In contrast, the woman's subjection to man was a punishment imposed upon a woman's soul or reason.

Thomas Aquinas, in *Summa Theologiae*, similarly identified three kinds of punishments affecting women but believed that all of them pertained exclusively to their bodies. While the first two concerned pregnancy and childbirth, the third chastisement was women's resistance and yet necessity to obey their husbands' will. For Aquinas, the actual male headship was not a punishment but instituted by God even before sin. It was the woman's original disobedience that had turned this divinely established hierarchy into a curse.

This view that Eve's subjection to her husband was part of the good, originally created order was traced back to Augustine and remained dominant in scholastic theology. This approach was also found in the medieval mystical tradition. For example, Bernard of Clairvaux associated Eve with "flesh"—inordinately curious, ignorant, foolish, and lacking wisdom. In contrast, Adam represented higher capacities of the soul, primarily reason. As reason ought to keep the body in subjection, Adam originally had the responsibility to instruct and lead Eve, and the failure of that led to the fall.[34] According to Mickey Mattox's analysis of scholarly commentaries on Genesis produced around Luther's time, the majority of early modern reformers preserved the belief in God's original establishment of gender hierarchy before the fall.

Merry Wiesner-Hanks has shown that early modern tradition typically defined the stages of a man's life by his changing involvement and growing responsibilities in his work and the affairs of his community. While sexual development was acknowledged as an aspect of adolescence viewed as its own stage of man's life, marriage and fatherhood typically did not merit inclusion among the factors defining the man's lifecycle.[35] In contrast, although usually not discussed as formally as men's lives, the stages of an early modern woman's life were determined through her relationship to man and her sexual status, seen as her progression from virginity to marriage to, perhaps, widowhood. While the marriage age varied across regions of Europe and especially by class, puberty commonly rendered girls marriageable. In most cases, early modern marriage meant the beginning of a continuing cycle of pregnancies and pregnancy losses, deliveries, long—up to two years—periods of lactation followed by another pregnancy, and the cycle repeated itself for most of a woman's reproductive life. Reproductive experiences were foundational to early modern perceptions of womanhood, at the core of which—predictably and irreversibly—was pain.

Many early modern women approached their frequent childbirths with apprehension and fear, viewing them as life-threatening and potentially debilitating events that certainly meant agonizing pain. At the same time, women also developed ways to cope, given the routine, mundane, and near-universal nature of such experiences. They used a variety of comforting resources available, including religious consolation, magical charms and rituals, and support from female relatives and friends. Mary Lindemann has estimated that the early modern rate of maternal demise was likely one to two cases per one hundred births, and Merry Wiesner-Hanks assessed the lifetime risk between five and seven percent.[36] While this rate might not seem as overwhelming as it is sometimes imagined today, most women gave multiple births, knew someone who died in childbirth, and perhaps even witnessed a maternal death during labor, which increased the sense of its proximity. More so than death, labor carried the risk of injury and complications, including uterine prolapses, severe vaginal tearing, and most complications associated with high-risk pregnancies for which treatments were unknown and which had devastating consequences for early modern women.

Unlike contemporary North American births, typically occurring with only the father and a midwife or hospital staff present, early modern births were communal affairs, with a number of participants, all of whom were other women. This gender-specific nature of the event reinforced the social connection between childbirth and womanhood, creating tangible and symbolic spaces connecting women's embodied and communal experiences. A woman approaching labor would prepare by choosing and inviting female friends and neighbors to assist her, which had both practical and social functions.[37] The father was never present at childbirth, unless the woman was dying. The rare appearance of a male surgeon was dreaded, as it indicated that the mother and/or infant were passing away, and the surgeon was called to dissect and remove a deceased infant from the mother's body. In the sixteenth century, the birth was commonly managed by a midwife, or in rural areas, by a skilled local woman, if a midwife was not available. Infections of the mother and newborn were rampant. Abnormal fetal presentation, especially if a child was emerging face- or arm-first, required significant skills to turn the fetus *in utero* to enable delivery; if unsuccessful, it was frequently deadly for both mother and child. Similarly, cesarean sections were very rare and almost always resulted in the woman's demise.

In early modernity, infant mortality remained high. For example, in Luther's native Germany, it was estimated at 154 newborn deaths for 1000 live births, the lowest rate among Western European countries.[38] With the exception of upper-class women who likely used wet nurses, many common born women nursed their children until they turned two. Breastfeeding also helped to somewhat space births due to its natural contraceptive effect. Artificial contraceptive methods were rare and underdeveloped, and most women continued to get pregnant until their early forties. Given their shorter-than-current life expectancy, many spent almost the entirety of their adult life raising children, further contributing to the strong early modern association of motherhood with womanhood.

Reproductive loss was common, though in the absence of pregnancy tests and ultrasounds, early modern women were not very aware of first-trimester miscarriages. Pregnancy was believed to be confirmed when a mother felt quickening (fetal movement in utero), which normally did not happen until the fourth or fifth month. A missed period was not regarded as a reliable sign of pregnancy, as most women did not have regular menstrual cycles due to extended breastfeeding. At the same time, delayed menstruation was considered harmful for female bodies, resulting in the common use of herbal remedies to induce periods. While the ingredients in these remedies and their concentration varied, their stronger kinds likely caused uterine contractions and potentially caused early miscarriages, which women would perceive as an expulsion of blood clots rather than as a pregnancy loss. As pregnancy progressed, the risk of stillbirth remained, contributing to the known dangers of childbirth. A barren marriage often caused profound suffering, intertwined with negative economic and relational consequences for the wife, typically considered the one at fault for her alleged inability to conceive or sustain pregnancy.

In this cultural context, in his lectures on Genesis, Luther contemplated what Eve's (and all subsequent women's) reproductive experiences would have been like, had the first mother not believed the serpent. Luther imagined that "just as a pretty girl, without any inconvenience, nay, even with great pleasure and some pride, wears on her head a beautiful wreath woven from flowers, so, if she had not sinned, Eve would have carried her child in her womb without any inconvenience and with great joy."[39] For Luther, the divine verdict upon Eve resulted in women's reproductive suffering that extended beyond labor, encompassing the entire cycle of pregnancy and continuing into the care of an infant.[40] The dangers began at conception, followed by months of discomfort and distress. Luther listed arduous and strange things routinely experienced by pregnant women as consequence of Eve's sin, including "very painful headaches, dizziness, nausea, an amazing loathing of food and drink, frequent and difficult vomiting, toothache, and a stomach disorder which produces a craving, called pica, for foods from which nature normally shrinks."[41] In addition, miscarriages, stillbirths, and infertility were all additional expressions of Eve's curse. Even when a pregnancy was successful, it culminated in an excruciating, perilous, and even life-threatening labor and delivery. While childbirth was the peak of reproductive suffering, even beyond it, Luther noted that the mother's pain and inconveniences went on in her continuing tasks of nourishing her children.

Moreover, according to Luther, Eve's (and all women's) reproductive punishment also included decreased fertility. Luther observed that birds, fish, dogs, cats, and pigs all produced large litters, while a woman—even the most fertile—was generally regrettably limited to birthing only one child per year. Certainly, such deviation of a woman's procreative abilities from the rest of the divinely created animal world must have been due to the consequences of sin! An occasional birth of twins, triplets, or even rare quadruplets happened as a remnant of her once robust fertility and served as a reminder of what would have been possible for a woman, had Eve not sinned.[42]

Luther's theology of bodily suffering consistently featured a theme of hope in the possibility of its alleviation also due to divinely originated healing provided through medicine. However, this emphasis was almost entirely absent from his engagements, specifically with women's reproductive pain. In Luther's historical context, very little help was available to women with pregnancy or labor complications, or even for normal labor pain management. Luther's writings on this subject were grave, acknowledging the inevitably overwhelming agony of women's childbearing experiences that were often life-threatening and anxiety-filled, while stressing God's mercy and grace as the sole sources of relief available to women. In his 1531 sermon, Luther vividly portrayed the increasing distress of a woman nearing childbirth.[43] The expectant mother was progressively apprehensive and vulnerable, unable to predict the severity of impending pain or the outcome of her labors. She could only acknowledge her complete helplessness and beg for God's help. Luther contrasted the spiritual certainty of Christians confident in their salvation with the uncertainty of a woman approaching labor. While God promised salvation on account of faith alone, he did not promise an easy or even moderately uncomfortable labor. On the contrary, God declared that he would greatly increase women's pain in childbearing, which remained true in Luther's era, just as it did in the time of Eve.

While Luther emphasized that the dangers and pains of pregnancy and childbirth were irreversible, he also advocated for behaviors believed in his early modern context to decrease dangers to the unborn child.[44] Pregnant women should be treated gently, never intentionally scared or exposed to potentially disturbing images or experiences, lest this negatively affect the fetus. Luther warned that infants were born with multiple birthmarks or red spots covering their bodies as a result of their pregnant mother getting excited or frightened and moving her hands over the unborn child's subsequently affected parts. He also cited an example of the Wittenberg resident born with the face of a corpse. The poor man believed that this unfortunate transfiguration of his face occurred in his mother's womb when she was startled by the sight of a dead body. An even stranger occurrence was reported in Luther's boyhood town where, seeking to scare mice away, a pregnant woman's neighbor attached a bell to a mouse. Unfortunately, the pregnant woman heard the rodent making music. She was so disturbed that she herself gave birth to a mouse!

These grotesque and outlandish stories were thoroughly rooted in the sixteenth-century understanding of the body. The twenty-first-century Western body, while certainly impacted by external factors, is perceived as an enclosed system in which internal processes are separated by a clear boundary from the outside world. In contrast, as Mary Lindemann argued based on Mikhail Bakhtin's work on Rabelais, an early modern European body was a "porous" system: open to and malleable by the outside world, with its internal processes intertwined with external physical and spiritual occurrences.[45] Unaware of the factors affecting fetal development, early modern thought ascribed congenital abnormalities or even unusual physical appearances of infants to external factors, such as the color of food a pregnant woman ate or the visual images she frequently saw or the animals to which she was exposed. Merry Wiesner-Hanks similarly showed the associations between a mother's consuming red wine and strawberries and red birthmarks in children, or between a pregnant mother's contact with a hare and her child being born with a cleft lip.[46] Efforts to control and prevent instances of potentially harmful interference on the part of the outside world into the female womb sought to avert a feared deformation of the fetus. In this light, Luther's bizarre instructions constituted a sixteenth-century attempt at prenatal care.

Furthermore, Luther's theological commitment of stressing grace over sin compelled him to look for ways in which God's grace ultimately mitigated women's reproductive punishment. Luther pointed out that God's chastisement of Eve could have been significantly harsher, yet she was shown mercy. God did not destroy Eve or altogether condemn her but allowed her to keep her sex and remain a woman. She was not separated from Adam and sentenced to loneliness but was allowed to remain in the company of her husband. Finally, although with greater pain, Eve was still able to reproduce and bear children.

Eve's retained reproductive power led to her and subsequent women's chance to exhibit what Luther repeatedly called the "glory of motherhood."[47] Luther frequently praised women's embodied abilities to nourish children: they were adept at keeping their unborn offspring warm and safe in their wombs, could nurse their infants with their breasts, and knew how to soothe and put to sleep even the fussiest of newborns. All of this was unlike men, who, in Luther's assessment, handled babies with the dexterity of clumsy dancing camels! In his earlier 1522 "Sermon on Married Life," Luther even claimed that if one were not born a woman, they should wish to become one in order to experience the amazing and godly work of childbirth, during which they would also suffer—and possibly die—albeit in a God-honoring way.[48]

Furthermore, Luther interpreted Genesis 3:16 as establishing the divine punishment on women, subjecting them to their husbands against their wills. He also believed that it was a strictly physical chastisement, imposed exclusively on the woman's body and having no bearing on her soul. For example, in his earlier Sermon on Genesis 3, Luther preached that,

> *He [God] gives the woman [Eve] her torment, but proceeds soberly and spares her, absolves her of spiritual misery, and lays the penalty upon her body as with Adam. He says to her, "I will give you much pain when you are pregnant," and after that, "You shall bear your children with sorrow," and thirdly, "You shall humble yourself before your husband, and he shall be your lord." In these three passages you see nothing that does not affect the body. The soul is already saved and has become a child of God. For that reason, God turns eternal punishment into a temporal and physical one.*[49]

Luther's insistence that all of Eve's condemnations solely affected Eve's body enabled him to construct a dialectic between God's physical punishments and spiritual blessings, which he saw pronounced in Genesis. In particular, Luther juxtaposed Eve's bodily punishment and her spiritual triumph by reading Genesis 3:16 alongside Genesis 3:14–15, declaring a curse upon the serpent to be stricken by the woman's offspring. He read this as a promise of Satan's defeat to come specifically through a woman's reproductive power to produce a child. For Luther, it was crucial that Genesis 3:15 identified the serpent's adversary as an offspring (or "seed" in Luther's translation) of a woman, not a man, as Luther thought would be more appropriate. Therefore, this had to be a direct allusion to Mary's role as the mother of Christ, who was not an offspring of a human father. Somehow, hearing God's condemnation on the serpent, Luther's Eve recognized in it a hope of resurrection and eternal life. For this reason, Luther repeatedly described Eve's punishment as "happy and joyful."[50] In fact, having been expelled from the garden, Luther's Eve did not get discouraged and would frequently comfort her husband with the reminders of God's mercy.

In his sermons on Genesis given in 1527, Luther occasionally followed the medieval Aristotelian tradition by describing women as innately less perfect than men, as the moon, albeit glorious, was less perfect than the sun. At the same time, in the same sermons, Luther stated that before the fall, Eve was not inferior to Adam, in either her mind or soul. This hermeneutical tension was resolved by the time of Luther's mature lectures on Genesis, which decisively stressed Eve's original equality with Adam. Unlike the Eve of medieval scholastics, before the fall, mature Luther's Eve "previously was very free and, as the sharer of all the gifts of God, was in no respect inferior to her husband."[51] Eve's subordination to Adam only came as a punishment as a result of her sin. Luther took it for granted that, as a consequence of Eve's disobedience, the woman's sphere of authority had subsequently been limited to household-related affairs and could not extend into the spheres of civic or ecclesial governance. Nevertheless, in his lectures on Genesis, Luther taught that

> *If Eve persisted in the truth, she would not only not have been subjected to the rule of her husband, but she herself would also*

have been a partner in the rule which is now entirely the concern of males."[52]

Thus, Luther departed from the dominant tradition in premodern theology, which considered women's subjugation to men as founded by God even before the fall. In contrast, Luther developed a radical claim for his context that women's subordinate status was neither based on their mental, spiritual, or character inferiority, nor was it part of God's originally established hierarchy. John Thompson has argued that in the history of late medieval and early modern theological tradition, Luther's assertion of the original equality of sexes stood out as the clearest one.[53] Furthermore, for Luther, a woman's subjugation was not imprinted upon her soul, which in Christ would become free and saved from the consequences of the fall. Rather, a woman's subordinate status had originated solely as a punishment for Eve's disobedience, which, as Luther earlier stressed, was exclusively temporal and physical. Luther's discontinuity with the preceding medieval tradition on gender inequality is remarkable. So is his reinterpretation of patriarchy from reflecting women's inherent spiritual status to instead serving as a purely external hierarchy. Both of these shifts could have become helpful in theologically resisting patriarchy and challenging the tradition of misogyny in Christian thought.

And yet Luther's interpretation of Genesis did not challenge patriarchy but reaffirmed it. He saw women's subordination to men as temporal, ending with their physical lives, but in this world, the condemnation was neither relieved nor mitigated. In Luther's context, this assumption was confirmed not only theologically but also experientially. With the preceding tradition, Luther regarded women's subjugation to men as part of a broader punishment imposed on the female body in Genesis 3, the other part being their reproductive suffering. From an early modern perspective, starting from Eve's pregnancies with Cain and Abel and continuing into the sixteenth century, the reality and intensity of women's reproductive suffering remained fundamentally unaltered. The pains of pregnancy and the agony and grave dangers of childbirth continued with dreadful inevitability and little hope of alleviation. For Luther, this was not due to the limitations of prescientific medicine but because female reproductive pain was unchangeably divinely decreed as a consequence of original sin. Similarly, alongside women's reproductive suffering, their subordinate status was also immutably established by the divine decree as punishment for the first transgression. With the unprecedented advances in obstetrics and pain relief in the twenty-first century, the challenge to Luther's patriarchal stance comes not only from contemporary exegesis but also from modern medicine.

5

CONTEMPORARY REFORMATIONS OF MEDICINE AND RELIGION

"MIGHT IT NOT be that only theology can save medicine?"[1] This question concludes Jeffrey Bishop's seminal work in the philosophy of modern medicine, which diagnoses its numerous crises. Posed over a dozen years ago, Bishop's call to engage theology for the reformation of medicine has not been fully heeded by scholars. Few studies that approached medicine with a theological lens primarily relied on early Christian thought, resources specific to the Catholic or Eastern Orthodox traditions, or their own exegesis of biblical passages.[2] Historical Protestant thought has remained an underutilized resource in engaging medicine theologically. While Martin Luther's theology cannot "save" medicine, this chapter contends that insights from his thought can serve as a valuable spiritual resource for addressing and reforming some of the pressing issues in the use and practice of contemporary US medicine.

My proposal to use Luther's early modern deliberations for confronting modern challenges might elicit initial skepticism. At first glance, his historical context at the dawn of scientific medicine is starkly different from our postmodern, highly technological medical landscapes. Moreover, Luther's anxieties over the devil's ubiquitous ploys, his vehement attacks on his theological opponents' healing practices, his patriarchal ideas about gendered suffering, and his literalist readings of Genesis are just a few aspects of his theology that might appear hopelessly anachronistic and frequently offensive to the twenty-first-century reader. Indeed, deeply permeated by early modern religious and medical assumptions, Luther's theology cannot simply be retrieved and applied to challenges within secularized US medicine. However, his thought offers interpretive insights, concepts, and contentions which, if creatively reimagined and put in conversation with current realities, can provide valuable tools for critically elucidating and constructively reforming the nonmaterial dimensions of individuals' experiences of suffering and healing in their relationship to contemporary medical practice. These spiritual resources can help positively transform engagements with medicine by Christian communities of faith, ultimately benefiting the broader state of health care and public health. Overall, my creative employment of early modern Christian thought will contribute to a broader intellectual project of "theological humanism," aiming to utilize religious traditions to enhance shared human experience in a pluralistic society.

In this chapter I develop three potential contributions of Luther's theology for reforming the use and practice of modern medicine. First, I will note the current lack of spiritual resources helping patients engage physical suffering in ways that account for both the historically unprecedented possibilities of modern Western medicine and its persistent limits. Premodern Christian approaches tended to overtly spiritually valorize and normalize pain. They were developed to provide comfort in their contexts marked by pervasive suffering, rudimentary medical knowledge, and basic known treatments. Such approaches are no longer spiritually sustainable in today's settings that offer significantly greater opportunities for relief and recovery due to technologically advanced medicine.

On the other hand, notable religious developments of twentieth-century Christianity, including the Pentecostal-Charismatic movement and liberation theology, have generally approached suffering as an evil to be resisted, with the goal of eventual healing and liberation. Additionally, modern American religiosity has embraced "moralistic therapeutic deism"—a set of beliefs assuming a sense of divine protection over the happiness and fulfillment of virtuous individuals. Overall, major expressions of contemporary Christian theology, practice, and popular spirituality offer limited resources for coping with suffering when it seemingly becomes permanent or irresolvable, such as in cases of chronic and degenerative conditions or terminal disease. I will suggest that Luther's thought can contribute to developing a balanced spirituality of physical suffering in contemporary clinical contexts, holding together its premodern acceptance and late modern resistance. Luther's approach encourages practical resistance to suffering, including through the use of medicine, while remaining spiritually equipped to meet the stubborn persistence of suffering and attentive to its potentially spiritually formative role.

The second contribution of Luther's thought is the reframing of a long-standing question in Christian history about the relationship between supernatural and natural, or medical, healing. Following the emergence of Pentecostal-Charismatic renewal over a hundred years ago, faith healing practices gained renewed and increasing prominence in twentieth- and twenty-first-century Christianity. The rapidly growing global Pentecostal-Charismatic movement regards the continuing availability of divine healing as central to its beliefs, worship, and evangelism. Consequently, it revived old questions about the role of medicine and whether medical healings are inherently spiritually inferior to miraculous ones. The perceived hierarchy between natural and faith healings may leave religious practitioners feeling spiritually defeated or distressed when faced with a seeming lack of divine intervention to heal them or others. It could also negatively impact their health outcomes due to a greater hesitancy in taking advantage of medical help, leading to delayed or inappropriately limited treatments. Luther's theology can disrupt the hierarchy between "natural" and "supernatural" healing, by presenting both types of healing as originated from the same divine source. If constructively appropriated, Luther's exegesis of biblical stories can help religious communities view God's healing distributed through a variety of created means but more commonly through medical ones.

Finally, Luther's theology of the idolatry of medicine can challenge US Christians to recognize their religious-like reliance on modern medicine. Interdisciplinary conversations in medical anthropology, sociology, history, bioethics, and religious studies have noted that present-day Western societies have transferred to medicine certain functions traditionally attributed to religion. Luther's thought challenges the new "healthism" in American culture, which renders individuals responsible for earning the good of health through virtuous health behaviors and portrays health failures as character failures on the part of "undeserving" populations. Furthermore, Americans increasingly rely on medicine to conquer suffering, provide reassurance amid health uncertainties, give hope for healing and restoration, and even defy death against biological odds. When interacting with health care systems, US patients pursue expensive, high-technology medical interventions more frequently, extensively, and with a greater intensity than in peer countries.

Nevertheless, the higher frequency and scope of high-tech medical consumption has failed to produce better clinical outcomes. In the United States, medicine has consistently demonstrated a "preferential option" for the white wealthy, with rising costs and eroding equity. Despite this, a strong cultural religious-like attachment to the "rescue fantasy" of medicine has contributed to a cultural resistance to health care reform, potentially entailing explicit limits or regulated access to some interventions.

In a culture that holds a quasi-religious perception of medicine, the idea of limiting medical interventions potentially available to oneself, even if it would result in greater access for others and not adversely affect one's own prospects of recovery, can be existentially threatening. In light of Scripture and tradition, Christian communities possess underutilized potential to become allies and leaders in the pursuit of a more equitable and just health care system. However, the cultural clinging to medicine for deliverance from suffering and death also affects communities of faith. Luther's concept of idolatry challenges North American Christians to critically examine the unacknowledged religious functions they may be attributing to medicine and to relinquish their idolatrous reliance on it as the primary source of protection and restoration of their vital needs. Luther's theology invites a reformation of Christian spiritualities of medicine, liberating communities of faith to support and work for its greater justice and equity.

A New Reformation of Physical Suffering

Theological reflections on the nature, significance, and implications of suffering constituted a major recurrent theme in the history of the first seventeen hundred years of Christian thought. Suffering was commonly attributed to the destructive effects of sin on humanity, but it was also viewed as spiritually beneficial. Suffering fulfilled Jesus's promise that servants were not greater than their master and that those who followed him must carry their own crosses. For premodern and early modern Christians, the imitation of Christ meant not only emulating his holiness but also being conformed to him in his suffering. Moreover, pain underscored human vulnerability and finitude. It reminded Christians of their status as mortal creatures, unlike that of their eternal divine Creator who punished the first humans for presumptuously attempting to breach that divide. By fostering humility and encouraging prayer, afflictions combated pride, identified since Augustine as humanity's first sin. Tribulations promoted an eschatological hope, by bringing to Christians a painful awareness that this world was not their true home. In a way, suffering was a theological lemon that produced in the life of a Christian a spiritually formative lemonade.

The experiences of physical suffering and bodily pain were seen as particularly conducive to Christian spiritual formation. Their endurance could externally manifest and internally encourage Christian spiritual transformation. In early Christianity, physical torments and death by martyrdom served as both a daunting possibility and the ultimate testimony of Christians perfected in their faith. In the early third century, Tertullian, one of the founders of the Latin theological tradition, taught that Christians should not flee persecution to avoid martyrdom, but instead remain with their communities, firmly prepared to endure in their bodies torture and executions.[3] Not much later in the East, Origen wrote an *Exhortation to Martyrdom*, vividly describing the torments of the body as a means of Christian exaltation and glorification of God.[4]

With the conversion of Constantine and the legalization of Christianity in the Roman Empire, which effectively ended martyrdom, asceticism emerged as a new way of physically embodying a more perfect Christian commitment, surpassing that of ordinary life. Initially practiced in the solitude of the Egyptian desert and later embraced in the West in a communal monastic form, Christian asceticism promoted spiritual excellence, including by means of mortifying or disciplining the body through harsh living conditions, sleep deprivation, celibacy, and fasting. The ascetic tradition evolved and remained prominent in various manifestations throughout the Middle Ages, emphasizing the positive spiritual impact of bodily deprivations for fortifying the spirit and bringing the passions of the flesh under control. In the early modern era of religious persecutions and wars, spiritualized interpretations of bodily suffering gained renewed hermeneutical prominence. In sum, while the history of Christian thought resists broad generalizations, its dominant spiritual ethos in approaching suffering during its first seventeen centuries was that the afflictions endured by the body constituted a painful but spiritually beneficial and essential dimension of human existence. For premodern and early modern Christians, it was not the persistent presence but the absence of suffering that would be cause for surprise.

A broad shift in Christian approaches to suffering began to occur in the eighteenth century, coinciding with the rise of a secular notion of progress as the gradual elimination of suffering in society.[5] While the connection between sin and suffering had always been present in the history of Christian theology, this connection increasingly meant that suffering became understood as evil to be eradicated, rather than as a divine instrument of spiritual correction and growth. Fast-forward to the twentieth century, and a new theological attention to resisting suffering became pivotal for two important developments of late modern Christianity—the emergence of the Pentecostal movement and liberation theology.

The Pentecostal movement, which originated in the early twentieth century, has been described as "the second Reformation," echoing the first Reformation of the early modern era. It has placed a central emphasis on the practices of divine healing and restoration.[6] This emphasis also resulted in a perception of suffering as an overall negative, even demonically induced experience to be spiritually resisted and ultimately defeated. The "prosperity gospel" movement promising health and wealth to its adherents has also been strongly associated with the Pentecostal tradition. While certainly not all Pentecostal Christians endorse the prosperity gospel, the Pentecostal tradition has been criticized, including from within by its own theologians, as struggling to offer a sustainable theological response to uncurable or persistent suffering, beyond devotionally attempting to fix it.[7] This is a significant critique for the fastest growing branch of twenty-first-century Christianity, which recently accounted for 656 million followers and for nearly 27 percent of world Christian population.[8]

At the same time, in the mid-twentieth century, liberation theologians embarked on a project of developing and promoting renewed exegetical and theological justifications for Christian social resistance to suffering with the goal of liberating oppressed communities. In the Latin American context, they stressed the imperative of actively opposing unjust structures and ushering in social change to free the poor and marginalized. Around the same time, in the United States, James Cone argued for the centrality of liberation to the Christian tradition, conceptualizing it as God's gift to those fighting oppression and violence. By drawing on African American religious experience, Scripture, and tradition, Cone grounded liberation in Christology and theologies of atonement. According to Cone, "because he [Jesus] was one with divinity and humanity, the pain of the cross was God suffering for and with us so that our humanity can be liberated for freedom in the divine struggle against oppression."[9] The oppressed must arrive at the realization that, in their pursuit of liberation, God is fighting alongside them. Jesus did not merely bear suffering on the Cross but fought and won against suffering and death on behalf of humanity, setting an example and a mandate for his followers.

While liberation theological production in its various forms has largely remained within the academy, there has been an increasing embrace of social liberation emphases among grassroots Pentecostal movements, approaching social oppression as a form of spiritual oppression to be terminated.[10] While liberation theology primarily addresses suffering resulting from social injustice, its foundational theological presuppositions, centered on the divine struggle against suffering, oppression, and death, align with the Pentecostal tradition's generally negative perspective on suffering as actively opposed by God.[11]

Both the Pentecostal tradition and liberation theology have exerted a significant positive influence on twenty-first-century Christianity and its role in society. They have introduced revitalized practices and theological perspectives centered around the resistance to suffering and the eradication of oppression. Much of this influential output, whether explicitly or implicitly, arose as a reaction to perceived Christian compliance in suffering, which could be traced to prevailing theological models of valorizing suffering in earlier eras. At the same time, in the late modern West, where substantial progress is being made in opposing suffering and promoting justice, there remains a noticeable dearth of new religious resources, appropriate for current contexts and addressing what to do when the struggle with suffering proves insurmountable.

Further exacerbating this theological trouble with suffering, a form of religiosity, termed "moralistic therapeutic deism" by sociologists Christian Smith and Melinda Lundquist Denton, has been increasingly popular among younger generations of Christians. "Moralistic therapeutic deism" imagines God as watching over and helping good people to have good lives, marked by happiness and fulfillment.[12] Unlike the Pentecostal tradition or liberation theology, the moralistic-therapeutic Christianity falls short to actively engage the practices of justice and healing. Often stemming from racial and class privilege, it assumes an eventual divine resolution of personal problems. Consequently, this form of religiosity becomes profoundly inadequate for resourcing and spiritually equipping its adherents when they are confronted with instances of severe and seemingly insurmountable suffering.

In sum, while the dominant ethos of premodern and early modern Christian approaches to suffering often stressed its inevitability and its positive spiritually formative role, prominent late modern Christian approaches tend to interpret persistent suffering either as evil to be resisted and ultimately eliminated, or as a theological surprise, which should not have impacted good people. None of these approaches is fully adequate for spiritually aiding those dealing with physical suffering in the twenty-first-century Western medical contexts.[13] Some contemporary Christian theologians have advocated the retrieval of the premodern tradition as providing valuable answers to modern questions about the suffering of the body. However, much of premodern Christianity's spiritualization and valorization of suffering, produced in the context of limited medical options, comes in conflict with remarkably greater opportunities for healing and relief now available due to the historically unprecedented advances in modern medicine. The emphasis on the positive formational role of suffering may also be conveniently interpreted as downplaying the imperative to actively resist societal injustices that contribute to health disparities.

At the same time, while late modern medicine has made significant achievements in prolonging life and partially improving symptoms, it has not been as successful in learning to fully cure numerous conditions. The reality of chronic and degenerative conditions, permanent disability, and terminal disease remains pervasive. If Christians prioritize resistance as their main reaction to afflictions, they will find themselves lacking spiritual resources when their bodies are confronted with expanding and seemingly unstoppable suffering. Many will lack the adequate theological tools to make sense of what they may perceive as both a failure of medicine and a failure of God to deliver them from the adversity of suffering.

Luther's thought offers spiritual resources for engaging physical suffering in ways that would be sensitive to both the historically unprecedented possibilities and the persistent limits of modern Western medicine. The hermeneutical spaciousness found in his theology of physical afflictions holds together their diverse interpretations and makes room for both acceptance and resistance to suffering. Luther was certainly not surprised by the enduring pervasiveness of suffering. On the contrary, he would have been alarmed by the absence of troubles and hardships in the lives of Christians, since it would indicate their feeble or misguided faith that the world and the devil would not perceive as a threat. For Luther, in some, but not all cases, physical calamities could be divinely imposed as divine discipline or bitter medicine for wayward believers. Christians also suffered due to offenses from the unfaithful world, the assaults of the devil, the pervasive consequences of sin since the fall, and their conformity to Christ. While the intransigent Luther might seem an unlikely candidate to offer a theological "middle way," through his theological distinction between the inner and the outer person, Luther retained the premodern spiritual validation of suffering while predating the late modern resistance to it.

Luther emphasized that Christians were called to suffering in their bodies to foster growth in faith, reliance on God, perseverance in prayer, and conformity to Christ. At the same time, Christians were also called to resist bodily suffering, including through the use of medicine, since by resisting suffering, the church opposed the devil and his forces of death and destruction.[14] In fact, according to Luther, it would be a sin for Christians to recklessly endanger their bodies, refuse an opportunity to faithfully alleviate their physical suffering or provide for the needs of their bodies. Luther's thought implores the sick to diligently and actively seek relief, including through the use of medicine, while remaining attentive to the potential spiritual growth spurs provided by afflictions. It resources Christians to expect the inevitable seasons of suffering, during which they should remain hopeful and persistent in their pursuits of healing, yet also spiritually prepared for the possibility that healing might not occur. In other words, his theological approach encourages Christians to diligently use medicine, but without placing their hope in its limited means.

Miraculous Healings and Modern Medicine

A belief in healing miracles has been a part of the Christian tradition since its inception. The Gospel accounts of Jesus's ministries record seventy-two instances of exorcisms and healings, with forty-one detailing distinct episodes.[15] The New Testament writings and early Christian texts also mention occurrences of miraculous recoveries. Concurrently, the early Christian tradition witnessed the development of a line of thought denouncing naturalistic medicine on religious grounds, although historians of Christianity have generally considered this to be a marginal tradition.[16] For instance, the second-century Gnostic leader Marcion considered the material world to be inherently evil. Marcion allegedly removed the phrase "beloved physician" from the description of Luke in the epistle to the Colossians. In the late second century, Tertullian initially affirmed the utility of medicine in some of his earlier works. However, in his later writings in the early third century, he seemed to view the use of medicine as largely pagan.[17] Simultaneously, in the East, Tatian, a second-century Syrian Christian thinker, promoted severe asceticism and condemned the use of medicine due to its material nature, juxtaposing it to spiritual healing by God. Likewise, in North Africa in the late second and early third centuries, Arnobius of Sicca contrasted medicine, based on human reason, with divine healing empowered by God without recourse to material means.

At the same time, these condemnations of medicine were developed as part of theological agendas that sharply opposed the material to the spiritual and that were eventually denounced as heterodox. For example, Marcion's dualist Gnostic teachings were deemed heretical, leading during his lifetime to his excommunication by the Church of Rome. Arnobius's beliefs were linked to Marcion's, and Tertullian's writings against medicine likely came after his conversion to the Montanist movement, also regarded as heterodox. Tatian was accused by Irenaeus of practicing Gnosticism and founding the Gnostic Encratite sect, which, in addition to medicine, reportedly forbade marriage, alcohol, and the consumption of meat. In contrast, prominent early and late antique thinkers, including Clement of Alexandria, Gregory of Nazianzus, Basil the Great, John Chrysostom, and Augustine, at different points expressed a positive view of medicine as part of God's good creation for the benefit of humanity.

Nevertheless, some theologians of prominent and unquestioned orthodoxy approached medicine as ultimately inferior to faith healing. Without rejecting medicine, they maintained a spiritual hierarchy between medical and miraculous faith cures. For example, Augustine and Gregory of Nazianzus, while commending medicine, considered miraculous healing to be even more excellent, since it unambiguously revealed the power of God.

Occasionally, this hierarchy between the supernatural and natural healing was developed to the point of discouraging or even prohibiting truly spiritual Christians from using medicine, and instead urging them to seek God's supernatural healing. For example, in the early third century, Origen delineated two approaches to medicine based on one's attainment of Christian perfection. For ordinary believers, the utilization of medical means was permissible and even recommended. However, Origen advised more perfect Christians to rely solely on God for healing. Origen drew an analogy between marriage and medicine: just as he regarded celibacy to be better than marriage, so reliance on God alone for healing was superior to the use of medicine. A similar perspective was outlined in the surviving fourth-century homilies whose contested authorship has been attributed to St. Macarius, a prominent figure in an ascetic movement in Egypt. These homilies discouraged monks from using medicine and claimed that, despite its usefulness and divine origin, medicine was intended for the people of the world. In contrast, devout monks must pursue ascetic practices and, if they become ill, place complete trust in God's healing.

This sentiment persisted two centuries later in the teachings of St. Barsanuphius, a Christian hermit from Palestine. In his letters of spiritual counsel, St. Barsanuphius asserted that consulting physicians indicated a weaker faith, while placing full hope in God's healing alone manifested a perfect faith in God, a state he conceded was attainable by only a few. The stance, relegating the use of medicine to spiritually weaker Christians and urging those with stronger faith to rely on God alone for healing, appears to have endured, at least in Eastern Christianity, into the late Middle Ages. For example, as late as the fourteenth century, the renowned Byzantine theologian St. Gregory of Palamas noted that it was customary among some spiritual fathers to forbid their monks from using medicine when they fell ill.

However, in the modern era, the questions about the alleged supremacy of miraculous healing over natural remedies diminished in relevance, under the influence of the rising skepticism toward ideas regarded as anti-intellectual and superstitious. During the Enlightenment with its emphasis on the primacy of reason, Christian theologians grappled with concerns over the perceived irrationality of Christian faith. For those striving to secure a greater alignment of Christianity with the intellectual tenets of the Enlightenment, beliefs in miracles became a theological liability to be addressed. For example, in his seminal work, *The Christian Faith*, Friedrich Schleiermacher developed a comprehensive critique of traditional beliefs in miracles on pragmatic, epistemological, and metaphysical grounds.[18] Schleiermacher's theology prepared the ground for many emphases of the ensuing emergence of liberal Protestant thought, including its suspicion of miracles. Subsequently, with the advent of the historical-critical method and the quest for the historical Jesus in nineteenth-century Western scholarship, scholars increasingly challenged their literal and traditional interpretations. Once prominent, questions about medical and supernatural cures were now relegated to the periphery of academic theological inquiry.

Moreover, while the authenticity of miraculous healings in the Christian tradition faced academic scrutiny, they also gradually diminished in significance within the life of the church. The Reformation's rejection of established practices for seeking wondrous healing through the intercession of saints disrupted longstanding religious customs without offering a clear Protestant alternative. Furthermore, following the Reformations, a new theological perspective on miracles, known as cessationism, had emerged. Originally associated with the Reformed tradition, cessationism spread beyond it and took firm root in many Protestant denominations. Cessationism posited that, while early miracles were genuine, they served to confirm the initial credibility of the teachings of Christ. At some point, with the conclusion of the apostolic age and the establishment of the biblical canon, miracles had fulfilled their intended role. They ceased during the first centuries of Christianity and were no longer available to the church.

However, miraculous healing attained a renewed significance for contemporary Christian practice following the emergence of the Pentecostal tradition in the early twentieth century.[19] Pentecostal Christianity emphasizes what Miroslav Volf characterized as the "materiality of salvation," manifested through tangible physical signs, including prophecy, glossolalia (speaking in tongues), exorcism, and divine healing, which is the preferred Pentecostal term for miraculous faith healing.[20] It has been argued that divine healing holds the central importance for Pentecostal religious expression, surpassing even the significance of the practice of glossolalia.[21] Healing has been functioning as a Pentecostal "sign of redemption," playing a conspicuous role in worship services and evangelism.

In light of its emphasis on healing miracles, from its inception the Pentecostal tradition has wrestled with the role of medicine. Rooted in the holiness movement and a series of revival meetings in the United States and globally, the public emergence of North American Pentecostalism happened at the Azusa Street revival that commenced on the eponymous street in Los Angeles in 1906. Its participants were reported to witness numerous miraculous signs, prominently including healings. The revival's presider William Seymour played a key role in shaping the theological direction of the emerging movement, including through the Azusa Street Mission's periodical *Apostolic Faith*. Seymour taught in the *Apostolic Faith* that "medicine is for unbelievers, but the remedy for the saints of God we will find in James 5:14." He also insisted that Jesus would provide divine healing "for all those who have faith in him."[22]

It is worth pointing out that Seymour did not condemn or reject medicine altogether. He believed it was useful, although for "unbelievers" who lacked Christian faith. This stance toward medicine echoed the attitudes of earlier Christian writers who taught that spiritually superior Christians had no need for medical interventions. This sentiment was not unique to Seymour, as early Pentecostals were documented to forbid their members from consulting physicians or using medicine.[23]

Over time, the tradition of explicitly prohibiting medicine among the faithful has significantly diminished within the Pentecostal movement, but a hierarchy between divine and medical healing has persisted. For instance, Aimee Semple McPherson, a leading Pentecostal celebrity evangelist of the twentieth century, would wear a nurse outfit at her revival meetings during which she performed faith healings.[24] This choice of nurse attire served to underscore the cultural significance of medicine as a symbol of healing while simultaneously highlighting its ultimate superfluousness compared to divine healing power. Even more recently, such as during and immediately following the COVID-19 pandemic, studies have indicated that, compared to the general population and other Christian denominations, Pentecostal communities worldwide exhibited greater hesitancy toward vaccination on religious grounds.[25]

Pentecostal (and its related Charismatic) movement has been experiencing explosive growth, projecting to reach one billion followers by 2050 and encompass a third of the world's Christians.[26] The rapid expansion of the movement underscores the ongoing vitality of questions surrounding medical and miraculous healing for twenty-first-century Christian communities of faith. Does the inability to receive divine healing signal one's lack of holiness or weakness of faith? Should a believer first seek supernatural recovery through prayer and anointing before resorting to medical means? The perceived hierarchy between natural and faith healings may leave Christians feeling spiritually defeated or distressed when they face an apparent lack of divine intervention to heal them or others. A greater hesitancy in taking advantage of medical help could also adversely affect medical outcomes, due to delayed or inappropriately limited treatments.

Luther's early modern theology of medicine speaks with insight to such enduring questions, which carry significant practical implications.[27] Influenced by the late medieval nominalist distinction between God's absolute and ordained power, Luther posited that God predominantly exercised the latter form of power, operating through the laws and means of nature, including providing healing through medicine. Luther did not deny the reality of healing miracles. According to him, the significantly less frequent occurrence of supernatural faith cures compared to natural, medical ones should not be interpreted as a manifestation of God's unwillingness to restore a petitioner's health or as a result of the petitioner's lack of faith. Rather, it reflected God's sovereign choice to govern the world through his ordained power, channeled within the bounds of the natural laws that God originally established through his absolute power. For Luther, God could certainly choose to exercise his absolute power, as instances of faith cures manifested, however experience indicated that God preferred to heal through medicine, not miracles.

Additionally, Luther's theology challenges a spiritual hierarchy between medical and miraculous faith healings. According to his logic, both forms of healing exhibited a parallel causal structure. In both cases, God acted as the primary, ultimate cause of healing, which was then distributed through God's chosen means. Usually, these means were divinely established, natural secondary causes, as seen in instances like Hezekiah's healing through the application of an anti-inflammatory poultice. More rarely, God healed through means naturally unfit for healing and only effective through God's absolute power, exemplified by the healing of the Israelites through looking at the Bronze Serpent. Consequently, it would be erroneous for a Christian to view miraculous healing as spiritually superior, since both miraculous and medical healing ultimately originated from the same divine source. Luther's model even implicitly questions the reference to miraculous healing as "divine healing" in the Pentecostal-charismatic tradition. For Luther, both natural and supernatural faith modes of healing were equally divine.

Moreover, Luther's thought challenges a tradition of Christian skepticism toward medicine, which suggests that, compared to expecting miraculous healing, using medicine signifies a weaker faith or a lack of trust in God. Luther vehemently insisted on the importance of relying for healing on God, not medicine. But what did reliance on God in matters of health practically entail? For some of Luther's—and of our own—contemporaries, it might imply trusting in God's provision of supernatural recovery. But for Luther, such an expression of trust would constitute a theologically misplaced reliance on God's absolute power while bypassing his ordained power. Moreover, it would contradict biblical teachings about the goodness and usefulness of the material world. According to Luther, proper Christian trust affirmed the original goodness of created means, as proclaimed by God, after God fashioned the world. Such trust acknowledged God's desire for humanity to utilize created means as partners in divine work, as evidenced by God delegating to the first people the task of tilling and cultivating his garden even before the fall. Far from indicating a lack of faith, using medicine represented a proper expression of trust in God.

A Spiritual Reformation of Medicine

Renowned medical ethicist Daniel Callahan once distinguished between two stages in the history of Western medicine, in relation to its evolving role and influence in society.[28] The first stage was that of prescientific medicine, wherein medical explanations were typically limited and often misguided. The earlier chapters of this book showed that diagnostic, treatment, and palliative tools during this period were quite rudimentary, and access to them was generally restricted to the affluent sick. In light of these realities, in the premodern West, Christianity assumed a significant role in assigning meaning to the persistent reality of suffering and offering devotional tools to respond to it. While prescientific medicine saw occasional advancements in its knowledge and practice, they were modest and sporadic. These advancements could not yet resource a narrative of sustained medical progress that emerged to define what Callahan termed the second stage of medicine.

Our current, second stage commenced with the beginning of the scientific transformation of medicine in early modernity. As previously noted, in the sixteenth century, Andreas Vesalius established that the direct study of the body through dissection was essential for anatomical knowledge. In the early seventeenth century, Francis Bacon's writings laid the theoretical foundations for assessing the veracity of knowledge by testing hypotheses through repeated experimentation. The principle of experimentation was soon brought to medicine by William Harvey, through his discovery of blood circulation and the function of the heart. The advent of the scientific method facilitated the pursuit of a new and ambitious agenda for medicine.

As Michel Foucault argued in his *Birth of the Clinic*, starting from the Enlightenment, scientific medicine in the West began to actively influence the philosophical view of the human person. Foucault's analysis of medical discourse in late-eighteenth and early-nineteenth-century France highlighted a paradigmatic shift in localizing and mapping of disease within the human body, informed by the emergence of a novel medical perspective on death. Death offered a new outlook on disease and the patient's body, now viewed as its living embodiment.[29] This perspectival transformation necessitated a reconfiguration of medical discourse around defining the reformed contours of modern medical visibility. It demanded that doctors adopt what

Foucault termed a "medical gaze," focusing on biomedical data while overlooking non-biomedical information from a patient's narrative.

According to Foucault, these paradigmatic shifts in physicians' perspectives on death, the patient's body, and the corresponding evolution in medical discourses were not merely advancements in medical scientific method; they also carried profound ontological implications. These shifts fundamentally altered Western engagements with finitude, signifying a cultural moment in Europe when henceforth "medical thought [became] fully engaged in the philosophical status of man."[30] Since the Enlightenment, medicine has actively participated in shaping humanity's quest for meaning. In particular, Western medicine has promoted the belief in the possibility of mastering nature. It fostered faith in the ever-expanding possibilities of science to diminish suffering, alter human bodies, and extend life. Such goals were both individually and socially desirable, and their advances appeared unstoppable.

Moreover, in the twentieth century, the emergence of new medical possibilities, coupled with medicine's involvement in the cultural production of meaning, led to what Callahan termed a "social expansionism" of late "second-stage" medicine. Medicine began assuming roles in society that were previously fulfilled by other practices. Even the definition of health itself has undergone evolution. Previously, concepts of health were primarily biomedical, focusing on normal bodily functions. However, in 1948 the World Health Organization transformed the definition of health by connecting it to overall well-being. It now defines health as "a state of complete physical, mental, and social well-being and not merely the absence of disease or infirmity."[31] This comprehensive understanding of well-being, now labeled "health," is the objective that "second-stage" medicine is tasked and trusted with achieving.

In light of these developments, scholars of medical anthropology, sociology, history, bioethics, and the study of religion have been exploring the question of whether and how contemporary Western medicine might have assumed functions traditionally attributed to religion.[32] For example, in his classic essay, "The Religious Features of Scientific Medicine," Harold Vanderpool argued that modern medicine exhibits seven out of ten phenomenological characteristics of religion.[33] For instance, medicine acts as a "protective screen," offering hope to shield and rescue those seeking its protection and intervention from the deeply feared experiences of pain, suffering, and even death. Moreover, even the awareness of the promise of medical interventions relieves anxiety and apprehension not only for those directly affected by health crises but also for society at large. According to Vanderpool, medicine metaphorically draws a curtain of separation between the realm of the healthy and the formidable domain of physical suffering.[34] Additionally, diseases, injuries, and other forms of physical suffering bring not only pain but also the dread of the unknown. By providing a diagnosis, medicine names a patient's suffering, alleviating this dread by transforming the unknown into something known and identified. When a patient asks, "What is wrong with me?" it becomes an existentially significant question to which medicine provides a naturalistic explanation and, akin to religion, may offer a path to healing as salvation.

Vanderpool noted that, similar to religion, modern medicine resists limiting hopes in what it can accomplish. Medical hope often refuses to be constrained by biomedical reality, by fostering optimism in new, experimental treatments or potentially overly aggressive uses of life-sustaining technology. This hope is conveyed and affirmed through religious-like symbols of set-apart clinical authority, such as red crosses or physicians' white coats. In clinical settings, finality is accepted with difficulty and proclaimed with reluctance, influenced by what Howard Broody described as the medical "rescue fantasy," driving physicians to employ every possible measure to defy a patient's death and encouraging patients and their loved ones to seek the same.[35] Similarly, societal discourse on medical progress frequently implies a defiance of its eventual limits.

In their book, *Hostility to Hospitality: Spirituality and Professional Socialization within Medicine*, Michael and Tracy Balboni contended that secular medicine's foundational structures mirror those of Christian religion.[36] For example, within the cultural imaginary, physicians act similar to priests, mediating access to health as the highly desired good. Hospitals operate as set-apart spaces, providing coveted access to healing, while therapies and medical interventions function as ritualized practices of restoration and defiance against death. Having established this parallel, the Balbonis argued that, while reflecting elements of Christianity, contemporary Western medicine divorced itself from all religious and metaphysical commitments, instead orienting its structures solely toward an utterly material telos located within itself. For the Balbonis, this orientation has had adverse practical consequences. The discourse of medical progress extols the alleviation of suffering, prolongation of life, and maximization of health as paramount values as well as goals worthy of growing societal and individual financial investment. At the same time, medicine itself assumes the responsibility for achieving these objectives. The role of patients has been reduced to trusting the aims, expertise, and benevolence of medical structures, while contributing financially to their prosperity.

Additionally, modern medicine frequently frames adherence to its guidelines not merely as a matter of prudence but as a moral choice. For example, abstaining from smoking, maintaining a healthy diet, managing weight, exercising regularly, and undergoing routine health checks are presented as integral to leading a good life. Conversely, failure to comply is increasingly viewed not just as imprudent behavior, but as ethically flawed and reflective of character deficiencies. This "medical guardianship," presenting health promotion in moral terms, is reinforced by public health campaigns advocating for specific behaviors and serving as medicine's evangelistic efforts for the greater good of public health.

In their essay, "Neither a Sinner, nor a Saint: Health as a Present-Day Religion in the age of Healthism," Swedish scholars Barbro Wijma and Britta Pelters highlighted the perceived role of medicine in Western societies as the chief mediator ensuring and maintaining access to the ultimate good of well-being.[37] Wijma and Pelters contend that while its stated goals are beneficial for public health, "modern scientific medicine has become a culturally powerful, propagation-aggressive religion of health establishment," which they termed "healthism."[38] They further analyzed how health choices are portrayed as ethical decisions, positioning individuals as moral agents who are ultimately responsible for deserving the good of health. Drawing parallels with Weber's seminal essay, "The Protestant Ethic and the Spirit of Capitalism," Wijma and Pelters suggested that "healthism" operates on a similar logic of personal moral effort. Moral "health character" is grounded in self-discipline, hard work, and obedience to medical scientific authority regarding what is beneficial. This character is seen as yielding the reward of good health. Conversely, one's refusal to walk in the spirit of healthism leads to medical impairments, for which individuals are considered accountable.

Capitalist "healthism" has proven to be deeply classist. It appeals to a sense of moral health superiority of the middle and upper classes, who possess necessary resources to practice healthism, over lower "health" classes. The perceived failures of the latter to maintain health are viewed as their personal character failures, while broader cultural issues involved are conveniently overlooked. In the United States, moralistic healthism has become pervasive. It has become culturally commonplace to question whether a cancer patient smoked, if a heart attack patient was overweight, or whether a mother of a differently abled child used alcohol or harmful medications during pregnancy. Even age-related frailties, once viewed as normal manifestations of growing older, are now medicalized. Individuals who manage to reach advanced age without developing common conditions like mobility issues or cognitive decline are now elevated not as rare examples but as role models for successful aging. The overarching framework of healthism is thoroughly grounded in the assumption that medical issues are earned consequences for one's irresponsible behaviors, while physical well-being is a due reward for health-controlled living. This framework reminds one of the religious view of health as a sign of righteousness, against which Luther vehemently argued in his lectures on Genesis.

Luther's theology of suffering and health challenges healthism with its notions of disease as punishment and of health as reward for virtuous behavior. While Luther allowed for an interpretation of suffering as a consequence of one's actions, he also emphasized that physical afflictions arose from various causes, often without blame falling on the sufferer. He stressed that while health was a divine gift and blessing, it should never be treated as a sign of righteousness. Luther's thought encourages the communities of faith to encounter those who suffer with grace, rather than with judgment or suspicion of health sin. His perspective also challenges healthism's classist stance, rendering those with limited resources for practicing it as health sinners responsible for their suffering.

Furthermore, in the United States, religious-like approaches to physical well-being and medicine have been driven by capitalist health care systems, with vested financial interest in promoting such attitudes to increase their profits. Indeed, unlike Luther's vision of the gospel promise of salvation, which was given freely and did not require human contributions, in the United States, medicine's promises of salvation, perfection, and alleviation of suffering primarily benefit the white rich. This reality has been corroborated by numerous studies on health disparities and inequalities across class and race.[39] For instance, it has been assessed that at the age of forty, the wealthiest one percent of Americans enjoy a life expectancy of ten to fifteen years greater (varying by gender) than the poorest one percent. Another study showed that Hispanic individuals were over two hundred and fifty percent more likely to be uninsured than non-Hispanics.[40] Moreover, three in ten adults between the ages of fifty and sixty-four reported having forgone essential expenses, including food, clothing, utilities, and over-the-counter drugs, in order to be able to pay for medical care, with the number especially high for women and African Americans.[41]

Despite these striking inequalities, for years, the United States spending on health care per capita has been the largest among wealthy countries. It was recently estimated to be over twice the average of other affluent nations.[42] However, these considerably greater investments have not translated into better health outcomes, which have lagged behind in common metrics, including life expectancy, infant mortality, and the management of conditions such as asthma and diabetes.[43]

Studies have identified a number of factors primarily responsible for the unsustainable costs of health care in America. These included inflated administrative expenses, lack of regulation on prescription drug prices, insufficient availability of primary care, and, importantly, high utilization of extensive high-tech care for medically redundant procedures and diagnostic tests.[44] Research has shown that when more privileged Americans do interact with health care, they embrace it with a remarkable degree of intensity, consuming a large volume of medical interventions.[45] This would be justifiable, if it resulted in better medical outcomes. However, multiple studies have shown that greater consumption of high-tech medical services does not correlate with an improved quality of care or superior health outcomes.[46] For example, heart disease has been the leading cause of mortality in the United States. Compared to Canada, the United States has four times more MRIs, three times more cardiac surgeons, and has documented a significantly higher rate of the performance of invasive cardiac testing and procedures following a heart attack.[47] However, despite this, the US heart attack survival rates within a year after the event have been virtually identical to those in Canada, while heart disease mortality rates have been rising.[48]

Moreover, while failing to produce better health outcomes, medical overconsumption has hurt health care access, equity, and affordability. While the American health care system over-provides expensive high-tech treatments and tests, it routinely under-provides cheaper routine and preventative services. Additionally, reflecting what has been termed "a paradox of plenty," access to clinical services have been hindered in the geographic regions of the United States with the most extensive medical resources and utilization.[49]

Health economists have noted that creating sustainable and cost-effective medicine would have to involve imposing certain limits or more regulated access to some interventions, following the example of peer countries that have successfully maintained a comparable or higher level of care while keeping costs manageable.[50] The United States health care system is already plagued by implicit rationing, which is ultimately less equitable, transparent, and cost-effective than a more explicit approach to health care resource allocation. However, despite the expanding crises of medical affordability and accessibility, culturally, the idea of introducing any form of explicit rationing into health care is met with strong resistance from a significant portion of the population.

This cultural resistance has been commonly interpreted through the lens of ethical concerns about resource allocation or philosophical differences in viewing health care as either a "privilege" or a "human right."[51] However, I propose that the quasi-religious functions assigned to medicine in American society also play a role. As Callahan observed long ago, "Americans are in love with healthcare" and "attach [to it] their ideals and hopes."[52] He argued that garnering public support for a meaningful reform would require a fundamental shift away from the belief in medicine as the primary conqueror of suffering, provider of comprehensive well-being, and defeater of death through the prolonging of physical life as much as biologically possible. Limiting medical interventions potentially available to oneself, even if it would not adversely affect one's prospects of recovery, can be existentially threatening in a culture that holds a quasi-religious perception of medicine.

When medicine is seen as the primary source of fulfilling one's most vital needs, there is a natural inclination to desire its highest availability for oneself, even if it comes at the expense of making it out of reach for others.

Christian communities possess an underutilized potential to become active allies in promoting efforts to achieve a more just and equitable access to medical resources. Christian Scripture strongly supports the moral imperative to extend healing to the wounded, hurting, sick, and oppressed. Likewise, the history of Christianity showcases a rich tradition of developing and contributing to the creation of institutions and initiatives providing health care especially to the poor and marginalized. However, the cultural clinging to medicine for deliverance from suffering and death also affects communities of faith. Expanding Christian efforts for medical justice first demands a reformation of Christian spiritualities of medicine.

I contend that the successful facilitation of such a reformation for Christian faith communities would benefit from exposing and addressing the religious functions implicitly assigned to medicine through an explicitly religious lens. Luther's theology of idolatry and its application to medicine provides valuable tools to illuminate and challenge assumptions about modern medicine and its role. A distinctive aspect of Luther's theology of idolatry is its departure from the traditional association of idolatry with misdirected worship to a definition of idolatry as misplaced reliance. An object of idolatry in itself may be good, as medicine is a good divine creation; however, improper emotional attachments can lead to its ultimate misuse.

Have Christians placed their ultimate hopes for healing, deliverance, and restoration in medicine? Have these attitudes contributed to the development of unjust health care systems driven by profit? Are they inhibiting efforts to bring healing to all who are sick, hurting, poor, and oppressed? North American Christians must critically examine their potentially idolatrous attachments to medicine and consider how these attachments might hinder their willingness to share its means with others. Instead, they should embrace their religious tradition's call to extend inclusive healing to their neighbors in need. Luther's theology invites a reformation of Christian spiritualities of medicine, liberating faith communities to contend for more just and equitable access to health care resources for all.

CONCLUSION

IN 1543, THREE years before Martin Luther's death, Flemish physician Andreas Vesalius began the scientific reformation of medicine with the publication of his *De humani corporis fabrica libri septem* (*On the Fabric of the Human Body in Seven Books*).[1] Composed as an anatomy textbook, Vesalius's work introduced numerous novel insights into the structural organization of the human body and some of the functions of its organs, thereby correcting previous understandings of medieval Galenic medicine.[2] Vesalius illustrated his groundbreaking arguments by intricate drawings and diagrams, informed by his meticulous dissections and the study of human cadavers. While dissections had previously been perceived as a repugnant task relegated to untrained assistants, Vesalius performed them personally, including in public demonstrations for educational purposes, thus establishing this practice as an integral part of early modern medical education.

Vesalius consistently justified his revolutionary claims by appealing to the human body, which he referred to as "the true book."[3] He responded to students' anatomical queries by encouraging them to examine and feel the dissected bodies for themselves. Although records of Vesalius's confessional affiliation have not survived, it has been suggested that a central commitment of Luther's reformation—restoring the supreme authority of Scripture in matters of faith—influenced Vesalius's method, with its emphasis on the body as the ultimate source of knowledge in matters of medicine.[4] Just as Luther insisted on testing the traditions and historical theologies of the church against the Bible, Vesalius similarly advocated measuring anatomical traditions and the writings of ancient authorities against the "true book" of the body. At the same time, neither the founder of the medical nor of the religious reformation initially intended for their agendas to spark a "revolution." Vesalius aimed to correct errors and restore the original principles of the ancient anatomical tradition, much like Luther sought to recover the original meaning of the gospel, as confessed by the early church.

Luther's closest ally and friend, theologian and religious reformer Philip Melanchthon, held Vesalius in high regard and was deeply influenced by the assertions of his new anatomy. In 1552, prompted by Vesalius's findings, Melanchthon revised and published his treatise *Liber de anima* (*the Book of the Soul*), originally composed in 1540 as a commentary on Aristotle's treatise on the soul.[5] Melanchthon saw new anatomical knowledge as directly relevant for theology; he even wrote a series of orations discussing the workings of the heart, trachea, and esophagus, based on Vesalius's teachings. For Melanchthon, anatomy testified of God as the creator of nature, offered insights into the place and operations of the soul within the human body, and provided a new avenue for attaining deeper knowledge of God, the original author of the body. Consequently, while at medieval universities anatomy had traditionally been taught exclusively to medical students, Melanchthon introduced it to students of arts and philosophy, ultimately ensuring that all students at the University of Wittenberg studied this subject.

The theological significance attributed to anatomy by Melanchthon and his colleagues also resulted in an expansion of the influence of Protestant religious thought on medical faculty at the University of Wittenberg. It eventually led Lutheran physicians to develop a distinct perspective on the human body, combining novel scientific insights and specific theological beliefs. Vivian Nutton termed this new perspective "Wittenberg anatomy."[6] The emergence of the reformation of medicine in early modern universities was marked by vigorous polemics between Galenists and proponents of Vesalius's new anatomy. Lutheran anatomists supported Vesalius's teachings, also perceived as theologically beneficial for understanding creation, mortality, and divine providence. The Lutheran "Wittenberg anatomy" spread to other Protestant universities, promoting new medical knowledge while maintaining its connections to particular theological presuppositions.[7]

This influential project of theological anatomy came after Luther. Until the end of his life, Luther refrained from openly lending the weight of his theological support to academic debates shaping the emerging medical science. He upheld his intention to leave the reformation of medical curricula to the medical faculty, as stated in his 1520 programmatic treatise issued at the dawn of the Reformation.[8] Rather than attempting to theologically assess competing anatomical claims, Luther focused on the Christian reception of medicine and the appropriate practical and affective engagements with physical suffering and modes of healing, in light of Protestant theological beliefs.

These engagements have constituted the main subject of this book, which has developed a threefold argument. First, I complicated the longstanding and vibrant scholarly tradition stressing the key spiritual, theological, and formational functions assigned to suffering in Luther's thought, which I contended has inadvertently obscured Luther's views on the responsibility to actively resist suffering. I demonstrated that while Luther advocated for an internal acceptance of the inevitability of physical suffering, he simultaneously encouraged, and even pastorally mandated, an outward resistance to suffering, including through the use of medicine. In his mature works, he interpreted the refusal to actively oppose bodily threats and afflictions as sin. Second, I offered a novel investigation into Luther's theological engagements with physical healing and medicine, contrasting them with late medieval Catholic and Radical Protestant approaches. I argued that Luther's theology of medicine and bodily healing was shaped by his theology of means, and especially his original interpretation of idolatry. Finally, I suggested ways in which Luther's early modern interpretation of physical suffering, his spiritual vision of miraculous and medical healings in the life of a Christian, and his concern with medical idolatry can serve as spiritual resources for addressing some of the tensions in the contemporary relationship between religion and medicine, as well as contemporary medicine's crises of equity and justice.

In her seminal study, titled *The Reformation of Feeling*, Susan Karant-Nunn argues that early modern clerics, including Martin Luther, sought to influence lived piety and their audiences' affective responses to suffering and death in ways that reflected what these spiritual leaders saw as appropriate religious beliefs. My book has shown that, in light of new Protestant religious concerns, Luther similarly sought to shape his audiences' emotional dispositions accompanying and guiding the use of medicine and other healing means. Indeed, at least in Luther's case, his theologically motivated "reformation of feeling" extended beyond death and suffering to also include a reformation of healing.

Luther's spiritual reformation of healing was firmly influenced by his reading of the Bible, where he found a sacred history of medicine and instructions regarding its use. His interpretations of biblical, and particularly Old Testament, narratives as teaching medical piety rested on his belief that, while specific contexts changed over time, starting from the tree of life with its medicinal fruit, the fundamental spiritual dynamics of this history remained the same. Sin continued to result in new forms of bodily suffering, the devil and angels remained engaged in a cosmic battle over the health of human bodies, and the divine Word still acted through ever-developing medical means. Throughout this sacred history, the religious conscience in a sick body remained a battlefield between idolatry and pious trust, whether that conscience belonged to an ancient Israelite gazing upon the bronze serpent in the wilderness, an early modern German peasant considering a pilgrimage to a saint's shrine in exchange for healing, or, Luther might say, a twenty-first-century patient placing their hope for delivery from suffering and death in advanced medical technology. Luther presented medicine as a spiritually significant practice, within which spiritual forces of evil and good acted through and upon drugs, doctors, and desperate desires for healing.

NOTES

Introduction

1 In this book, I use the following standard abbreviations: WA: *D. Martin Luthers Werke: Kritische Gesamtausgabe, Schriften*, 73 vols. (Weimar: Böhlau, 1883–); WATR: *D. Martin Luthers Werke, Tischreden*, 6 vols. (Weimar: Böhlau, 1912–1921); WABr: *D. Martin Luthers Werke: Kritische Gesamtausgabe, Briefwechsel*, 18 vols. (Weimar: Böhlau, 1930–1948); LW: Jaroslav Pelikan and Helmut T. Lehmann, ed., *Luther's Works*, 55 vols. (Concordia Publishing House/Fortress Press, 1955–). The treatise *To the Christian Nobility of the German Nation Concerning the Reform of the Christian Estate* is found in WA 6.381.404–469; LW 44:117–219.

2 WA 6.459.1; LW 44:202.

3 "Medice vivere est misere vivere." WATR 3:628, no. 3801; LW 54:277. The German term for Luther's "Table Talk" is *Tischreden*. While Luther's "Table Talk" remarks are used in Luther scholarship, including occasionally in this book, the authenticity of Luther's purported "Table Talk" statements is not consistently reliable; therefore, they should be considered with a greater degree of historical caution.

4 On Luther's alleged theological indifference toward medicine, see Richard Toellner, "Die medizinischen Fakultäten unter dem Einfluß der Reformation," in *Renaissance—Reformation: Gegensätze und Gemeinsamkeiten*, ed. Andreas Buck (Harrassowitz, 1984), 287–297. Toellner argued that "in Wittenberg findet ein Einfluß der Reformation auf die Medizinische Fakultät nicht statt," ("Die medizinischen Fakultäten," 297).

5 See Vivian Nutton, "Wittenberg Anatomy," in *Medicine and the Reformation*, ed. Ole Peter Grell and Andrew Cunningham (Routledge, 1993), 11–32; Mitchell Lewis Hammond, "'Ora Deum & Medico Tribus Locum': Medicine in the Theology of Martin Luther and Philipp Melanchthon," in *Religion und Naturwissenschaften im 16. und 17. Jahrhundert*, ed. Kaspar von Greyerz, Thomas Kaufmann, Kim Siebenhüner, and Roberto Zaugg (Gütersloher Verlagshaus, 2010),

33–50. Nutton showed that, with Luther's support, Philip Melanchthon reformed the study of anatomy at the University of Wittenberg, including by incorporating into the art curriculum the works by the founder of modern anatomy, Andreas Vesalius. Challenging Toellner's conclusion, Lewis Hammond argued that the different degrees of attentiveness shown by Luther and his Wittenberg colleague and friend Philip Melanchthon toward medicine were a matter of personal interest rather than that of evaluative judgment.

6 Scholarship on Luther's theology of the cross is abundant. Classic studies include Walther von Loewenich, *Luther's Theologia Crucis* (Kaiser, 1954); Alister E. McGrath, *Luther's Theology of the Cross: Martin Luther's Theological Breakthrough*, 2nd rev. ed. (Blackwell, 2011). More recent contributions include the following: Gerhard Forde, *On Being a Theologian of the Cross: Reflections on Luther's Heidelberg Disputation, 1518* (Eerdmans, 1997); Carl E. Braaten and Robert W. Jenson, eds., *Union with Christ: The New Finnish Interpretation of Luther* (Eerdmans, 1998); Jens Wolff, *Metapher und Kreuz: Studien zu Luthers Christusbild* (Mohr Siebeck, 2005); Robert Kolb, "Luther's Theology of the Cross Fifteen Years after Heidelberg: Luther's Lectures on the Psalms of Ascent," *Journal of Ecclesiastical History* 61 (2010): 69–85. For constructive interpretations of Luther's theology of the cross, see also Mary M. Solberg, *Compelling Knowledge: A Feminist Proposal for an Epistemology of the Cross* (SUNY Press, 1997); Vítor Westhelle, *The Scandalous God: The Use and Abuse of the Cross* (Fortress Press, 2006).

7 Susan Karant-Nunn, *The Reformation of Feeling* (Oxford University Press, 2010). Karant-Nunn's analysis focuses on Luther's sermons on the Passion. See especially 78–83, 250–255. In addition to Luther and early modern Lutheranism, Karant-Nunn also analyzes attempts to reform emotions in early modern Protestant Reformed and Catholic traditions.

8 Ronald Rittgers, *The Reformation of Suffering: Pastoral Theology and Lay Piety in Late Medieval and Early Modern Germany* (Oxford University Press, 2012), especially 85–86.

9 By describing Luther's Protestant project of reforming religious experience of suffering, Ronald Rittgers provided the following comprehensive summary of Luther's new perspective on suffering: "Luther introduced a new doctrine of suffering into early modern Christianity, and this new doctrine was central to his larger effort to reform the church of his day. As we have seen, he wanted Christians to embrace suffering as a divine gift that mortified their sinful nature, conformed

them to Christ, created empathy for fellow sufferers, and, especially, tested their faith. Luther wished to strip Christians of the means they had traditionally employed to understand and cope with suffering, largely because he thought that these means were essentially pagan in origin; that is, he believed that they relied on human reason to make sense of suffering and on human moral strength to appease or barter with God in the midst of it. The true Christian (*Christianus*) was what Luther later called a 'Crosstian' (*Crucianus*), that is, a person who willingly took up the cross and suffered with Christ; like Job, Crosstians obediently submitted to divinely imposed suffering, even though it confounded their reason and threatened to shatter their window of dim faith. . . . Crosstians did not seek out suffering, but when it came, they accepted it and were content to stand before God on the basis of faith alone." Rittgers, *The Reformation of Suffering*, 121.

10 Vincent Evener, *Enemies of the Cross: Suffering, Truth, and Mysticism in the Early Reformation* (Oxford University Press, 2020). In this study analyzing Luther's theology of suffering alongside the theologies of suffering of his contemporary Radical reformers, Vincent Evener concludes that "Luther, Karlstadt, and Müntzer, in their respective claiming and dismissing of the cross, drew upon and clashed within a shared paradigm of the Christian as sufferer: they agreed that fallen, self-assertive human beings had to suffer to become receptive to true doctrine, faith, and life, perceptive about the truth or falsehood of doctrines, teachers, and their own experiences, and active in the world in ways pleasing to God. The true experience of God and God's work brought suffering both spiritual and visible for fallen human beings; the true doctrine proclaimed this suffering; and true Christians were remade by the divinely worked mortification or even annihilation of their fallen self-will to discern whether and where God's message was being heard and obeyed." Evener, *Enemies of the Cross*, 6. Evener further argued that "Christians were to accept suffering in its many forms, from disease to persecution, as God's work 'under a contrary.'" Evener, *Enemies of the Cross*, 8.

11 Jeffrey Bishop, *The Anticipatory Corpse: Medicine, Power, and the Care of the Dying* (University of Notre Dame Press, 2011), 313.

12 See David E. Klemm and William Schweiker, *Religion and the Human Future: An Essay on Theological Humanism* (Blackwell, 2008).

13 William Bouwsma, *A Usable Past: Essays in European Cultural History* (University of California Press, 1990), 172.

Chapter 1: The Early Modern Reformation of Salvation

1 In the Middle Ages, prostitution was legalized. Most late medieval cities maintained at least one brothel, viewed as an unfortunate yet necessary outlet for men's sexual desires, aimed at keeping them away from virgin maidens, honorable matrons, and sodomy. Later, Protestant authorities abolished legal prostitution within their territories.

2 This discussion of late medieval soteriologies primarily depends on the following sources: Steven E. Ozment, *The Age of Reform (1250–1550): An Intellectual and Religious History of Late Medieval and Reformation Europe* (Yale University Press, 1980); Heiko Augustinus Oberman, *The Harvest of Medieval Theology: Gabriel Biel and Late Medieval Nominalism* (Harvard University Press, 1963); Heiko Augustinus Oberman, *The Dawn of the Reformation: Essays in Late Medieval and Early Reformation Thought* (T&T Clark, 1986, reprinted 1992); Steven E. Ozment, "Home Viator: Luther and Late Medieval Theology," in *The Reformation in Medieval Perspective*, ed. Steven E. Ozment (Quadrangle Books, 1971), 1422; and Johan Huizinga, *The Autumn of the Middle Ages* (University of Chicago Press, 1997).

3 Thomas Aquinas, *Summa Theologiae*, vol. 40, ed. T. F. O'Meara and M. J. Duffy (Cambridge University Press, 2006), hereafter *ST*. *ST Suppl.* Q.12, A3. All subsequent citations from the *Summa Theologiae* are from this edition.

4 Unless quoted directly from LW or other early modern sources, all biblical citations are from the New Revised Standard Version Updated Edition (NRSVUE). National Council of Churches of Christ in the United States of America, 2021.

5 During the debates at the Council of Trent, the Franciscans requested to include congruous merits into the final decrees of the Council, and a subsequent change in theological language was done in response to this request. The Tridentine theology of justification ended up favoring the Scotist-Nominalist view of merits; however, the language of Trent was deliberately left vague to allow for the rival schools within the early modern Catholicism to nevertheless preserve their respective teachings.

6 See Oberman, *The Dawn of the Reformation*, 213. On Bradwardine, also see selections from Thomas Bradwardine's "The Cause of God against the Pelagians" in Heiko Augustinus Oberman, *Forerunners of the Reformation: The Shape of Late Medieval Thought* (Rinehart and Winston, 1966), 151–164. On Staupitz, see selections from Johann von Staupitz's "Eternal Predestination and Its Execution in Time" in

Oberman, *The Dawn of the Reformation*, 175–201. For a summary of Staupitz's theology, see David C. Steinmetz, *Misericordia Dei: The Theology of Johannes Von Staupitz in Its Late Medieval Setting* (E. J. Brill, 1968), and David C. Steinmetz, *Luther and Staupitz: An Essay in the Intellectual Origins of the Protestant Reformation* (Duke University Press, 1980).

7 The Parisian condemnations of 1270 and 1277 rejected the radical Aristotelian philosophy of the Muslim scholar Averroes and its influence on Christian scholasticism of the time. Averroes taught that God was removed from the world, which had come to existence by necessity, and that human will was passive and actualized from the outside. He also denied the immortality of individual souls. The Parisian condemnations affected the prominence of the Thomistic school and prompted the rise of "the Franciscan alternative." After the condemnation of Averroes's teachings, a group of late medieval Franciscans, known as Nominalists, largely reacted against the radical determinism of Averroism, by theologically embracing a renewed emphasis on the freedom of both human and divine wills.

8 Gabriel Biel, "The Circumcision of the Lord" in Oberman, *Forerunners of the Reformation*, 168.

9 On Biel's theology, see Gabriel Biel, "The Circumcision of the Lord" in Oberman, *The Forerunners of the Reformation*, especially 165–73. See also Oberman, *The Harvest of Medieval Theology* and Ozment, "Home Viator."

10 In his classic essay, "Iustitia Christi and Iustitia Dei: Luther and the Scholastic Doctrines of Justification," Oberman disproved objections to the claims of a radical break of Luther's soteriology from the late medieval Catholic ones. According to such objections, late Nominalist and especially Biel's soteriology presented a remarkable and unfortunate deviation from a typical medieval Roman Catholic understanding of salvation, while Luther's soteriology existed in a significant continuity with the late medieval Augustinian perspective, due to the importance that they both placed on the doctrine of the bondage of the will. On the contrary, Oberman demonstrated that, at the heart of Luther's doctrine of justification was the equation of *iustitita Christi* with *iustitia Dei.* For Luther, one was fully justified at the moment when one trusted God's promise of salvation by faith alone. At this moment, the righteousness of Christ became imputed to this new Christian, whom God since reckoned as righteous. See Heiko Augustinus Oberman, "'Iustitia Christi' and 'Iustitia Dei': Luther and the Scholastic

Doctrines of Justification," *The Harvard Theological Review* 59, no. 1 (1966): 1–26.

11 See Susan Elizabeth Schreiner, *Are You Alone Wise? The Search for Certainty in the Early Modern Era*, Oxford Studies in Historical Theology (Oxford University Press, 2011), especially chapter 2, "Abba! Father! The Certainty of Salvation," 37–77.

12 The following discussion on the medieval view of faith depends on Berndt Hamm, *The Reformation of Faith in the Context of Late Medieval Theology and Piety: Essays by Berndt Hamm*, ed. Robert James Bast (Brill, 2004). In this work, Hamm discussed theologies of faith summarized by Gabriel Briel and Johann Staupitz as distinctly representative of late medieval Catholicism. For an earlier comprehensive presentation of various types of faith produced in the Middle Ages, see Aquinas, *ST*, IIaIIae 2.5.

13 Norman P. Tanner, ed., *Decrees of the Ecumenical Councils* (Sheed & Ward; Georgetown University Press, 1990), 245–246.

14 There were exceptions, when the circumstances prevented the reception of the sacrament. For example, martyrs were believed to die in a state of grace, even though they might not have had a chance to partake in the sacrament. Similarly, baptism restored to a state of grace those who were baptized and subsequently died in infancy.

15 The ensuing discussion depends on Darrel W. Amundsen, *Medicine, Society, and Faith in the Ancient and Medieval Worlds* (Johns Hopkins University Press, 1996), 196–221, and especially on 203–205.

16 Quoted in Jonathan Sumption, *Pilgrimage: An Image of Mediaeval Religion* (Rowman & Littlefield, 1976), 80.

17 As argued by Amundsen, *Medicine, Society, and Faith*, 205.

18 Humbert de Romans, *Sermon 40*, quoted by Jarrett Bede, *Social Theories of the Middle Ages 1200–1500*, Rep. edition (Newman Book, 1942), 223.

19 The following discussion depends on Thomas Benedek, "The Image of Medicine in 1500: Theological Reactions to 'The Ship of Fools,'" *Bulletin of the History of Medicine* 38, no. 4 (1964): 329–342.

20 Geiler delivered the sermon in 1498 on the Tuesday before Easter. Nine weeks later, he preached a subsequent one, titled "Of Foolish Physicians," based on verse fifty-five of "The Ship of Fools." In this later sermon Geiler attacked physicians' vices, most prominently avarice and incompetence.

21 Benedek, "The Image of Medicine in 1500," 5.

22 Benedek, "The Image of Medicine in 1500," 5.

23 Benedek, "The Image of Medicine in 1500," 5.

24 The following discussion especially depends on Amundsen, *Medicine, Society, and Faith*, 206–207; Hildegard, *Hildegard of Bingen, On Natural Philosophy and Medicine: Selections from Cause et Cure*, trans. Margret Berger, Library of Medieval Women (D. S. Brewer, 1999), 9–12; and Pearl Kibre, "The Faculty of Medicine in Paris, Charlatanism, and Unlicensed Medical Practices in Later Middle Ages," *Bulletin of the History of Medicine* 27, no. 1 (February 1953): 1–20.

25 See Keith Thomas, *Religion and the Decline of Magic* (Scribner, 1971), especially chapter 1, "The Magic of the Medieval Church," 25–31.

26 On medieval uses and distinctions between the spiritually legitimate and illegitimate uses of natural means for healing and the use of astrology see Richard Kieckhefer, *Magic in the Middle Ages* (Cambridge University Press, 2000), 85, 120–31.

27 Aquinas, *ST*, IIaIIae Q96.A2.

28 Kieckhefer, *Magic in the Middle Ages*, 67–68, 80.

29 The ensuing discussion of saints depends on André Vauchez, *Sainthood in the Later Middle Ages*, trans. Jean Birrell (Cambridge University Press, 2005); André Vauchez, "Saints and Pilgrimages: New and Old" in *The Cambridge History of Christianity*, ed. Miri Rubin and Walter Simons, Cambridge History of Christianity (Cambridge University Press, 2009), 324–339; Amanda Porterfield, *Healing in the History of Christianity* (Oxford University Press, 2005); Ronald C. Finucane, *Miracles and Pilgrims: Popular Beliefs in Medieval England* (Rowman and Littlefield, 1977); and Robert Norman Swanson, *Religion and Devotion in Europe, C.1215-c.1515* (Cambridge University Press, 1995).

30 I used the English translation: Vauchez, *Sainthood in the Later Middle Ages*. The following paragraph depends on Vauchez, especially chapter 14, "'*Virtus*:' The Language of the Body," 427–443 and chapter 15, "The Structures and Expansion of the Field of the Miraculous," 444–477, as well as on Gabor Klaniczay, chapter 13, "Using Saints: Intercession, Healing, Sanctity" in John Arnold, *The Oxford Handbook of Medieval Christianity*, Oxford Handbooks (Oxford University Press, 2014), 217–237.

31 See, for example, the treatise *De Laude Sanstorum* by Victricius, bishop of Rouen. See a discussion in Klaniczay, "Using Saints," 218.

32 Vauchez, *Sainthood in the Later Middle Ages*, 466.

33 On medieval Christian pilgrimage, see Swanson, *Religion and Devotion in Europe, c.1215-c.1515*, especially pp. 193–206; and Finucane,

Miracles and Pilgrims. See also Marcus Bull, "Pilgrimage," in ed. John Arnold, *The Oxford Handbook of Medieval Christianity* (Oxford University Press, 2014), 201–216.

34 See, among others, Amundsen, *Medicine, Society, and Faith*, 212.

35 Swanson, *Religion and Devotion in Europe*, 153–155.

36 Marcus Bull argued that in contrast to other religious traditions, for example, Islam, where pilgrimage is a requirement, in Christianity pilgrimages were never seen as necessary religious obligations. This explains a relatively smooth process of their decline in the Middle Ages. See Bull, "Pilgrimage," 211.

37 Finucane, *Miracles and Pilgrims*, 83–100.

38 Vauchez, *Sainthood in the Later Middle Ages*, 468–470.

39 On the survey of these developments see Vauchez, *Sainthood in the Later Middle Ages*, 472–477.

40 The following discussion depends on Philip Soergel, "Miracle, Magic and Disenchantment in Early Modern Germany," in *Envisioning Magic: A Princeton Seminar and Symposium*, ed. Peter Schäfer and Hans Kippenberg (Brill, 1997), 215–234, especially 220–221.

41 Vauchez, *Sainthood in the Later Middle Ages*, 476.

42 This paragraph primarily depends on Klaniczay, "Using Saints," 221–222, 227; Vauchez, *Sainthood in the Later Middle Ages*, 439–443.

43 See Raymond of Capua, *The Life of St. Catherine of Siena*, trans. George Lamb (Harvill Press, 1960), especially 35–36.

44 Raymond, *The Life of St. Catherine of Siena*, 36.

45 The motivations and religious significance behind late medieval female mystics voluntary torturing of their bodies have been debated by scholars. This phenomenon was likely exacerbated by the fact that women in the late medieval context were largely limited to using the language of their bodies to publicly express their religious experiences or claim spiritual authority. In his work *Holy Anorexia*, Rudolph Bell explores life accounts of two-hundred and sixty-one "holy" women in Italy, starting from the thirteenth century, and prominently focusing on the life of St. Catherine of Siena. Based on contemporary clinical understandings of the eating disorder known as anorexia, or voluntary self-starvation, Bell argued that undiagnosed anorexia—rather than supernatural spiritual experiences—was the true reason behind Catherine and her followers' motivations to starve themselves. See Rudolph M. Bell, *Holy Anorexia* (University of Chicago Press, 1985). Bell's argument is disputed by Caroline Walker Bynum in her classic work *Holy Feast and Holy Fast: The Religious Significance of Food to Medieval*

Women. Bynum challenges scholarly interpretations, including Bell's, that reduce medieval women's extreme fasting to clinical eating disorders or mechanisms for coping with social systems restricting women's agencies. In contrast, Bynum demonstrates that food had profound religious significance in the Middle Ages, when eating was "the most basic and literal way of encountering God." (Bynum, *Holy Feast and Holy Fast,* 2). For Bynum, holy fasting and holy feasting were empowering and deeply symbolic ways for medieval women to express their pieties and religious identities. See Caroline Walker Bynum, *Holy Feast and Holy Fast: The Religious Significance of Food to Medieval Women* (University of California Press, 1987).

46 The ensuing discussion about the major developments in the history of medicine in this era chiefly depends on William Bynum, *The History of Medicine: A Very Short Introduction* (Oxford University Press, 2008) and Andrew Wear, Roger Kenneth French, and Iain M. Lonie, eds., *The Medical Renaissance of the Sixteenth Century* (Cambridge University Press, 1985).

47 The ensuing overview of the Black Death primarily depends on chapter 2, "Plagues and Peoples" in Mary Lindemann, *Medicine and Society in Early Modern Europe*, 2nd ed, New Approaches to European History (Cambridge University Press, 2010), 55–58. See also Laura A. Smoller, "Of Earthquakes, Hail, Frogs, and Geography: Plague and the Investigation of the Apocalypse in the Later Middle Ages" in *Last Things: Death and the Apocalypse in the Middle Ages* (University of Pennsylvania Press, 2000), 156–187, as well as chapter 7, "Caring and Curing in the Medieval Catholic Tradition," and chapter 10, "Medical Deontology and Pestilential Disease in the Late Middle Ages," in Amundsen, *Medicine, Society, and Faith*.

48 Lindemann notes that these symptoms were developed in modern cases of plague. It remains insufficiently established how these symptoms might have been manifested differently in early modernity. See Lindemann, *Medicine and Society*, 56.

49 "Chronicle of Angolo di Tura", quoted in William M. Bowsky, *The Black Death: A Turning Point in History?* (Holt, Rinehart and Winston, 1971), 13–14.

50 *ST* II.IIae.Q32.A4.

51 *ST* II.IIae.Q71, especially A1 and 4.

52 These criteria were taken from Augustine, *De Doctrine Christiana* (i.28), which says that "since one cannot do good to all, we ought to consider those chiefly who by reason of place, time, or any other

circumstance, by a kind of chance are more closely united to us," as quoted by Thomas, *ST*, IIaIIae. Q71. A1.

53 A similar sentiment was expressed in Humbert de Romans's sermon quoted earlier in the chapter: "So let them [physicians] deal faithfully with their patients as to cause them as little expense as possible; let them take a moderate fee that their conscience not be hurt." As quoted in Amundsen, *Medicine, Society, and Faith*, 204.

54 The following discussion depends on *ST* II.IIae.Q32, especially A2.

55 In *ST* II.IIae.Q32.A2 Aquinas broadened the meaning of "visiting the sick" in his reply to Objection 2. He included leading the blind or providing support to "the lame" as other examples of "visiting the sick." He also mentioned that financially assisting the poor is directly related to meeting these needs. For St. Thomas's theology of charity see *ST* IIaIIae.Q23–46.

56 Aquinas noted that, in some particular instances, it was better to give corporeal than spiritual alms. For example, it was preferable to give a hungry man food, not instruction. See *ST* II.IIae.A32.Q3.

57 *ST* II.IIae.Q32.A4.

58 *ST* II.IIae.Q32.A4. Aquinas made a similar point in his discussion of the possibility of a person meriting the first grace for another person in *ST* IaIIae.Q114.A6. For the summary of St. Thomas's theology of merit, see *ST* IaIIae.A114.

59 See Amundsen, *Medicine, Society, and Faith*, 198–205 and Darrel W. Amundsen and Gary B. Ferngren, "Philanthropy in Medicine: Some Historical Perspectives," in *Beneficence and Health Care*, ed. Earl E. Shelp, vol. 11 (Springer Netherlands, 1982), 1–31, especially 22–23.

60 The following paragraph primarily relies on Martin Brecht, *Martin Luther: His Road to Reformation, 1483–1521* (Fortress Press, 1993), 46–50. Numerous academic biographies of Martin Luther have been produced, using various interpretive lenses. Prominent examples include Heiko Augustinus Oberman, *Luther: Man Between God and the Devil*, trans. Eileen Walliser-Schwarzbart (Yale University Press, 1990); Martin Brecht, *Martin Luther*, vol. 3 (Calwer Verlag, 1986); Roland H. Bainton, *Here I Stand: A Life of Martin Luther* (Abingdon Press, 1990); Heinrich Bornkamm, *Martin Luther in Der Mitte Seines Lebens: Das Jahrzehnt Zwischen Dem Wormser Und Dem Augsburger Reichstag* (Vandenhoeck & Ruprecht, 1979); James M. Kittelson, *Luther the Reformer: The Story of the Man and His Career* (Augsburg Publishing House, 1986), Martin E. Marty, ed., *Martin Luther: A Life*, Penguin Lives (Penguin Books, 2008) and Lyndal Roper, *Martin*

Luther: Renegade and Prophet, (Random House, 2016). For Luther's own account of his life, see his "Preface" to the complete edition of his Latin writings in WA 54.179–187; LW 34:327–337.

61 For the place of the Observant Hermits of St. Augustine within the late medieval religious landscape, see Eric Leland Saak, *High Way to Heaven: The Augustinian Platform between Reform and Reformation, 1292–1524*, Studies in Medieval and Reformation Thought 89 (Brill, 2002). For Luther as an observant Augustinian Hermit, see also Eric Leland Saak, *Luther and the Reformation of the Later Middle Ages* (Cambridge University Press, 2017).

62 There are two competing views on the timing of Luther's "evangelical discovery." The first approach traces it back to Luther's earlier lectures on the Psalms, while the second—and more widely accepted one—dates it to 1518.

63 WATR 2, no. 1681, cited in Oberman, *Luther: Man Between God and the Devil*, 155.

64 WA 54.186.4–9; LW 34:337

65 Numerous works have provided summaries and in-depth discussion of major themes and aspects of Martin Luther's exegesis, in relation to the prior history of Christian thought and Luther's own historical location and experiences. For more recent sources of reference, surveying key elements of Luther's thought and its connections to broader contexts, see David M. Whitford, ed., *Martin Luther in Context* (Cambridge University Press, 2018) and Derek R. Nelson, and Paul R. Hinlicky, eds., *The Oxford Encyclopedia of Martin Luther* (Oxford University Press, 2017). See also Donald K. McKim, ed., *The Cambridge Companion to Martin Luther. Cambridge Companions to Religion* (Cambridge University Press, 2003).

66 For Luther's own account of his exegetical method, see his "Brief Introduction on What to Look for and Expect in the Gospels" in WA 10.8–18; LW 35:117–123, his sermon "How Christians Should Regard Moses" in WA 16.363–393; LW 35: 161–174 as well as his various prefaces to the books of the Bible.

67 For Luther's description and defense of his approach to translating the New Testament and the Old Testament see respectively his open letter "On Translating" in WA 30.II.632–646; LW 35:180–202 and "Defense of the Translation of the Psalms" in WA 38.9–17; LW 35.209–223.

68 "Ibi continuo alia mihi facies totius scripturae apparuit" WA 54.186.9–10; LW 34:337.

69 For the regulations of the Code of Justinian regarding gifts in marriage, see https://www.uwyo.edu/lawlib/blume-justinian/ajc-edition-2/books/book5/Book%205-16rev.pdf
70 On the comparison between medieval Catholic and Luther's understandings of faith, see Hamm, *The Reformation of Faith*, especially chapter 5, "Why did 'Faith' become for Luther the Central Concept of the Christian Life?" See also David C. Steinmetz, *Luther in Context*, 2nd edition (Baker Academic, 2002), chapter 4, "Abraham and the Reformation", especially 33, 40–41.
71 According to Hamm, for Luther, faith, "combined with the biblical Word becomes the Christocentric relational concept for participation in Christ" (Hamm, *The Reformation of Faith*, 173). In this chapter, Hamm also demonstrates that receptive and relational characteristics of faith in Luther's thought were informed by late medieval soteriological assumptions. While preserving these qualities of faith, Luther transformed their meaning to argue for its soteriological function.
72 On the connection between Luther's soteriology and pneumatology, see Schreiner, *Are You Alone Wise?*, 57. The following discussion relies on chapter 2, "'Abba! Father!' The Certainty of Salvation," especially 56–58.
73 For Luther's discussion of Abraham's faith in the context of exegeting Genesis 15:6 see WA 42:561–569; LW 3:18–29.
74 For Luther's discussion of Noah's faith see LW 2:87–89; WA.42.323–325. For Luther, Noah's loneliness in his faith and his righteousness in the face of his mockers was akin to his own loneliness in his righteous upholding of the gospel against the assaults and mockery of his Catholic, Anabaptist, and Sacramentalist opponents.
75 "Itaque Mundus stolidissimum indicavit Noah, qui talia crederet, et risit eum ac aedificium eius sine dubio exagitavit." WA 42.312.15–17; LW 2.71

Chapter 2: Martin Luther's Reformation of Physical Suffering

1 *The Sermon on Cross and Suffering* is found in WA 32:28–39, LW 51:197–209.
2 Rittgers, *Reformation of Suffering*, 86.
3 WA 30.I. 253:8–15; Martin Luther, "Small Catechism (1529)," in *The Book of Concord: The Confessions of the Evangelical Lutheran Church,*

ed. Robert Kolb, Timothy J. Wengert, and Charles P. Arand (Fortress Press, 2000), 357, IV: 14.

4 WA.46.84; LW 24:392.

5 WA6.119.34–120.6; LW 42:144.

6 The following discussion depends on WA.31.68–74; LW 14:47–49, WA.45.649–651; LW 24:207–208, WA.20.13–14; LW15:11.

7 WA.31.73; LW 14:49.

8 "Dispergit bona sua, dat aurum, argentum, fruges, pacem, bonam valetudinem etiam ingratis et pessimis hominibus." WA 44.371.25–26; LW 7:97.

9 The following discussion relies on WA 43.51–53, LW 3:247–249. Luther also mentioned that Sodom's prosperity was not a sign of divine favor elsewhere in his lectures on Genesis, such as in his exegesis of the story of Joseph in Genesis 39:40 whose misfortunes he juxtaposed to Sodom's alleged abundance.

10 The treatise *On the Councils and Churches* is found in WA.50.509–653; LW 41:6–178. The following discussion draws upon Oberman's discussion of suffering and the church's everyday martyrdom. See Heiko Augustinus Oberman, *Luther: Man Between God and the Devil*, trans. Eileen Walliser-Schwarzbart (:Yale University Press, 1990), especially 184–185, 255, 263–265. Evener points out that in one of Luther's last sermons he argues that endurance of suffering and persecution distinguished true Christians from all "other religions and faiths." See Evener, *Enemies of the Cross*, 2. He further discusses ways in which, influenced by different uses of the inherited medieval mystical tradition, Luther, Thomas Müntzer, and Andreas Carlstadt produced theological demarcations between "true" and "false" suffering, tied to their distinctions between "true" and "false" Christians and Christian doctrines. See also Vincent Evener, "The 'Enemies of God' in Luther's Final Sermons: Jews, Papists, and the Problem of Blindness to Scripture," *Dialog* 55, no. 3 (September 2016): 229–238, https://doi.org/10.1111/dial.12259.

11 WA 50.641.35–642.7, cited in Oberman, *Luther*, 255.

12 Evener identifies three categories of false suffering in Luther's thought: 1) Suffering as punishment to the wicked who could not bear it properly, 2) Suffering that was unexpected but falsely embraced in order to win human or divine approval, and 3) Self-chosen suffering. See Evener, *Enemies of the Cross*, 6.

13 For Luther, not only Catholic, but his Protestant theological opponents, such as Radical reformers, sought and experienced "counterfeit"

suffering. This included suffering due to their persecution by Catholic authorities. However, since, for Luther, such suffering did not stem from their allegiance to the gospel, it could not have been genuine.

14 Oberman, *Luther*, 185.

15 WA 10.ii.295:18–26; LW 45:39. For Luther's theological rejection of monastic life, in particular the prohibition to marry, see "The Judgment of Martin Luther on Monastic Vows" in WA 8.564–669; LW 44: 245–401. WA includes its accompanying letter to Luther's Father; for its English translation see LW 48: 328–336. There is abundant literature on Luther's monastic life; for a representative analysis see chapter 14, "Luther's Dispute with the Monastic Ideal" in Bernhard Lohse, *Martin Luther's Theology: Its Historical and Systematic Development* (Fortress Press, 1999), 116–121. See also Christoph Bultmann, Volker Leppin, and Andreas Lindner, eds., *Luther Und Das Monastische Erbe: Spätmittelalter, Humanismus, Reformation.* Studies in the Late Middle Ages, Humanism and the Reformation 39 (Mohr Siebeck, 2007). For a summary of the ideals of medieval monastic theology, against the context of which Luther's critique emerged see Jean Leclercq, *The Love of Learning and the Desire for God* (Fordham University Press, 1961). On the influence of Luther and early Reformation on German monasticism and its ensuing transformation see Eike Wolgast, *Die Einführung Der Reformation Und Das Schicksal Der Klöster Im Reich Und in Europa*, 1. Auflage, Quellen Und Forschungen Zur Reformationsgeschichte, Band 89 (Gütersloher Verlagshaus, 2014).

16 "Itaque non videmus in Historiis horum Patriarcharum ieiunia certorum dierum, abstinentiam ab oeconomia, politia, macerationem carnis." WA 44.527.14–15; LW 7:307.

17 WA6.165.20–25; LW 39:39–40.

18 WA10.iii.36:10–37.8; LW 51:86–87.

19 Luther's lectures on Genesis 13:5–12 are in WA 42.501–508; LW 2:335–345.

20 "Ne quidem si vitam miseri hominis una buccella carnis servare possent, id facerent." WA 42.504.11–12; LW 2:339.

21 "Arithmetic" and "geometric proportio" are explained in WA 43.641:19–33; LW 5:308–309. Luther's lectures on Genesis 29:28 are in WA 43.640–642; LW 5:306–310 and his lectures on Genesis 48:17–18 are in WA 44:701–706; LW 8:168–174. In his commentary on Genesis 48:18 Luther credited Aristotle for the importance of geometric application in ethics as well as Augustine for sustaining this principle in his own rule.

22 "Multos tetrica illa abstinentia necarint, quos uno iusculo gallinae, aut frusto carnis, aut veste mundiore potuissent servare." WA 44.705.1–11; LW 8:172.
23 The following discussion depends on WA 47.51–64; LW 22:322–337.
24 WA 47.62.34:36; LW 22:335–336.
25 WA 51.89.20–23 quoted in Oberman, *Luther*, 147.
26 WABr 1:525–527; LW 48:69 cited in John Wilkinson, *The Medical History of the Reformers* (The Handsel Press, 2001), 13.
27 WA 44.383:4–5; LW 7:113.
28 The following discussion depends on Oberman, *Luther*, 325–326.
29 Cited in Oberman, *Luther*, 326.
30 For the history and a comprehensive online collection of the Cranachs' paintings of Luther, see the Cranach Digital Archive, https://lucascranach.org. For a collection of art sources, see *Martin Luther Und Die Reformation in Deutschland*, Exhibition Catalog (Germanisches Nationalmuseum, 1983). For the Cranachs' portraits of Luther see Steven E. Ozment, *The Serpent & the Lamb: Cranach, Luther, and the Making of the Reformation* (Yale University Press, 2011); Bonnie Noble, *Lucas Cranach the Elder: Art and Devotion of the German Reformation* (University Press of America, 2009); and Martin Warnke, *Cranachs Luther: Entwürfe Für Ein Image*, Originalausg, Kunststück (Fischer, 1984). For a general survey, see Joseph Leo Koerner, *The Reformation of the Image* (University of Chicago Press, 2004).
31 "Ein feisten doctor," WA TR. 6:302.12–14, No. 6975.
32 See Peter Newman Brooks, ed., *Seven Headed Luther: Essays in Commemoration of a Quincentenary 1483–1983* (Clarendon, 1983).
33 See Hanne Kolind Poulsen, "Between Convention, Likeness and Iconicity: Cranach's Portraits and Luther's Thoughts on Images," in Andreas Tacke, ed., *Lucas Cranach, 1553/2003: Wittenberger Tagungs-Beitraǧe Anlaššlich Des 450. Todesjahres Lucas Cranachs Des a ̉lteren* (Leipzig, 2003), 205–216. For a summary of themes central to Luther's representations see Robert Kolb, *Martin Luther as Prophet, Teacher, Hero: Images of the Reformer, 1520–1620* (Baker Books, Paternoster Press, 1999).
34 See Lyndal Roper, "Martin Luther's Body: The 'Stout Doctor' and His Biographers," *The American Historical Review* 115, no. 2 (April 2010): 351–384, https://doi.org/10.1086/ahr.115.2.351. For a summary of the significance of Luther's changing images see especially 381–382.
35 Roper, "Martin Luther's Body," 357–362.
36 Roper, "Martin Luther's Body," 364.

37 The following discussion focused on Luther's lectures on Genesis 39:19–23 depends on WA 44.370–378; LW 7:96–106.
38 "Da cumpt nun Christus, und leucht in die Hell hinein mit gnesigen Augen." WA 44.373.29–30; LW 7:100.
39 "En adsum Ioseph, suffciat tibi mea inspection." WA 44.373.40–41; LW 7:100.
40 "Gementibus, eiulantibus, frementibus." WA 44.374.335; LW 7:101.
41 "Martyr" in WA 44.375.30 and elsewhere.
42 For a summary of Luther's theology of God's alien work, see Alister E. McGrath, *Luther's Theology of the Cross: Martin Luther's Theological Breakthrough*, 2nd edition (Wiley-Blackwell, 2011), 223–232. On God's hiddenness see chapter 3, "Luther and the Hidden God," in Steinmetz, *Luther in Context*, 23–31; and B. A. Gerrish, *The Old Protestantism and the New: Essays on the Reformation Heritage* (University of Chicago Press, 1982); and chapter 7, "Men Should Be What They Seem: Appearances and Reality" in Schreiner, *Are You Alone Wise?*, 323–390.
43 As discussed by Steinmetz, *Luther in Context*, 29–31.
44 This point was developed in McGrath, *Luther's Theology of the Cross*, 224–228; Rittgers, *The Reformation of Suffering*, 118.
45 For a recent discussion on the interconnectedness between Luther's developing theology of the Cross with his emerging Protestant view of human suffering see chapter 5, "Suffering and the Theology of the Cross" in Rittgers, *The Reformation of Suffering*, 111–124.
46 See Evener, *Enemies of the Cross*, especially chs. 2 and 3, pp. 75–162.
47 The discussion of *Anfeschtung* in Luther's theology is primarily dependent upon McGrath, *Luther's Theology of the Cross*, 224–228. See also Horst Beintker, *Die Uberwindung Der Anfechtung Bei Luther: Eine Studie Zu Seiner Theologie Nach Den Operationes in Psalmos 1519–21* (Evangelische Verlagsanstalt Berlin, 1954), 58–66. Beintker, *Die Uberwindung Der Anfechtung Bei Luther: Eine Studie Zu Seiner Theologie Nach Den Operationes in Psalmos 1519–21*, 58–66; Paul Theophil Bühler, *Die Anfechtung Bei Martin Luther* (Zwingli Verlag, 1944); Helmut Appel, *Anfechtung Und Trost Im Spätmittelalter Und Bei Luther* (SVRG, 1938); Von Friedrich Karl Schumann, *Gottesglaube Und Anfechtung Bei Luther* (Deichert'sche Verlagsbuchhandlung, 1938).
48 As argued by Beintker, *Die Überwindung*, 86–87 cited in Rittgers, *The Reformation of Suffering*, 313.
49 Vincent Evener also argued that, in addition to its spiritually formative role, the role of suffering in Luther's theology was extended to one's

ability to discern truth. This encompassed leading sinners to embrace the gospel through despair over their inadequate abilities, as well as discerning between false pseudo-Christian teachings and genuine evangelical truths. Thus, for Luther, Christian suffering, including bodily suffering, became an essential instrument for both believing and living faithfully. This also applied to perspectives on suffering held by Luther's theological opponents, Thomas Müntzer and Andreas Carlstadt. See Evener, *Enemies of the Cross*, 6.

50 "Initium operationis divinae hoc est, quod avertit faciem suam, nec videtur esse Deus, sed Diabolus. Sic in praesenti historia facies eius conversa est ad meretricem et tyrannum, hos solos fovet neglecto Ioseph. Sicut Hieremias quoque queritur: 'Prope es tu ori eorum.' Ideo iactitant Deum sibi adesse propitium et faventem. *Sie wonet Gott*, sprechen sie. Sed Ioseph, Iacob, Abraham, non habent in se conversam hanc faciem. Da heists, hie wont der Deuffel, 'Faciem meam non videbis' etc. Quia sic consuevit Deus ducere et gubernare suos. Sicut in cantico Habacuc describitur: 'Semitae tuae in aquis multis, et vestigia tua non cognoscuntur.' Item Esaiae 36 [sic!] 'Et erunt oculi tui videntes praeceptorem tuum, et aures tuae audient verbum post tergum momentis.' Et Christus ad Petrum inquit: 'Quod ego facio tu nescis modo, scies autem postea.' "Du wilt mir in faciem sehen, vis me facere quod tibi commodum et bonum videtur. Verum sic agam, ut videatur tibi fatuus aliquis haec fecisse, non Deus. Du solt mir in ruken sehen, nicht in das angesicht. Non debes videre opera et consilia mea quibus te fingo et refingo in beneplacitum meum. Es soll dich nerrich schunden. Non aliter ea accipies et intelliges, ac si essent mors et Diabolus ipse." WA 44. 376.1–18; LW 7:103–104.

51 "Claude oculos et sustento te verbo." WA 44.378.4–5; LW 7:106.

52 Rittgers, *The Reformation of Suffering*, especially 85–86.

53 Rittgers, *The Reformation of Suffering*, 83.

54 Rittgers, *The Reformation of Suffering*, 85–86, 206. For a summary of Rittgers's argument about Luther's new theology of suffering, see especially 121–123.

55 As mentioned by Rittgers, *The Reformation of Suffering*, 131. "A Sermon on Indulgence and Grace" is in WA 1:243–246. The English translation used is from Martin Luther, *Sermon von Ablass und Gnade* [Sermon on indulgences and grace], ed. Howard Jones, Martin Kessler, Henrike Lähnemann, and Christina Ostermann, Treasures of the Taylorian: Series one, Reformation pamphlets 2 (Taylor Institution Library, 2018), 2–31.

56 WA 1.244.15–24.
57 WA 1.244.40–245.4.
58 For example, as noted by Rittgers, *The Reformation of Suffering*, 131.
59 "Trials" or "temptations." "Eodem vero modo gerit se Deus erga sanctos in tentationibus, ut Ioseph erga fratres." WA 44.466.13–14; LW 7:225.
60 "Ludus" in WA 44.466.22; LW 7:225 and elsewhere. Luther uses the same word to describe Joseph's "game" ("ludus") with his brothers, such as in WA 44.466.10; LW 7:225.
61 Luther made an exception regarding the retributive function of suffering as a form of satisfaction for crime within the penal legal system of civil society. While he recognized this as a reasonable function of suffering when imposed by the government in civic society, Luther maintained that this could never be its proper theological function. See WA 44:467–468; LW 7:227.
62 See especially WA 44.470–472; LW 7:231–232; WA 44.487–488; LW 7:254–255.
63 "Vides ergo quo animo Christus puniat suos, quam sit ibi ardens caminus charitatis, non tantum spiritualis, sed etiam carnalis." WA 44.492.20–21; LW 7:260.
64 Whipping or beating ("verberare,"), chastise ("castigare") with a rod ("virga"). See, for example, WA 44.472.26–30; LW 7:233, WA 44:471; LW 7:231–232, and elsewhere.
65 Rittgers, *Reformation of Suffering*, 119.
66 "Sic Deus adfligit nos variis calamitatibus, non ut puniat, quanquam revera poena est, sed non delectatur ea." WA 44.468.22-23; LW 7:228.
67 See, for example, WA 44.468.32–33; LW 7:228, WA 44.470.26–27; LW 7:231, WA 44.489.17; LW 7:256 and elsewhere.
68 "Quaerant ipsi sanitatem et purgationem." WA 44.468.20–21; LW 7:228.
69 "Itaque ad manifestandam et purgandam eam utitur Deus remediis violentis et acerbic." WA 44.468.32–33; LW 7:228.
70 See WA 44.468.33–36; LW 7:228, WA 44.475.15–16; LW 7:237 and elsewhere.
71 See, for example, WA 44.475.15–16; LW 7:237: "secet, urat, purget Deus reliquias fermenti originalis"; "you will long for God to cut, burn, and purge away the remnants of the original yeast."
72 *Whether One May Flee from a Deadly Plague* is in WA 23:323–379; LW 43:115–138. For a modern annotated edition, helping understand this treatise in its original contexts, see Martin Luther, *Fleeing Plague:*

Medieval Wisdom for a Modern Health Crisis. Introduction and notes Anna Marie Johnson (Fortress Press, 2023).

73 For Luther's contribution to the emerging Protestant efforts of health care relief, see Harold J. Grimm, "Luther's Contributions to Sixteenth-Century Organization of Poor Relief," *Archiv Für Reformationsgeschichte—Archive for Reformation History* 61, no. jg (December 1, 1970): 222–234, https://doi.org/10.14315/arg-1970-jg11; Carter Lindberg, "'There Should Be No Beggars Among Christians:' Karlstadt, Luther, and the Origins of Protestant Poor Relief," *Church History* 46 (1977): 313–334. See also, Carter Lindberg, "Luther on Poverty," *Lutheran Quarterly* 15, no. Spring (2001): 85–101.

74 "Graviter peccant." WA 44:528.4; LW 7:308.

75 The following discussion of Luther's lectures on Genesis 40:12–15;16–19 depends on WA.44.381–385; 389–390; LW 7:112–116; 122–123.

76 "Singulari studio hanc opportunitatem captavit." WA 44.383.41; LW 7:114.

77 "Sed est exemplum eius doctrinae quam tradit Paulus 1. Corinthiorum 7: 'Si servus vocatus es, non sit tibi curae, sed si potes tieri liber, magis utere. Non enim nobis ipsi accersere mala et pericula debemus. Sed quando vel casu, vel divina voluntate adfligimur, ibi constanter et magno animo et auxilia, quibus possumus liberari. Est enim tentatio Dei, contemnere oblata remedia malorum divinitus monstrata." WA 44:382.33–40; LW 7:113.

78 *The Freedom of a Christian* is in WA.7.42–73; LW 31:331–377.

79 WA 7.22.3–4; LW 31:344.

80 Developed in 1523 treatise *Temporal Authority: To What Extent It Should Be Obeyed* in WA 11.229–280; LW 45:77–133. Luther's dialectic of the two kingdoms reflected Augustine's teachings on the two kingdoms outlined in the City of God. Luther's theological innovation was his insistence on separate spheres of authority for the two kingdoms, thus establishing for the first time a Protestant theological

Chapter 3: Early Modern Reformations of Medicine

1 The following paragraphs consulted the preface to the *Sermon on Keeping Children in School* by Charles M. Jacobs and Robert C. Schultz in LW 46: 209–213. The sermon is found in WA30ii.517–588; LW 46:213–259.

2 WA 30.II.60–63; LW 46:211.

3 WA 15:9–53; LW 45:339–378.

4 For Luther's discussion of medicine in the *Sermon on Keeping Children in School,* see WA30ii.580.27–582.22; LW 46:252–254.
5 See note 3 to the Introduction.
6 "Medice vivere est misere vivere." WATR 3:628, no. 3801; LW 54:277.
7 See, for example, WATR 1:150–151, no. 360; LW 54:53–54, WATR 3:578–579, no. 3733; LW 54:266.
8 WA 6.459.1; LW 44:202.
9 For example, Richard Toellner argues that Luther viewed medicine as ultimately irrelevant for theology, eventually resulting in the Reformation's lack of influence on the medical faculty in Wittenberg. See note 4 to the Introduction.
10 See Vivian Nutton, "Wittenberg Anatomy," in *Medicine and the Reformation*, ed. Ole Peter Grell and Andrew Cunningham (Routledge, 1993), 11–32; Mitchell Lewis Hammond, "'Ora Deum & Medico Tribus Locum': Medicine in the Theology of Martin Luther and Philipp Melanchthon," in *Religion und Naturwissenschaften im 16. und 17. Jahrhundert*, ed. Kaspar von Greyerz, Thomas Kaufmann, Kim Siebenhüner, and Roberto Zaugg (Gütersloher Verlagshaus, 2010), 33–50. For a summary of this discussion see note 5 to the Introduction. Johann Anselm Steiger's *Medizinische Theologie* remains the only major investigation into Luther and medicine, focusing on Luther's and early modern Lutheranism's use of medical imagery and metaphors in broader theological discussions. In contrast, I focus on Luther's theology of medicine and instructions regarding its proper use.
11 On the role of astrology in the early modern era, see Robin Barnes, *Astrology and Reformation* (Oxford University Press, 2016).
12 See Thomas, *Religion and the Decline of Magic*, especially chapter 1, "The Magic of The Medieval Church," 25–31; and Kieckhefer, *Magic in the Middle Ages.*
13 See Andrew Cunningham, and Ole Peter Grell, eds., *Health Care and Poor Relief in Protestant Europe, 1500–1700* (Routledge, 1997) and Carter Lindberg, *Beyond Charity: Reformation Initiatives for the Poor* (Fortress Press, 1993).
14 For Galen's anatomy see chapter 3, "Leaned Medicine," especially 86–97, in Lindemann, *Medicine and Society*; and chapter 1, "The Ancients of Anatomy," especially 25–32, in Andrew Cunningham, *The Anatomical Renaissance: The Resurrection of the Anatomical Projects of the Ancients* (Routledge, 1997).
15 Despite this, Galen himself likely never dissected a human cadaver. As a Greek practicing in Rome where human dissection was prohibited

at his time, he instead performed dissections on both living and dead animals, primarily apes.

16 On challenging the myth of religious prohibition of dissection in medieval and Renaissance Europe (with a focus on Italy) and the centrality of gender for the development of early modern anatomy see Katharine Park, *Secrets of Women: Gender, Generation, and the Origins of Human Dissection* (Zone Books, 2006).

17 At the era when human corpses for dissection were in short supply, Vesalius was allegedly able to obtain an unprecedented amount of human remains for his study due to the generosity of a local magistrate who supplied him with bodies of executed criminals.

18 On challenging the thesis of Vesalisus's *Fabrica* as radically breaking with the tradition of medieval anatomy, see chapter 4, "Vesalius: The Revival of Galenic Anatomy," in Cunningham, *The Anatomical Renaissance*, 88–143. Similarly, in the second quarter of the sixteenth century Swiss physician Paracelsus (Theophrastus von Hohenheim) vehemently attacked Galen's system. While presently recognized as a pivotal figure in the development of early modern medicine, the degree of influence of his highly eclectic and radical teachings on his contemporaries was likely more limited.

19 Lindemann, *Medicine and Society*, 26.

20 On the importance of constitution and individualized treatments, see Lindemann, *Medicine and Society*, 23–24.

21 Recent research has highlighted the central role played by women in early modern healing and health. For a summary, see Lindemann, *Medicine and Society*, 243. On household medicine, see Lindemann, *Medicine and Society*, 121–124.

22 The following discussion depends on chapter 4, "Learning to Heal" in Lindemann, *Medicine and Society*, 121–157. See also Jonathan Sawday, *The Body Emblazoned: Dissection and the Human Body in Renaissance Culture* (Routledge, 1995). For general surveys of the development of science in Luther's era, see Marie Boas Hall, *The Scientific Renaissance 1450–1630* (Dover, 1994) and Allen G. Debus, *Man and Nature in the Renaissance*, Cambridge History of Science (Cambridge University Press, 1978). For the sixteenth-century medicine, see also Andrew Wear, Roger Kenneth French, and Iain M. Lonie, eds. *The Medical Renaissance of the Sixteenth Century* (Cambridge University Press, 1985) and Charles Webster, ed., *Health, Medicine, and Mortality in the Sixteenth Century* (Cambridge University Press, 1979).

23 For Luther's lectures on Isaiah 38, see WA 31.ii.246–257; LW 16:332–345. While Luther's lecture followed verse by verse the text of Isaiah 38, his overall reconstruction of the story more closely reflected its presentation in 2 Kings 20:1–7, with the exception of Hezekiah's song of praise found only in Isaiah 38.

24 "Domine, si sic vivitur." WA 31.ii.255.5; LW 16:341. Luther disputed the addition of "if" (si) in his translation near the beginning of this verse.

25 "Ita hie experiencia sentit rex nullam medicinae efficaciam sanandi esse, sed in verbo, sicut non in pane et cibo consistit alimentum, sed in verbo. Mirabilia facit verbum in corpore humano, non medicinae et victus, sed solum verbum. Si omnia medicinae genera devorarentur, nihil efficiunt sine verbo." WA 31.ii.255.9–13,15–17; LW 16:341–42.

26 For a brief summary of Luther's theology of the Word, see Steinmetz, *Luther in Context*, 115–116.

27 Steinmetz, *Luther in Context*, 115.

28 "Gott ist in der creatur, die wirckt vnd schafft er. Aber wir achtens nicht vnd suchen dieweyl secundas vnd philosophicas causas." WATR 5:17, no. 5227, quoted in Steiger, *Medizinische Theologie*, 40. Also see WATR 5:17 ("secundae causae obscurant primas"), quoted in Steiger, *Medizinische Theologie,* 40–41. Steiger makes a similar interpretation of Luther's view of causality (39–41).

29 "Utere medicinis, sed noli illis confidere, sed deo." WA 31.ii.256.7–8; LW 16:343.

30 Cling ("haerere"), trust ("confidere"), and rely ("fidere"). Luther's use of the term *haerere* follows Augustine's abundant use of this concept in his narrations on the Psalms and elsewhere.

31 The "ungodly" ("impii") or more commonly "fanatics" or "enthusiasts" (designated by Luther with a pejorative German word *Schwärmerei*) were members of other Protestant reform movements, typically referred to as spiritualists and Radical reformers (term coined by George Huntston Williams, in contrast to magisterial reformers, like Luther, whose programs of reform were conducted with the support of city magistrates). Although encompassing diverse groups, Radical reformers shared a key emphasis on the theological importance of subjective spiritual experience and the direct knowledge of God from the Holy Spirit to the human spirit, unmediated by external means. In contrast, Luther stressed that the knowledge of God had to be mediated by the Word and Sacrament. For the most comprehensive, classic work on the theologies and histories of Radical reformer groups,

see George Huntston Williams, *The Radical Reformation*, 3rd. ed., rev. and expanded, Sixteenth Century Essays & Studies 15 (Truman State University Press, 2000). Since the *Schwärmerei* were fellow Protestants who borrowed many of Luther's theological teachings, prominently including justification by faith alone, Luther perceived them as "false brethren," (Gal. 2:4), deceived by a satanic spirit and promoting disunity within the church. For a classic study of Luther's polemics with other Protestant reformers, see Mark U. Edwards, *Luther and the False Brethren* (Stanford University Press, 1975). See also Wilhelm Maurer, *Luther Und Die Schwärmer* (Lutherisches Verlagshaus, 1952).

32 In response to Karlstadt's rumored teachings against medicine, Luther's "table talk" recorded him drawing a comparison between using medicine when sick to eating when hungry. "Sicut respondi dem Hondorff, qui cum ex Carlstadio audisset non licere uti medicina et me interrogaret, dixi ad eum: Esset yhr auch, wenn euch hungert?" WATR 1:151–152, no. 360. This connection also is suggested in Johann Anselm Steiger, *Medizinische Theologie.*

33 For Karlstadt's biography see Hermann Barge, *Andreas Bodenstein von Karlstadt*, 2 vols. (B. De Graaf, 1968). While this work has been criticized for displaying an anti-Luther bias and errors in periodization, it still remains unsurpassed as Karlstadt's most authoritative biography. For a survey of Karlstadt's thought see, Ronald J. Sider, *Andreas Bodenstein von Karlstadt: The Development of His Thought, 1517–1525*, Studies in Medieval and Reformation Thought 11 (Brill, 1974), a standard work albeit criticized for diminishing the distinction between Luther and Karlstadt's theological positions. For historical sources outlining Luther and Karlstadt's polemics, see Andreas Karlstadt, Martin Luther, and Ronald J. Sider, eds., *Karlstadt's Battle with Luther: Documents in a Liberal-Radical Debate* (Augsburg Fortress Press 1978; Wipf and Stock, 2001), and for the analysis of Karlstadt's theological controversy with Luther, see Amy Nelson Burnett, *Karlstadt and the Origins of the Eucharistic Controversy: A Study in the Circulation of Ideas*, Oxford Studies in Historical Theology (Oxford University Press, 2011). For a survey of scholarly research on Karlstadt and the ongoing reassessment of his contributions and legacy, see Martin Kessler, *Das Karlstadt-Bild in Der Forschung*, Beiträge Zur Historischen Theologie 174 (Mohr Siebeck, 2014).

34 This is Karlstadt's second significant engagement with the concept of *Gelassenheit*. The first one was his 1520 treatise, titled *On the Supreme Virtue of Gelassenheit.*

35 Strictly speaking, the term "mysticism," if applied to the sixteenth century theology, is anachronistic. What is now termed as mystical thought or tradition within Western Christianity exercised considerable influence throughout the Middle Ages, however, was not formally recognized as such. Only in the early seventeenth century, the French term *la mystique* first became used in conjunction with identifying a particular mode of Christian endeavors to attain intimate knowledge and unity with the divine at knowing God. The distinction of mysticism as a part of Christian theology in its own right marked a crucial development in the history of Western mystical tradition. See Michel de Certeau, *The Mystic Fable*, vol. 1, *The Sixteenth and Seventeenth Centuries* (University of Chicago Press, 1992). Bernard McGinn's seven-volume study, *The Presence of God: A History of Western Christian Mysticism* (Crossroad, 1991–) provides an extensive investigation into Christian mystical tradition in the West. For more on the mystical German notion of Gelassenheit, see the latest volume (number 5) in this series, *The Varieties of Vernacular Mysticism, 1350–1550.*

36 See Steven Ozment, *Mysticism and Dissent: Religious Ideology and Social Protest in the Sixteenth Century* (Yale University Press, 1973) for a discussion of the medieval mystical theology, in particular as expressed in *Theologica Germanica* (to which Ozment refers by its German title, *Theologia Deutsch*), in the Reformation religious ideologies of dissent.

37 The extent to which Luther's views on suffering became influenced by post-Eckhartian mysticism remains a matter of scholarly disagreement. Recently, Vincent Evener has argued for the former view. See "Introduction" in Evener, *Enemies of the Cross*, esp. 3–4. Evener also notes that Luther likely owed his interest in Tauler to his own Augustinian mentor, Johann von Staupitz. See also Volker Leppin, "Mystische Erbe auf getrennten Wegen: Überlegungen zu Karlstadt und Luther," in Christoph Bultmann, Volker Leppin, and Andreas Lindner, eds., *Luther Und Das Monastische Erbe: Spätmittelalter, Humanismus, Reformation*. Studies in the Late Middle Ages, Humanism and the Reformation 39 (Mohr Siebeck, 2007), 154–162. An alternative view stresses that Luther's appreciation of mystical theology of suffering was primarily based on his finding it to be in agreement with his traditional sources of theological authority, the Bible and Augustine. For a survey of the reception of medieval mysticism by early modern Protestants, see Ronald K. Rittgers and Vincent Evener, eds., *Protestants and Mysticism in Reformation Europe*, St Andrews Studies in Reformation History (Brill, 2019). For an argument for Luther's deep personal

embrace of mysticism, see Bengt R. Hoffman, *Luther and the Mystics: A Reexamination of Luther's Spiritual Experience and His Relationship to the Mystics* (Augsburg, 1976). For an important, earlier work on the general relationship between Luther and mysticism, see "Simul genitus et raptus. Luther und die Mystik" in Heiko Augustinus Oberman, *Die Reformation: Von Wittenberg Nach Genf* (Vandenhoeck & Ruprecht, 1986).

38 For an overview of Luther's editions of *Theologia Germanica* and of the relationship between his early thought and the ideas of these treatises see chapter 2 of Ozment, *Mysticism and Dissent,* especially 17–25. For a lengthier analysis of Luther's engagement with the treatise see Bengt Hoffman, *The Theologia Germanica of Martin Luther* (Paulist Press, 1980). For a historical introduction to *Theologica Germanica*, see Bernard McGinn, *The Presence of God*, vol. 4, *The Harvest of Mysticism in Medieval Germany* (Crossroads, 2005), 392–404.

39 Andreas Karlstadt, "The Meaning of the Term Gelassen and Where in Holy Scripture It Is Found," in *The Essential Karlstadt: Fifteen Tracts,* trans and ed. Edward J. Furcha (Herald Press, 1995), 133–168. For the discussion of food, see especially 141,150, 153. On pleasure as sin apart from God, see 137–139.

40 Karlstadt, "The Meaning of the Term Gelassen," 150.

41 Karlstadt, "The Meaning of the Term Gelassen," 153.

42 Karlstadt, "The Meaning of the Term Gelassen," 153

43 Karlstadt, "The Meaning of the Term Gelassen," 153.

44 Karlstadt, "The Meaning of the Term Gelassen," 138.

45 Andreas Karlstadt, "Regarding the Sabbath and Statutory Holy Days," in *The Essential Karlstadt: Fifteen Tracts,* 317–338.

46 Luther's works contain multiple discussions of the role of created means. For a good summary of Luther's view of causality and the role of means in his lectures on Genesis, see WA 43.68–73; LW 3:270–277.

47 For the context of this issue, see Steiger, *Medizinische Theologie*, 39–41. For a substantial analysis of this issue, see David Steinmetz, "Scripture and the Lord's Supper in Luther's Theology," in *Luther in Context,* 72–85.

48 The discussion depends on WA 40.ii.77–79; LW 1:101–103.

49 The following discussion depends on WA 43.68–73; LW 3:270–277.

50 "Potentia absoluta" as absolute power and "ordinata" as the ordained or "ordered" one.

51 On the discussion of God's power see *ST*.I.Q25. For a survey of medieval theology of God's absolute and ordained power see Francis

Oakley, "The Absolute and Ordained Power of God in Sixteenth- and Seventeenth-Century Theology." *Journal of the History of Ideas* 59, no. 3 (1998): 437–461. https://doi.org/10.2307/3653896

52 The following discussion depends on Oberman, *The Harvest of Medieval Theology*, 257–261; 45–46.

53 The following discussion depends on WA 42.316–317; LW 2:75–77.

54 For example, after encouraging his audience to use means, Luther counseled that "ubi igitur haec mediorum seu creaturarum copia vel deest vel cessat, ibi aut patere, aut expecta auxilium a Domino. Sicut Iudaei faciebant, quos ad mare constitutos et ab hoste a tergo cinctos nulla amplius industria sublevare poterat. Quare aut miraculosa liberatio speranda, aut certa mors subeunda erat" (WA 42.317.8–12). "When the supply of these means or creatures is either lacking or depleted, then you must either suffer or wait for help from the Lord, as did the Jews, whom no further effort could sustain when they were standing at the sea and were surrounded by the enemy in their rear. In these circumstances they were obliged either to hope for a miraculous deliverance or to endure certain death" (LW 2:77).

55 "Si volet me Deus servare, tempore famis aut pestis ero superstes, etiam sine cibo aut medicina. Sin fuerit pereundum, nihil proderunt illa omnia." WA 44.527.26-28; LW 7:308

56 "Nobis enim ad ordinatam potestatem respiciendum, et ex ea iuditium sumendum est;" "[Haec fuit potentia Dei absoluta, secundum quam tum agebat], sed secundum hane nihil nos iubet. Vult enim nos facere secundum ordinatam potentiam." WA 43.71.18–19, 26–28; LW 3:274.

57 The extent to which Luther believed in the continuing possibility of miraculous healing in his own era has been debated. See, for instance, D. P. Walker, "The Cessation of Miracles," in *Hermeticism in the Renaissance*, ed. Ingrid Merkel and Allen G. Debus (Folger, 1988), 110–124; Philip Soergel, "Luther on Miracles," in *Miracles and the Protestant Imagination: The Evangelical Wonder Book in Reformation History* (Oxford University Press, 2012), esp. 38–46. Based on Luther's sermon on Matthew 8:1–14, Walker's influential essay concludes that Luther (at least sometimes) explicitly taught the cessation of miracles in the post-apostolic era, thus establishing the foundation for the later Protestant doctrine of cessationism. The same sermon on Matthew 8:1–14 was also part of Soergel's comprehensive, more recent analysis of the development of Luther's theology of miracles. Soergel argues that while Luther acknowledged that prayer and faith could still potentially

bring about miracles of healing even in his own time, he was nevertheless inclined to teach that the "miracles of the body" had generally ceased, a conviction that Soergel linked to Luther's polemics against the medieval cult of saints. On the other end of the spectrum, Bengt Hoffman's exploration of mystical dimensions of Luther's thought and ministry all but presented Luther as a faith healer of the body (Bengt Hoffman, *Theology of the Heart: The Role of Mysticism in the Theology of Martin Luther* (Lutheran University Press, 2003, 46–52)). According to Hoffman, "this theologian [Luther] who, in many descriptions has become the prototype for earth-bound spiritual power, was, in the case of spiritual healing, an advocate of reliance on power from higher realms" (46). For Luther's history with healing rites and their subsequent use in Lutheranism, including the contemporary era, see Kyle K. Schiefelbein-Guerrero "Healing Rites for a Post-Pandemic World," *CrossAccent* (Summer 2020): 50-59. In sum, the contested interpretations of Luther's attitudes toward miraculous healing highlighted a remarkable tension in Luther's thought between his desire to downplay a continuing reality of miracles (including healing miracles) in his own era and his acknowledgment that such miracles still could be (and were) possible on account of prayer and strong faith of the petitioner.

58 "Deus utitur mediis certis, et sua miracula sic temperat, ut tamen ministerio naturae et mediis naturalibus utatur." WA 42–316.23–25; LW 2:76. An alternative, more precise translation for "tones down" is "tempers" or "moderates."

59 "Sic Medicinae usus licitus est, imo necessarius: est enim conditum medium ad conservandam valetudinem." WA.42.316.37–39; LW 2:77.

60 The relationship between Luther's theology of medicine and created means has been explored by other scholars whose conclusions were similar yet distinct from mine, due to different interpretive strategies and the selection of primary sources. Most notably, Steiger in *Medizinische Theologie* (esp. 7–8) and elsewhere, grounded what he calls Luther's medical theology in his theology of creation and providential action, but ultimately in Luther's "medical Christology." According to Steiger, Luther's *Christologia medicinalis* was rooted in his soteriological embrace of the Chalcedonian Christology of the two natures of Christ, which showed Christ to be the perfect physician of both the soul and the body. Steiger also noted the relationship between this and the promise of Exodus 15:26. Hammond made a similar connection

between Luther's theology of medicine and divine providential power in creation (Hammond, "Ora Deum," 37).

61 While the theme of idolatry in the Reformations has traditionally been explored primarily in relation to John Calvin and the Reformed tradition, recent scholarship has emphasized Luther's original understanding of idolatry and its importance for his thought. See, for instance, Michael Lockwood, *The Unholy Trinity: Martin Luther against the Idol of Me, Myself, and I* (Concordia, 2016); Tae Jun Suk, "The Theology of Martin Luther between Judaism and Roman Catholicism: A Critical-Historical Evaluation of Luther's Concept of Idolatry" (PhD diss., Drew University, 1999). The following works also engage particular aspects of Luther's theology of idolatry: Carlos M. N. Eire, *War Against the Idols: The Reformation of Worship from Erasmus to Calvin* (Cambridge University Press, 1986), 65–73; Vilmos Vajta, *Luther on Worship* (Muhlenberg Press, 1954), 67–84, 125–148; Heinrich Bornkamm, *Luther and the Old Testament,* trans. Eric W. Gritsch and Ruth C. Gritsch, ed. Victor I. Gruhn (Fortress, 1969), 46–55; Randall C. Zachman, "The Idolatrous Religion of Conscience," in *The Assurance of Faith: Conscience in the Theology of Martin Luther and John Calvin* (Fortress, 1993), 19–39.

62 WA 30.I.133.1–8; 135, 9–16; Martin Luther, "Large Catechism" in Kolb and Wengert, ed., *The Book of Concord*, 386, I:2–3; 388, I:21.

63 See, for example, WA 31.ii.273–275, 282–283; LW 17:17,19, 29.

64 WA 47.64.34–76, 19; LW 22:337–350.

65 WA 47.64.34–65, 6; LW 22:337–338.

66 WA 47.65.24–27; LW 22:338.

67 WA 47.65.29–31; LW 22:339.

68 "Den das ansehen hats nicht gethan, sondern der Glaube an das wortt hatt geholffen." WA 47:66.2–3; LW 22:339.

69 WA 47.73.38–74, 4; LW 22:348.

70 Reports from *Table Talk* about natural medicinal means included discussions about allegedly curative properties of various kinds of animal feces, which, as Luther marveled, God did not despise to use as a means for healing (WATR 1.29.21–25, no. 78, quoted in Steiger, *Medizinische Theologie*, 39). Steiger analyzes this as a pharmacological-theological application of Luther's theology of the cross: the Word did not despise working even through the lowliest means (*Medizinische Theologie*, 40). Furthermore, in addition to the means of "naturalistic" medicine, including herbs, plants, and even feces, Steiger discussed other alternative forms of administering the medicine of the Word of

God in Luther's theology, such as through the Lord's Supper, the blood of Christ, and pastoral preaching and consolations (*Medizinische Theologie*, 22–24).

71 See Soergel, "Miracle, Magic and Disenchantment in Early Modern Germany," 220–221.

72 Vauchez, *Sainthood in the Later Middle Ages*, 476. For Protestant dismissal of the medieval and development of alternative perspectives on sainthood, see Robert Kolb, *For All the Saints: Changing Perceptions of Sanctity in the Lutheran Reformation* (Mercer University Press, 1987). For changing popular views, see Paul Russell, *Lay Theology in the Reformation: Popular Pamphleteers in Southwest Germany*, 1521–1525 (Cambridge University Press, 1986).

73 Luther himself stated precisely that in his commentaries on the Gospel of John, where he defined the purpose of what he saw as false healing miracles to have people "seduced into idolatry" and "transfer their trust from God to his [Satan's] lies" (WA 45.528; LW 24:74–75).

74 WA 47.73.2–23; LW 22:346–347.

75 "Eine Abgötterei." WA 47.73.20–21; LW 22:347.

76 Oberman, *Luther*.

77 For Lohse's discussion of the devil in Luther's theology, see Bernhard Lohse, *Martin Luther's Theology: Its Historical and Systematic Development* (Augsburg Fortress, 1999), 195–196.

78 Luther was recorded to have made this point in WATR 1:150–151, no. 360; LW 54:53–54.

79 WATR 1:265, no. 577; LW 54:102–103.

80 Schreiner, *Are You Alone Wise?*, 294. On the devil's disguises in Luther's theology, see 294–303.

81 As discussed by Oberman, *Luther*, 106.

82 WA 14.647.5–648, 37; LW 9:129–131; WA 14.685.6–20; LW 9:189.

83 The following discussion relies on WA 14.685.6–20; LW 9:189.

84 For the function of angels as divine agents to preserve the world as a theme in Luther's lectures on Genesis, see John A. Maxfield, *Luther's Lectures on Genesis and the Formation of Evangelical Identity* (Truman State University Press, 2008), 181–185. For the observation that scholarly interest in the demonic in early modern sources had marginalized the study of angels in Protestant piety until recently, see Scott Hendrix, "Angelic Piety in the Reformation: The Good and Bad Angels of Urbanus Rhegius," in *Frömmigkeit—Theologie—Frömmigkeitstheologie: Contributions to European Church History. Festschrift für Berndt Hamm zum 60. Geburtstag*, ed. Gudrun Litz, Heidrun Munzert, and

Ronald Liebenberg (Brill, 2005), 385–394. For a welcome change in recent scholarship that has highlighted new significance assigned to angels in the Protestant Reformations and influenced my discussion, see Philip Soergel, "Luther on the Angels," in *Angels in the Early Modern World*, ed. Peter Marshall and Alexandra Walsham (Cambridge University Press, 2006), 64–82; Rittgers, *Reformation of Suffering*, 208–210. By recovering and expanding functions attributed to angels in earlier Christian tradition, Protestant reformers augmented the roles of angels in order to forge a popular spiritual substitute for the medieval devotion to saints. While Protestants rejected medieval practices of seeking saintly intercessors, they saw angels as a biblically supported alternative for the provision of spiritual assistance, fulfilling an important pastoral need. At the same time, early Protestant views of angels were deeply grounded in medieval religious culture, especially in its beliefs surrounding intercession and death: Bruce Gordon, "Placing the Dead in Late Medieval and Early Modern Europe," in *The Place of the Dead: Death and Remembrance in Late Medieval and Early Modern Europe*, ed. Bruce Gordon and Peter Marshall (Cambridge University Press, 2000), 1–16. Protestant angels were protectors, guardians, comforters, and even intercessors.

85 The following is a summary of Soergel, *Luther on the Angels*, 64–82.

86 Et quod nascentibus novis morbis nova remedia ostenduntur: non hominum ea industria est, sed Angelorum ministerium, qui artificum animos gubernant et impellunt, sicut Sathan etiàm suos." WA 43.69.5–8; LW 3:271.

Chapter 4: The Genesis of Medicine and Gendered Pain

1 This inference is drawn from the absence of childhood health troubles mentioned in Luther's own writings or in others' accounts, which otherwise contain multiple descriptions of his health issues later in life. The ensuing discussion of Luther's health depends on John Wilkinson, *The Medical History of the Reformers: Luther, Calvin and Knox* (Handsel Press, 2001), especially 20–29, Oberman, *Luther*, 327–330, and Roper, "Martin Luther's Body: The 'Stout Doctor' and His Biographers." For suggested connections between Luther's health problems and his spiritual struggles, see Martin Brecht, *Martin Luther: Shaping and Defining the Reformation: 1521–1532*, trans. James L. Schaaf, vol. 2 (Fortress Press, 1990), 204–206.

2 Wilkinson, *The Medical History of the Reformers*, 20–21.

3 WABR 2:357; LW 48:257 cited in Wilkinson, *The Medical History of the Reformers*, 26.
4 Oberman, *Luther*, 328. As noted by Lyndal Roper, sharing such an explicit account of one's bowel movement was not out of the ordinary in Luther's less private, more openly physical sixteenth-century context. See Lyndal Roper, "Drinking, Whoring and Gorging: Brutish Indiscipline and the Formation of Protestant Identity," in *Oedipus and the Devil: Witchcraft, Sexuality, and Religion in Early Modern Europe* (Routledge, 1994), 145–170.
5 Quoted in WATR 3.578, no. 3733; LW 54:266
6 WATR 3:304, no. 3395c., cited in Wilkinson, *The Medical History of the Reformers*, 28.
7 Wilkinson, *The Medical History of the Reformers*, 23.
8 There is no surviving record of Luther's own written version of these lectures, which he delivered orally to his students, several of whom transcribed them. These transcripts were subsequently edited and published in four volumes in 1544 by his former student Veit Dietrich. The fact that Luther's Genesis lectures were preserved for the subsequent editions based on student notes rather than his own writings sparked a scholarly conversation about their full reliability. There has been a general agreement that, although with some exceptions, in their current form, these lectures overall accurately reflected Luther's exegetical approach and theological emphases. For a survey of the debate regarding the reliable character of Luther's lectures on Genesis, see J. A. Nestingen, "Luther in the Front of the Text: The Genesis Commentary," *Word and World* 14 (1994), 186–194.
9 Oberman, *Luther*, 166–167.
10 See chapter 4 "Scripture and Tradition" in Jaroslav Pelikan and Martin Luther, *Luther the Expositor: Introduction to the Reformer's Exegetical Writings*, Companion Volume (Concordia, 1959), 71–88.
11 For Luther's view of the historicity and interpretation of the Old Testament, see John A. Maxfield, *Luther's Lectures on Genesis and the Formation of Evangelical Identity*, vol. 80, Sixteenth Century Essays and Studies (Truman State University Press, 2008), especially 10–72, and Heinrich Bornkamm, *Luther and the Old Testament*, ed. Victor I. Gruhn, trans. Eric W. Gritsch and Ruth C. Gritsch (Fortress, 1969); for Luther's view of history, see especially 64–87 and chapter 4, "The Old Testament as Word of God", 81–218. For additional perspectives, see Mickey Leland Mattox, *Defender of the Most Holy Matriarchs: Martin Luther's Interpretation of the Women of Genesis in*

the Enarrationes in Genesin, 1535–45, Studies in Medieval and Reformation Thought 92 (Brill, 2003), Kenneth Hagen, *Luther's Approach to Scripture as Seen in His "Commentaries" on Galatians, 1519–1538* (Mohr, 1993), and Scott H. Hendrix, "Luther Against the Background of the History of Biblical Interpretation," *Interpretation: A Journal of Bible and Theology* 37, no. 3 (July 1983): 229–239, https://doi.org/10.1177/002096438303700302.

12 The ensuing discussion depends on WA 42.70.10–74.2; LW 1:92–97; 102. In particular, on Adams's perpetual youthfulness before the fall and the tree of life serving as a medicine preserving youth and vigor, see WA 42.70.17–29; LW 1:92; 102.

13 "Pharmacum" in WA 42.70.27–29; LW 1:92; "remedium" in WA 42.71:12; LW 1:93.

14 Changes in female fertility in this and the following paragraph are discussed by Luther in WA 42:162:1–21; LW 1:216–217. For Luther's vivid descriptions of pregnancy discomforts, see WA 42:149:29–150:3; LW 1:200.

15 "Virtute verbi." WA 42.73:13–15; LW 1:96, and further in WA 42.73:32-33; LW 1:96.

16 See WA 42:162:1–21; LW 1:216–217.

17 WA 42.70:34–35; LW 1:93.

18 The following paragraph of Genesis as the history of the church primarily depends on Pelikan, chapter 5 "The History of the People of God" in Pelikan and Luther, *Luther the Expositor*, 89–108 and Maxfield, chapter 4 "The Reconstruction of the Christian Past" in *Luther's Lectures on Genesis and the Formation of Evangelical Identity*, 141–179. See also Bornkamm, *Luther and the Old Testament*, 209–222.

19 See Maxfield, *Luther's Lectures on Genesis and the Formation of Evangelical Identity*, 176–179. Maxfield acknowledged that Luther was sharply critical of humanist biblical interpretation, yet he contends that, at the same time, Luther was influenced by the humanist methods and agenda for historiography. (178).

20 "A verbo Dei abduxit . . . ad Idolatriam." WA.42.112.31–32; LW 1:149.

21 For Luther's interpretation of the fall as the original idolatry, see Luther's lectures on Genesis 3:1–6 in WA 42.106–122; LW 1. 141–162. For a discussion of Luther's approach to idolatry as trust in deceptive appearances, see Susan Schreiner, *Are You Alone Wise?*, 325–327.

22 "Quasi dicat: Profecto bene fatui estis, si cogitatis Deum noluisse, ut de hac arbore comederetis, qui super omnes Paradisi arbores vos

constituit dominos. Imo vestra causa eas condidit. Quomodo, qui favit vobis omnia, huius unius arboris fructus invidere vobis potest tarn iucundos et suaves? Eo enim respicit Satan, quomodo eis verbum eripiat et cognitionem Dei, ut statuant: non est haec voluntas Dei, Deus hoc non praecipit." WA 42.115.1–6; LW 1:152

23 "Ne forte moriamur." WA 42.116.38–39; LW 1:155.

24 "Facile itaque esset eum cavere. Sed hic cum verbum aliud proponit, cum disputat de voluntate Dei, cum opponit nomen Dei, Ecclesiae et populi Dei, ibi tam facile caveri non potest." WA 42.112.11–13; LW 1:148.

25 "Adorant cogitationes suas relicto verbo." WA 42.112.28–29; LW 1:149.

26 As argued by Maxfield, *Luther's Lectures on Genesis and the Formation of Evangelical Identity*, 157–163.

27 The following discussion depends on chapter 5 "The History of the People of God," in Pelikan and Luther, *Luther the Expositor*, 91–95.

28 Donald Mowbray, *Pain and Suffering in Medieval Theology: Academic Debates at the University of Paris in the Thirteenth Century* (Boydell Press, 2009), 49, 51. The following discussion depends on Mowbray, 47–61.

29 On Luther's pre-flood human history as a golden age of humanity see John M. Headley, *Luther's View of Church History*, vol. 6, Yale Publications in Religion (Yale University Press, 1963). Also see Maxfield, *Luther's Lectures on Genesis and the Formation of Evangelical Identity*, 148–151.

30 The following discussion depends on Headley, *Luther's View of Church History*, 118–124.

31 The ensuing discussion depends on WA 42.153:8–155:14; LW 1:205–208.

32 For an exhaustive collection of primary sources on Luther's theological engagements with women, see Susan C. Karant-Nunn and Merry E. Wiesner-Hanks, eds., *Luther on Women: A Sourcebook* (Cambridge University Press, 2003). The most extensive discussion of women in early modern Germany is found in Heide Wunder, *He Is the Sun, She Is the Moon: Women in Early Modern Germany*, trans. Thomas Dunlap (Harvard University Press, 1998), which also provides a bibliography of sources in many languages. For surveys of the history of women and gender in early modern Germany, see Ulinka Rublack, ed., *Gender in Early Modern German History*, Past and Present Publications (Cambridge University Press, 2002) and Merry E. Wiesner-Hanks, *Women*

and Gender in Early Modern Europe, 3rd ed., New Approaches to European History 41 (Cambridge University Press, 2008). For detailed studies of women's societal roles see Joel F. Harrington, *Reordering Marriage and Society in Reformation Germany* (Cambridge University Press, 1995); Sheilagh C. Ogilvie, *A Bitter Living: Women, Markets, and Social Capital in Early Modern Germany* (Oxford University Press, 2003); and Lyndal Roper, *The Holy Household: Women and Morals in Reformation Augsburg*, Oxford Studies in Social History (Oxford University Press, 2001). See also Margaret Brannan Lewis, *Infanticide and Abortion in Early Modern Germany*, The Body, Gender and Culture 19 (Routledge Taylor & Francis Group, 2016).

33 The following discussion depends on Mowbray, *Pain and Suffering in Medieval Theology*, 47–61. For the discussion of the nature of Eve's punishment see 55–56. For the evolution of medieval approaches to Adam and Eve in the sixteenth century, see Cathleen M. Crowther, *Adam and Eve in the Protestant Reformation* (Cambridge University Press), 2013.

34 For Bernard of Clairvaux's exegesis of Genesis 3, see Madison Krahmer Shawn, "Adam, Eve, and Original Sin in the Works of Bernard of Clairvaux," *Cistercian Studies Quarterly* 37, no. 1 (2002): 3.

35 Wiesner-Hanks, *Women and Gender in Early Modern Europe*, 55–56. The ensuing discussion of early modern reproductive pain depends on Lindemann, *Medicine and Society*, especially 34–36 and 268–272, and Wiesner-Hanks, *Women and Gender in Early Modern Europe*, especially 55–100.

36 See Lindemann, *Medicine and Society in Early Modern Europe*, 35 and Wiesner-Hanks, *Women and Gender in Early Modern Europe*, 87.

37 See Wiesner-Hanks, *Women and Gender in Early Modern Europe*, 83–87. Wiesner-Hanks also points out that women feared anger and curses of uninvited neighbors, which were at times linked to witchcraft.

38 See Michael Flinn, *The European Demographic System, 1500–1820* (Brighton, 1981), 16–17 cited in Lindemann, *Medicine and Society in Early Modern Europe*, 34.

39 "Sicut enim elegans puella sine molestia, imo cum magna voluptate et superbia quadam pulchram Coronam ex floribus contextam in capite gestat, Ita sine omni molestia et cum magna voluptate Heua, si non peccasset, in utero gestasset foetum." WA 42.151.17–20; LW 1:202

40 This paragraph depends on Luther's discussion of women's reproductive pain in WA 42.147–152; LW 1:198–203.

41 "Statim suboriuntur acerrimi dolores capitis, vertigo, nausea et fastidium mirabile cibi et potus, crebrae et difficiles vomitiones, dolor dentium, et ventriculi vicium, quod Kittam excitat, quam picam vocant, cum tales cibos appetunt, a quibus incolumis natura abhorret." WA 42.149.34–37; LW 1:200.
42 See WA 42.162; LW 1:217.
43 WA 36.351-352; English translation is in Karant-Nunn and Wiesner-Hanks, *Luther on Women*, 173.
44 See WA 43.690–692; LW 5:380–382.
45 Lindemann, *Medicine and Society*, 25.
46 Wiesner-Hanks, *Women and Gender in Early Modern Europe*, 84.
47 "Gloriam maternitatis." WA 42.148.29; LW 1:199, see also WA 42.150.28; LW 1:201.
48 See WA 10.ii.296; English translation in Karant-Nunn and Wiesner-Hanks, *Luther on Women*, 172–173.
49 WA 24.96–104; English translation in Karant-Nunn and Wiesner-Hanks, *Luther on Women*, 23.
50 "Laeta et hilaris." WA 42.148.4; LW 1:198, also LW 42.148.23; LW 1:199.
51 "Antea liberrima et nulla in parte Viro inferior erat, socia omnium donorum Dei." WA 42.151.22–23; LW 1:202.
52 "At si Heua in veritate stetisset, non solum non subiecta imperio Viri esset, sed ipsa quoque socia gubernationis fuisset, quae nunc sola masculorum est." WA 42.151.34–36; LW 1:203.
53 John Lee Thompson, *John Calvin and the Daughters of Sarah: Women in Regular and Exceptional Roles in the Exegesis of Calvin, His Predecessors and His Contemporaries*, Travaux d'Humanisme et Renaissance 259 (Librairie Droz, 2014), 136–144.

Chapter 5: Contemporary Reformations of Medicine and Religion

1 Bishop, *The Anticipatory Corpse*, 313.
2 Notable existing studies include Daniel P. Sulmasy, *The Healer's Calling: A Spirituality for Physicians and Other Health Care Professionals* (Paulist Press, 1997); Jean-Claude Larchet, *The Theology of Illness* (St Vladimir's Seminary Press, 2002); Daniel P. Sulmasy, *A Balm for Gilead: Meditations on Spirituality and the Healing Arts* (Georgetown University Press, 2006); Joel Shuman and Brian Volck, *Reclaiming the Body: Christians and the Faithful Use of Modern Medicine* (Brazos Press,

2006). See also Therese M. Lysaught, "Medicine as Friendship with God: Anointing the Sick as a Theological Hermeneutic." *Journal of the Society of Christian Ethics* 29, no. 1 (2009): 171–191.

3 The text is available in the Tertullian Project, "Tertullian: De Fuga in Persecutione (with Critical Apparatus)," accessed March 1, 2024, https://www.tertullian.org/latin/de_fuga_app.htm.

4 See Origen, "An Exhortation to Martyrdom," in Origen, *Selected Writings: An Exhortation to Martyrdom, Prayer, First Principles, Book IV, Prologue to the Commentary on the Song of Songs, Homily XXVII on Numbers*. Classics of Western Spirituality Series (Paulist Press, 1979).

5 As discussed, for example, in Jean-Claude Larchet, *The Theology of Illness* (SVS Press, 2002), 12.

6 For the discussion of the Pentecostal movement as the "second reformation" in the history of Christianity and the centrality of divine healing for this tradition, see Candy Gunther Brown, ed., *Global Pentecostal and Charismatic Healing* (Oxford University Press, 2011), especially xvii–xix.; 6–11. On the preference of the term "divine healing" over "faith healing" or "spiritual healing" for the study of Pentecostalism, see 4–5.

7 For internal critique of Pentecostal theologians' lack of robust theological responses to suffering see, for example, Veli-Matti Kärkkäinen, "Theology of the Cross: A Stumbling Block to Pentecostal Spirituality?," in *The Spirit and Spirituality: Essays in Honour of Russell P. Spittler*, ed. Wonsuk Ma, Robert P. Menzies, and Russell P. Spittler, Journal of Pentecostal Theology 24 (T&T Clark International, 2004), 150–163; Gabriel Reuben Louis, "Response to Dr. Wonsuk Ma's 'Towards an Asian Pentecostal Theology.'" *Cyberjournal for Pentecostal-Charismatic Research* (July 1998), http://www.pctii.org/cyberj/cyberj4/louis.html. See also David Courey, *What Has Wittenberg to Do with Azusa? Luther's Theology of the Cross and Pentecostal Triumphalism* (T&T Clark, 2015).

8 The most recent data available is from 2021. See Gina A. Zurlo, Todd M. Johnson, and Peter F. Crossing, "World Christianity and Mission 2021: Questions about the Future," *International Bulletin of Mission Research* 45, no. 1 (January 2021): 15–25, https://doi.org/10.1177/2396939320966220. Also see Pew Research Center, "Global Christianity—A Report on the Size and Distribution of the World's Christian Population," in *Christian Movements and Denominations* (blog), December 19, 2011, https://www.pewresearch.org/religion/2011/12/19/global-christianity-movements-and-denominations/.

9 James H. Cone, *God of the Oppressed* (Seabury Press, 1975), 139. See also 156.

10 For the description of "progressive Pentecostalism" increasingly absorbing aspects of liberation theologies see Donald E. Miller and Tetsunao Yamamori, *Global Pentecostalism: The New Face of Christian Social Engagement* (University of California Press, 2007), 15–39.

11 Few attempts have been undertaken to apply liberation theology specifically to medical justice. For example, the founder of Latin American liberation theology Gustavo Gutiérrez and Harvard professor Paul Farmer coauthored a volume that remains a leading practice-oriented guide for putting Christian liberation theology in conversation with social justice work in medicine. See Michael P. Griffin and Jennie Weiss Block, eds., *In the Company of the Poor: Conversations between Dr. Paul Farmer and Fr. Gustavo Gutierrez* (Orbis Books, 2013). See also Lysaught, "Medicine as Friendship with God," 171–191. Further theological production is needed to continue developing this important area of research.

12 See Christian Smith and Melinda Lundquist Denton, *Soul Searching: The Religious and Spiritual Lives of American Teenagers* (Oxford University Press, 2009), iv. Also see Kenda Creasy Dean, *Almost Christian: What the Faith of Our Teenagers Is Telling the American Church* (Oxford University Press, 2010).

13 On the lack of adequate contemporary theological response to illness see Larchet, *The Theology of Illness*, especially 9–15. Larchet's project retrieves early Eastern Christian writers' theological interpretations of illness. See also Stanley Hauerwas, "Should Suffering Be Eliminated?" in *The Hauerwas Reader*, ed. John Berkman, and Michael Cartwright (Duke University Press, 2001), 556–576. See also "Why Medicine Needs the Church" in *The Hauerwas Reader*, 539–555. Important approaches specifically to the experiences of permanent disability have been developed by disability theologies; for a classic study in liberation disability theology, see Nancy L. Eiesland, *The Disabled God: Toward a Liberatory Theology of Disability* (Abingdon Press, 1994).

14 As also observed in Oberman, *Luther*, 330.

15 Porterfield, *Healing in the History of Christianity*, 21.

16 The following discussion of the attitudes toward medicine in early Christianity depends on Amundsen, *Medicine, Society, and Faith*, 127–175; Larchet, *The Theology of Illness*, 109–14; Gary B. Ferngren, *Medicine and Religion: A Historical Introduction* (Johns Hopkins University Press, 2014), 100–130.

17 As noted in Larchet, *The Theology of Illness*, 109. In contrast, Amundsen does not accept the position that Tertullian seemed to have rejected medicine later in his career. See Amundsen, *Medicine, Society, and Faith*, 146. With agreement with Amundsen, see also Gary B. Ferngren and Ekaterina N. Lomperis, *Essential Readings in Medicine and Religion* (Johns Hopkins University Press, 2017), 101–111.

18 For the exposition of Schleiermacher's critique of miracles, see William A. Dembski, "Schleiermacher's Metaphysical Critique of Miracles," *Scottish Journal of Theology* 49, no. 4 (November 1996): 443–465, https://doi.org/10.1017/S003693060004850X.

19 I use the term Pentecostal-Charismatic Christian as an umbrella term for a diverse tradition, emphasizing the continuing availability and practice of divine healing in the Christian church. The term Pentecostal is used in reference to classical Pentecostal denominations whose histories go back to the early twentieth-century revivals and which, alongside healing, stress the centrality of glossolalia for salvation. Unlike Pentecostal, second- and third-wave Charismatic Christians generally do not privilege glossolalia in their emphasis on the continuing reality of the supernatural gifts (*charisms*) of the Holy Spirit and can belong to a variety of Christian denominations and traditions.

20 Miroslav Volf, "Materiality of Salvation: An Investigation in the Soteriologies of Liberation and Pentecostal Theologies," *Journal of Ecumenical Studies* 26, no. 3 (1989): 447–467.

21 Brown, *Global Pentecostal and Charismatic Healing*, 3. Brown references a Pew study that found that, in eight out of ten surveyed countries, more than 70 percent of Pentecostal Christians either personally witnessed or experienced an episode of divine healing of the body. For more on the centrality of practice of divine healing in Pentecostal tradition, see also Kimberly Ervin Alexander, *Pentecostal Healing: Models in Theology and Practice*, Journal of Pentecostal Theology Supplement Series 29 (Blandford Forum: Deo, 2006); James Robinson, *Divine Healing: The Holiness-Pentecostal Transition Years, 1890–1906: Theological Transposition in the Transatlantic World* (Pickwick, 2013); Joseph W. Williams, *Spirit Cure: A History of Pentecostal Healing* (Oxford University Press, 2013).

22 Azusa Street Mission, "Questions Answered," *Apostolic Faith 1.11*, October 1907–January 1908 edition: 2. On divine healings during the revival, see also Azusa Street Mission, "Beginning of World Wide Revival," *Apostolic Faith 1.5*, January 1907 edition: 1.

23 See Williams, *Spirit Cure*, 81–97.

24 Leah Payne, *Gender and Pentecostal Revivalism* (Palgrave Macmillan, 2015), 70–73.

25 See for example Chinedu Anthony Iwu et al., "Prevalence and Predictors of COVID-19 Vaccine Hesitancy among Health Care Workers in Tertiary Health Care Institutions in a Developing Country: A Cross-Sectional Analytical Study," ed. Francesco Chirico, *Advances in Public Health* 2022 (March 22, 2022): 1–9, https://doi.org/10.1155/2022/7299092; Simona-Nicoleta Vulpe and Sorina Vasile, "Unvaccinated, Just Like Everybody Else. Vaccine Hesitancy in a Romanian Religious Community," *European Review of Applied Sociology* 16, no. 26 (June 1, 2023): 16–24, https://doi.org/10.2478/eras-2023-0003; Peter White, "Pentecostal Spirituality in the Context of Faith and Hope Gospel (Prosperity Preaching): African Pentecostal Response to the COVID-19 Pandemic," *Dialog* 61, no. 2 (June 2022): 148–155, https://doi.org/10.1111/dial.12727.

26 The most recent data available is from 2021. See Zurlo, Johnson, and Crossing, "World Christianity and Mission 2021," 15–25. Also see Pew Research Center, "Global Christianity—A Report on the Size and Distribution of the World's Christian Population." For the projection of Pentecostal-Charismatic growth, see Dale M. Coulter, "What Is Pentecostal-Charismatic Christianity?," *Firebrand*, November 9, 2021, https://firebrandmag.com/articles/what-is-pentecostal-charismatic-christianity.

27 There has been sparse theological engagement with Luther by scholars working within the Pentecostal tradition. Frank Maccia and Veli-Matti Kärkkäinen discuss the integration of Pentecostal emphases on the Holy Spirit with Luther's model of justification. See Frank Maccia, *Justified in the Spirit: Creation, Redemption, and the Triune God* (Eerdmans, 2010); Veli-Matti Kärkkäinen, *One with God: Salvation as Deification and Justification* (Liturgical Press, 2004). For Pentecostal scholars' engagements with Luther's theology of the Cross, see Courey, *What Has Wittenberg to Do with Azusa?*

28 The following discussion depends on Daniel Callahan, *False Hopes: Why America's Quest for Perfect Health Is a Recipe for Failure* (Simon & Schuster, 1998), 25–33.

29 Michel Foucault, *The Birth of the Clinic: An Archaeology of Medical Perception* (Vintage Books, 1994). For a summary of Foucault's argument see "Conclusion," 195–199. Foucault famously stated that, "It is when death became the concrete a priori of medical experience that death

could detach itself from counter-nature and become embodied and the living bodies of individuals" (196).

30 Foucault, *The Birth of the Clinic*, 198.

31 "Constitution of the World Health Organization," accessed April 5, 2024, https://www.who.int/about/accountability/governance/constitution.

32 On medicine as a new religion see Harold Y. Vanderpool, "The Religious Features of Scientific Medicine," *Kennedy Institute of Ethics Journal* 18, no. 3 (September 2008): 203–234, https://doi.org/10.1353/ken.0.0199; Margaret P. Wardlaw, "American Medicine as Religious Practice: Care of the Sick as a Sacred Obligation and the Unholy Descent into Secularization," *Journal of Religion and Health* 50, no. 1 (March 2011): 62–74, https://doi.org/10.1007/s10943-010-9320-4. See also Larchet, *The Theology of Illness*, 9–15. See also Michael J. Balboni and Tracy A. Balboni, *Hostility to Hospitality: Spirituality and Professional Socialization within Medicine* (Oxford University Press, 2019), chs. 10–12, especially, 178–198.

33 Vanderpool, "The Religious Features of Scientific Medicine." Prior analysis of religious functions of scientific medicine included Roy Branson, "The Secularization of American Medicine," *Studies—Hastings Center* 1, no. 2 (1973): 17–28. Branson argued that, under the influence of secularization, medicine's religious qualities were disappearing. Talcott Parsons, Renee C. Fox, and Victor M. Lidz, "The 'Gift of Life' and Its Reciprocation," in *Death in American Experience*, ed. Arien Mack, Schocken Books 409 (Schocken Books, 1973), 1–49 spoke of sacred dimensions in medicine. William May in his classic works discussed religious-like dimensions of medical imagery and their bearing on medical ethics. See especially William F. May, *The Physician's Covenant: Images of the Healer in Medical Ethics*, 2nd ed. (Westminster John Knox Press, 2000). Later, Foster contended that religious dimension was present in medical practice, without dedicating an extensive discussion to this claim. See Daniel W. Foster, "Religion and Medicine: The Physician's Perspective," in *Health/Medicine and the Faith Traditions: An Inquiry into Religion and Medicine*, ed. Martin E. Marty and Kenneth L. Vaux (Fortress Press, 1982), 245–270. See also an essay by Vanderpool's graduate student Daniel S. Goldberg, "Religion, the Culture of Biomedicine, and the Tremendum: Towards a Non-Essentialist Analysis of Interconnection," *Journal of Religion and Health* 46, no. 1 (2007): 99–108. For an argument that religious features of secular medicine merit a positive assessment, Margaret P. Wardlaw, "American

Medicine as Religious Practice: Care of the Sick as a Sacred Obligation and the Unholy Descent into Secularization," *Journal of Religion and Health* 50, no. 1 (March 2011): 62–74, https://doi.org/10.1007/s10943-010-9320-4.

34 Vanderpool, "The Religious Features of Scientific Medicine," 216. In his use of the imagery of "protective screen" and curtain, Vanderpool draws on Howard Brody, *The Healer's Power* (Yale University Press, 1992) and Goldberg, "Religion, the Culture of Biomedicine, and the Tremendum," 13–42, 139–153.

35 Brody, *The Healer's Power*, 139–152 cited in Vanderpool, "The Religious Features of Scientific Medicine," 217.

36 Balboni and Balboni, *Hostility to Hospitality*, 178–218. The following discussion is the summary of the Balbonis' argument.

37 Britta Pelters and Barbro Wijma, "Neither a Sinner nor a Saint: Health as a Present-Day Religion in the Age of Healthism," *Social Theory & Health* 14, no. 1 (February 2016): 129–148, https://doi.org/10.1057/sth.2015.21.

38 Vanderpool, "The Religious Features of Scientific Medicine," 220 cited in Pelters and Wijma, "Neither a Sinner nor a Saint: Health as a Present-Day Religion in the Age of Healthism," 141.

39 For the most recent statistics on health disparities in the United States, see regularly updated statistics, "About Disparities Data," Healthy People 2030, https://health.gov/healthypeople/objectives-and-data/about-disparities-data#highest.

40 At the age of forty, expected age at death increased for individuals in the top income quartile at a rate of about 2.5 times that for individuals in the bottom income quartile. The life expectancy gap between income groups keeps widening: From 2001 to 2014, in the United States, the richest individuals acquired approximately three years in longevity, while the poorest had no gains. See Raj Chetty et al., "The Association Between Income and Life Expectancy in the United States, 2001–2014," *JAMA* 315, no. 16 (April 26, 2016): 1750, https://doi.org/10.1001/jama.2016.4226. See also JAMA Health Disparities project https://sites.jamanetwork.com/health-disparities/, and the Health Inequality Project, https://healthinequality.org/. Additionally, while Black Americans represent approximately 13 percent of the US population, they account for 16 percent of the uninsured. See Arielle Bosworth, Kenneth Finegold, and Joel Ruhter, "The Remaining Uninsured: Geographic and Demographic Variation," *Washington, DC: Office of the Assistant Secretary for Planning*

and Evaluation, U.S. Department of Health and Human Services, no. HP-202106 (March 23, 2021), https://aspe.hhs.gov/sites/default/files/private/pdf/265286/Uninsured-Population-Issue-Brief.pdf. See also Latoya Hill, Samantha Artiga, and Anthony Damico Published, "Health Coverage by Race and Ethnicity, 2010–2022," *KFF*, January 11, 2024, https://www.kff.org/racial-equity-and-health-policy/issue-brief/health-coverage-by-race-and-ethnicity/.

41 Nicole Willcoxon, "Majorities Rate Cost, Equity of U.S. Healthcare Negatively," *Gallup.com*, October 6, 2022, https://news.gallup.com/poll/402191/majorities-rate-cost-equity-healthcare-negatively.aspx. See also Nicole Willcoxon, "Older Adults Sacrificing Basic Needs Due to Healthcare Costs," *Gallup.com*, June 15, 2022, https://news.gallup.com/poll/393494/older-adults-sacrificing-basic-needs-due-healthcare-costs.aspx.

42 See annual health statistics released by the Organization for Economic Co-operation and Development, available here, "OECD Health Statistics 2023—OECD," https://www.oecd.org/els/health-systems/health-data.htm.

43 The medicine's "preferential option for the rich" is even more apparent on a global scale. While Western medicine invests millions in developing niche treatments, many in the two-thirds world struggle with insufficient medical resources to address relatively easily preventable and treatable conditions. Over the past decade, ninety-nine percent of deaths occurring in children before their fifth birthdays were recorded in low- and lower-middle-income countries. Most of these children succumbed to complications related to prematurity, pneumonia, birth asphyxia, birth trauma, and diarrhea—conditions that could have been prevented with access to vaccines, skilled neonatal care, community health centers, improved nutrition, and basic healthcare education. These resources and interventions, readily available to many in the West, remain scarce in a significant portion of the majority world. The data provided by the World Health Organization (2012 most currently available at that time of access), accessed November 1, 2016, http://www.who.int/mediacentre/factsheets/fs310/en/index2.html.

44 There are numerous scholarly discussions of the matter. For public-oriented summaries, see James E. Dalen, "We Can Reduce US Health Care Costs," *The American Journal of Medicine* 123, no. 3 (March 2010): 193–194, https://doi.org/10.1016/j.amjmed.2009.12.011; David Cutler, "The World's Costliest Health Care," *Harvard Magazine*, April 10, 2020, https://www.harvardmagazine.com/node/70802;

Elliott Fisher et al., *Health Care Spending, Quality, and Outcomes: More Isn't Always Better*, The Dartmouth Atlas of Health Care (The Dartmouth Institute for Health Policy and Clinical Practice, 2009); Also see Shakeel Ahmed, "How To Cut Healthcare Costs," *Forbes*, November 1, 2023, https://www.forbes.com/sites/forbesbusinesscouncil/2023/11/01/how-to-cut-healthcare-costs/.

45 Fisher et al., *Health Care Spending, Quality, and Outcomes*. This reflects the phenomenon termed "supply-sensitive care," distinct from "effective care" (shown to result in improved health outcomes) or "preference-sensitive care" (elected procedures posing explicitly defined risks and benefits). In contrast, "supply-sensitive care" is discretionary and provided due to the availability of medical resources to supply more frequent and extensive medical interventions. Other factors that had been identified as contributing to the overutilization of medical services in the United States included "defensive medicine," when physicians overprescribed tests out of fear of lawsuits. It has also been also tied to the fee-for-service system, encouraging physicians to order more procedures.

46 See, for example, John E. Wennberg et al., "Inpatient Care Intensity and Patients' Ratings of Their Hospital Experiences," *Health Affairs* 28, no. 1 (January 2009): 103–112, https://doi.org/10.1377/hlthaff.28.1.103; Brenda E. Sirovich et al., "Regional Variations in Health Care Intensity and Physician Perceptions of Quality of Care," *Annals of Internal Medicine* 144, no. 9 (May 2, 2006): 641, https://doi.org/10.7326/0003-4819-144-9-200605020-00007; Elliott S. Fisher et al., "The Implications of Regional Variations in Medicare Spending. Part 1: The Content, Quality, and Accessibility of Care," *Annals of Internal Medicine* 138, no. 4 (February 18, 2003): 273, https://doi.org/10.7326/0003-4819-138-4-200302180-00006; Katherine Baicker and Amitabh Chandra, "Medicare Spending, the Physician Workforce, and Beneficiaries' Quality of Care: Areas with a High Concentration of Specialists also Show Higher Spending and Less Use of High-Quality, Effective Care.," *Health Affairs* 23, no. Suppl1 (January 2004): W4-184-W4-197, https://doi.org/10.1377/hlthaff.W4.184; Jonathan S. Skinner, Douglas O. Staiger, and Elliott S. Fisher, "Is Technological Change In Medicine Always Worth It? The Case of Acute Myocardial Infarction: Waste and Inefficiency Are Not Inevitable by-Products of Technological Growth.," *Health Affairs* 25, no. Suppl1 (January 2006): W34–47, https://doi.org/10.1377/hlthaff.25.w34.

47 See Alexis Pozen and David M. Cutler, "Medical Spending Differences in the United States and Canada: The Role of Prices, Procedures, and Administrative Expenses," *INQUIRY: The Journal of Health Care Organization, Provision, and Financing* 47, no. 2 (May 2010): 124–134, https://doi.org/10.5034/inquiryjrnl_47.02.124, and Jack V. Tu et al., "Use of Cardiac Procedures and Outcomes in Elderly Patients with Myocardial Infarction in the United States and Canada," *New England Journal of Medicine* 336, no. 21 (May 22, 1997): 1500–1505, https://doi.org/10.1056/NEJM199705223362106, cited in Cutler, "The World's Costliest Health Care."

48 See Tu et al., "Use of Cardiac Procedures and Outcomes in Elderly Patients with Myocardial Infarction in the United States and Canada." cited in Cutler, "The World's Costliest Health Care."

49 Fisher et al., *Health Care Spending, Quality, and Outcomes.*

50 For example, Canada places a limit on the total available amount of high-tech care. In the example discussed above, Canadian governments ration the available number of MRI scanners that can be purchased and the number of hospitals with open-heart surgery facilities. Within the established amount, physicians perform the allocation of the services. Cutler, "The World's Costliest Health Care." In 2019 a JAMA editorial identified greater explicit rationing as inevitable to control soaring health care costs. See Howard Bauchner, "Rationing of Health Care in the United States: An Inevitable Consequence of Increasing Health Care Costs." *JAMA* 321, no. 8 (2019): 751–752, https://doi.org/10.1001/jama.2019.1081.

51 Howard Bauchner, "Health Care in the United States: A Right or a Privilege." *JAMA* 317, no. 1 (2017): 29, https://doi.org/10.1001/jama.2016.19687.

52 See Callahan, *False Hopes*, 26.

Conclusion

1 Debates persist over whether the changes of the "Scientific Revolution" were truly "revolutionary," representing a displacement of inherited knowledge, or whether this period produced new knowledge through the gradual transformation of inherited paradigms. However, it is clear that this period witnessed the unprecedented development of new insights into the laws of nature, the emergence of a new scientific method rooted in experimentation, and ultimately resulted in the scientific reformation of the premodern view on the natural world. The idea of the Scientific Revolution happens due to paradigm shifts

understood as transformation of foundational concepts and methods, and creative displacement of inherited knowledge was developed in the classic monograph by Thomas S. Kuhn, *The Structure of Scientific Revolutions*, 3rd ed. (University of Chicago Press, 1996). For alternative approaches see Paul Thagard, *Conceptual Revolutions* (Princeton University Press); Howard Margolis, *Paradigms and Barriers: How Habits of Mind Govern Scientific Beliefs* (University of Chicago Press, 1993); Davis Baird, *Thing Knowledge: A Philosophy of Scientific Instruments* (University of California Press, 2004). Also see Rogier De Langhe, "A Comparison of Two Models of Scientific Progress," *Studies in History and Philosophy of Science*, 46 (June 2014): 94–99.

2 Around the same time, Vesalius also published an abridged version of the treatise, which contained more extensive illustrations and was titled *De Humani Corporis Fabrica Librorum Epitome* [Abridgement of the on the fabric of the human body].

3 As cited in Cunningham, *The Anatomical Renaissance*, 226

4 The following paragraph depends on Cunningham, *The Anatomical Renaissance*, 224–236.

5 For a summary of Philip Melanchthon's engagements with anatomy see Mitchell Lewis Hammond, "Ora Deum & Medico Tribus Locum: Medicine in the Theology of Martin Luther and Philipp Melanchthon," in *Religion und Naturwissenschaften im 16. und 17. Jahrhundert*, ed. Kaspar von Greyerz, Thomas Kaufmann, Kim Siebenhüner, and Roberto Zaugg (Gütersloher Verlagshaus, 2010), especially 38–50.

6 See Vivian Nutton, "Wittenberg Anatomy," in Ole Peter Grell and Andrew Cunningham, eds. Medicine and the Reformation (Routledge, 1993), 11–32. Also see Jürgen Helm, "Protestant and Catholic Medicine in the Sixteenth Century? The Case of Ingolstadt Anatomy," *Medical History* 45, no. 1 (January 2001): 83–96.

7 For a broader discussion of the theological influence of early Protestantism on the emergence of science, see Peter Harrison, *The Bible, Protestantism, and the Rise of Natural Science* (Cambridge University Press, 2001) and *The Fall of Man and the Foundations of Science* (Cambridge University Press, 2009).For the subsequent historical relationship between the Lutheran theology and medicine, see Crater Lindberg, "The Lutheran Tradition," in *Caring and Curing: Health and Medicine in the Western Religious Traditions*, ed. Ronald L. Numbers, and Darrel W. Amundsen (Macmillan, 1986), 173–204.

8 WA 6.459.1; LW 44: 202.

BIBLIOGRAPHY

Ahmed, Shakeel. "How To Cut Healthcare Costs." *Forbes*, November 1, 2023. https://www.forbes.com/sites/forbesbusinesscouncil/2023/11/01/how-to-cut-healthcare-costs/.

Alexander, Kimberly Ervin. *Pentecostal Healing: Models in Theology and Practice.* Journal of Pentecostal Theology Supplement Series 29. Blandford Forum: Deo, 2006.

Amundsen, Darrel W. *Medicine, Society, and Faith in the Ancient and Medieval Worlds.* Johns Hopkins University Press, 1996.

Amundsen, Darrel W., and Gary B. Ferngren. "Philanthropy in Medicine: Some Historical Perspectives." In *Beneficence and Health Care*, edited by Earl E. Shelp. Springer Netherlands, 1982. https://doi.org/10.1007/978-94-009-7769-3_1.

Appel, Helmut. *Anfechtung und Trost im Spätmittelalter und bei Luther.* SVRG, 1938.

Aquinas, Thomas. *Superstition and Irreverence.* Vol. 40 (2a2æ. 92–100). Edited by Thomas F. O'Meara and Thomas Gilby. Cambridge University Press, 2006.

Arnold, John. *The Oxford Handbook of Medieval Christianity.* Oxford Handbooks. Oxford University Press, 2014.

Azusa Street Mission. "Beginning of World Wide Revival." *Apostolic Faith* 1, no. 5 (January 1907).

Azusa Street Mission. "Questions Answered." *Apostolic Faith* 1, no. 11 (October 1907–January 1908).

Baicker, Katherine, and Amitabh Chandra. "Medicare Spending, The Physician Workforce, And Beneficiaries' Quality of Care: Areas with a High Concentration of Specialists Also Show Higher Spending and Less Use of High-Quality, Effective Care." *Health Affairs* 23, Suppl 1 (January 2004): W4-184–W4-197. https://doi.org/10.1377/hlthaff.W4.184.

Bainton, Roland H. *Here I Stand: A Life of Martin Luther.* Abingdon Press, 1990.

Baird, Davis. *Thing Knowledge: A Philosophy of Scientific Instruments.* University of California Press, 2004.

Balboni, Michael J., and Tracy A. Balboni. *Hostility to Hospitality: Spirituality and Professional Socialization within Medicine*. Oxford University Press, 2019.

Barge, Hermann. *Andreas Bodenstein von Karlstadt*. 2 vols. B. De Graaf, 1968.

Barnes, Robin Bruce. *Astrology and Reformation*. Oxford University Press, 2016.

Bauchner, Howard. "Health Care in the United States: A Right or a Privilege." *JAMA* 317, no. 1 (2017): 29. https://doi.org/10.1001/jama.2016.19687.

Bauchner, Howard. "Rationing of Health Care in the United States: An Inevitable Consequence of Increasing Health Care Costs." *JAMA* 321, no. 8 (2019): 751–752. https://doi.org/10.1001/jama.2019.1081.

Bede, Jarrett. *Social Theories of the Middle Ages 1200–1500*. Newman Book, 1942.

Beintker, Horst. *Die Überwindung der Anfechtung bei Luther: Eine Studie zu seiner Theologie nach den Operationes in Psalmos 1519–21*. Evangelische Verlagsanstalt, 1954.

Bell, Rudolph M. *Holy Anorexia*. University of Chicago Press, 1985.

Benedek, Thomas. "The Image of Medicine in 1500: Theological Reactions to 'The Ship of Fools.'" *Bulletin of the History of Medicine* 38, no. 4 (1964): 329–342.

Bishop, Jeffrey P. *The Anticipatory Corpse: Medicine, Power, and the Care of the Dying*. University of Notre Dame Press, 2011.

Bornkamm, Heinrich. *Luther and the Old Testament*. Edited by Victor I. Gruhn. Translated by Eric W. Gritsch and Ruth C. Gritsch. Fortress Press, 1969.

Bornkamm, Heinrich. *Martin Luther in Der Mitte Seines Lebens: Das Jahrzehnt Zwischen Dem Wormser Und Dem Augsburger Reichstag*. Vandenhoeck & Ruprecht, 1979.

Bosworth, Arielle, Kenneth Finegold, and Joel Ruhter. "The Remaining Uninsured: Geographic and Demographic Variation." Office of the Assistant Secretary for Planning and Evaluation, U.S. Department of Health and Human Services. Brief no. HP-202106, March 23, 2021. https://aspe.hhs.gov/sites/default/files/private/pdf/265286/Uninsured-Population-Issue-Brief.pdf.

Bouwsma, William J. *A Usable Past: Essays in European Cultural History*. University of California Press, 1990.

Bowsky, William M. *The Black Death: A Turning Point in History?* Holt, Rinehart and Winston, 1971.

Braaten, Carl E., and Robert W. Jenson, eds. *Union with Christ: The New Finnish Interpretation of Luther*. Eerdmans, 1998.

Branson, Roy. "The Secularization of American Medicine." *Hastings Center Studies* 1, no. 2 (1973): 17–28.

Brecht, Martin. *Martin Luther.* Vol. 3. Calwer Verlag, 1986.

Brecht, Martin. *Martin Luther: Shaping and Defining the Reformation, 1521–1532.* Vol. 2. Translated by James L. Schaaf. Fortress Press, 1990.

Brecht, Martin. *Martin Luther: His Road to Reformation, 1483–1521.* Fortress Press, 1993.

Brody, Howard. *The Healer's Power.* Yale University Press, 1992.

Brooks, Peter Newman, ed. *Seven-Headed Luther: Essays in Commemoration of a Quincentenary, 1483–1983.* Clarendon Press. Oxford University Press, 1983.

Brown, Candy Gunther, ed. *Global Pentecostal and Charismatic Healing.* Oxford University Press, 2011.

Buck, August, and Wolfenbütteler Arbeitskreis für Renaissanceforschung, eds. *Renaissance, Reformation: Gegensätze und Gemeinsamkeiten: Vorträge.* Wolfenbütteler Abhandlungen zur Renaissanceforschung, Bd. 5. Wiesbaden: In Kommission bei O. Harrassowitz, 1984.

Bühler, Paul Theophil. *Die Anfechtung bei Martin Luther.* Zwingli Verlag, 1944.

Bull, Marcus "Pilgrimage." In *The Oxford Handbook of Medieval Christianity,* edited by John Arnold. Oxford University Press, 2014.

Bultmann, Christoph, Volker Leppin, and Andreas Lindner, eds. *Luther Und Das Monastische Erbe: Spätmittelalter, Humanismus, Reformation.* Studies in the Late Middle Ages, Humanism and the Reformation 39. Mohr Siebeck, 2007.

Burnett, Amy Nelson. *Karlstadt and the Origins of the Eucharistic Controversy: A Study in the Circulation of Ideas.* Oxford Studies in Historical Theology. Oxford University Press, 2011.

Bynum, Caroline Walker. *Holy Feast and Holy Fast: The Religious Significance of Food to Medieval Women.* University of California Press, 1987.

Bynum, William. *The History of Medicine: A Very Short Introduction.* Oxford University Press, 2008.

Callahan, Daniel. *False Hopes: Why America's Quest for Perfect Health Is a Recipe for Failure.* Simon & Schuster, 1998.

Certeau, Michel de. *The Mystic Fable,* vol. 1, *The Sixteenth and Seventeenth Centuries.* University of Chicago Press, 1992.

Chetty, Raj, Michael Stepner, Sarah Abraham, et al. "The Association Between Income and Life Expectancy in the United States, 2001–2014." *JAMA* 315, no. 16 (April 26, 2016): 1750–1766. https://doi.org/10.1001/jama.2016.4226.

Crowther, Cathleen M. *Adam and Eve in the Protestant Reformation.* Cambridge University Press, 2013.

Cone, James H. *God of the Oppressed.* Seabury Press, 1975.

"Constitution of the World Health Organization." Accessed June 27, 2024. https://www.who.int/about/governance/constitution.

Coulter, Dale M. "What Is Pentecostal-Charismatic Christianity?" *Firebrand,* November 9, 2021. https://firebrandmag.com/articles/what-is-pentecostal-charismatic-christianity.

Courey, David. *What Has Wittenberg to Do with Azusa? Luther's Theology of the Cross and Pentecostal Triumphalism.* Bloomsbury T&T Clark, 2015.

Cunningham, Andrew. *The Anatomical Renaissance: The Resurrection of the Anatomical Projects of the Ancients.* Routledge, 1997.

Cunningham, Andrew, and Ole Peter Grell, eds. *Health Care and Poor Relief in Protestant Europe, 1500–1700.* Routledge, 1997.

Cutler, David. "The World's Costliest Health Care." *Harvard Magazine,* April 10, 2020. https://www.harvardmagazine.com/node/70802.

D. Martin Luthers Werke: Kritische Gesamtausgabe, Schriften, 73 vols. Weimar: Böhlau, 1883–.

D. Martin Luthers Werke: Kritische Gesamtausgabe, Tischreden, 6 vols. Weimar: Böhlau, 1912–1921.

D. Martin Luthers Werke: Kritische Gesamtausgabe, Briefwechsel, 18 vols. Weimar: Böhlau, 1930–1948.

Dalen, James E. "We Can Reduce US Health Care Costs." *The American Journal of Medicine* 123, no. 3 (March 2010): 193–194. https://doi.org/10.1016/j.amjmed.2009.12.011.

De Langhe, Rogier. "A Comparison of Two Models of Scientific Progress." *Studies in History and Philosophy of Science Part A* 46 (June 2014): 94–99. https://doi.org/10.1016/j.shpsa.2014.03.002.

Dean, Kenda Creasy. *Almost Christian: What the Faith of Our Teenagers Is Telling the American Church.* Oxford University Press, 2010.

Debus, Allen G. *Man and Nature in the Renaissance.* Cambridge History of Science. Cambridge University Press, 1978.

Dembski, William A. "Schleiermacher's Metaphysical Critique of Miracles." *Scottish Journal of Theology* 49, no. 4 (November 1996): 443–465. https://doi.org/10.1017/S003693060004850X.

Edwards, Mark U. *Luther and the False Brethren.* Stanford University Press, 1975.

Eiesland, Nancy L. *The Disabled God: Toward a Liberatory Theology of Disability.* Abingdon Press, 1994.

Eire, Carlos M. N. *War Against the Idols: The Reformation of Worship from Erasmus to Calvin*. Cambridge University Press, 1986.

Evener, Vincent. "The 'Enemies of God' in Luther's Final Sermons: Jews, Papists, and the Problem of Blindness to Scripture." *Dialog* 55, no. 3 (September 2016): 229–238. https://doi.org/10.1111/dial.12259.

Evener, Vincent. *Enemies of the Cross: Suffering, Truth, and Mysticism in the Early Reformation*. Oxford University Press, 2020.

Ferngren, Gary B. *Medicine and Religion: A Historical Introduction*. Johns Hopkins University Press, 2014.

Ferngren, Gary B., and Ekaterina N. Lomperis. *Essential Readings in Medicine and Religion*. Johns Hopkins University Press, 2017.

Finucane, Ronald C. *Miracles and Pilgrims: Popular Beliefs in Medieval England*. Rowman and Littlefield, 1977.

Fisher, Elliott, David Goodman, Jonathan Skinner, and Kristen Bronner. *Health Care Spending, Quality, and Outcomes: More Isn't Always Better*. The Dartmouth Institute for Health Policy and Clinical Practice, 2009. http://www.ncbi.nlm.nih.gov/books/NBK586761/.

Fisher, Elliott S., David E. Wennberg, Thrse A. Stukel, Daniel J. Gottlieb, F. L. Lucas, and Étoile L. Pinder. "The Implications of Regional Variations in Medicare Spending. Part 1: The Content, Quality, and Accessibility of Care." *Annals of Internal Medicine* 138, no. 4 (February 18, 2003): 273–287. https://doi.org/10.7326/0003-4819-138-4-200302180-00006.

Forde, Gerhard O. *On Being a Theologian of the Cross: Reflections on Luther's Heidelberg Disputation, 1518*. W.B. Eerdmans, 1997.

Foster, Daniel W. "Religion and Medicine: The Physician's Perspective." In *Health/Medicine and the Faith Traditions: An Inquiry into Religion and Medicine*, edited by Martin E. Marty and Kenneth L. Vaux. Fortress Press, 1982.

Foucault, Michel. *The Birth of the Clinic: An Archaeology of Medical Perception*. Vintage Books, 1994.

Furcha, Edward J., ed. *The Essential Karlstadt: Fifteen Tracts*. Translated by Edward J. Furcha. Herald Press, 1995.

Gerrish, B. A. *The Old Protestantism and the New: Essays on the Reformation Heritage*. University of Chicago Press, 1982.

Goldberg, Daniel S. "Religion, the Culture of Biomedicine, and the Tremendum: Towards a Non-Essentialist Analysis of Interconnection." *Journal of Religion and Health* 46, no. 1 (2007): 99–108.

Gordon, Bruce, and Peter Marshall, eds. *The Place of the Dead: Death and Remembrance in Late Medieval and Early Modern Europe*. Cambridge University Press, 2000.

Grell, Ole Peter, and Andrew Cunningham, eds. *Medicine and the Reformation.* Routledge, 1993.

Greyerz, Kaspar von, Thomas Kaufmann, Kim Siebenhüner, and Roberto Zaugg, eds. *Religion und Naturwissenschaften im 16. und 17. Jahrhundert.* Gütersloher Verlagshaus, 2010.

Griffin, Michael P., and Jennie Weiss Block, eds. *In the Company of the Poor: Conversations between Dr. Paul Farmer and Fr. Gustavo Gutierrez.* Orbis Books, 2013.

Grimm, Harold J. "Luther's Contributions to Sixteenth-Century Organization of Poor Relief." *Archiv Für Reformationsgeschichte—Archive for Reformation History* 61 (December 1970): 222–234. https://doi.org/10.14315/arg-1970-jg11.

Hagen, Kenneth. *Luther's Approach to Scripture as Seen in His "Commentaries" on Galatians, 1519–1538.* Mohr Siebeck, 1993.

Hall, Marie Boas. *The Scientific Renaissance 1450–1630.* Dover, 1994.

Hamm, Berndt. *The Reformation of Faith in the Context of Late Medieval Theology and Piety: Essays by Berndt Hamm.* Edited by Robert James Bast. Brill, 2004.

Hamm, Berndt, Gudrun Litz, Heidrun Munzert, and Roland Liebenberg, eds. *Frömmigkeit, Theologie, Frömmigkeitstheologie: Contributions to European Church History: Festschrift für Berndt Hamm zum 60. Geburtstag.* Studies in the History of Christian Traditions 124. Brill, 2005.

Hammond, Mitchell Lewis. "'Ora Deum, et Medico Tribuas Locum': Medicine in the Theology of Martin Luther and Philipp Melanchthon." In *Religion und Naturwissenschaften im 16 Und 17. Jahrhundert.* Edited by Kaspar von Greyerz, Thomas Kaufmann, Kim Siebenhüner, and Roberto Zaugg. Gütersloher Verlagshaus, 2010.

Harrington, Joel F. *Reordering Marriage and Society in Reformation Germany.* Cambridge University Press, 1995.

Harrison, Peter. *The Bible, Protestantism, and the Rise of Natural Science.* Cambridge University Press, 2001.

Harrison, Peter. *The Fall of Man and the Foundations of Science.* Cambridge University Press. 2009.

Hauerwas, Stanley, John Berkman, and Michael G. Cartwright. *The Hauerwas Reader.* Duke University Press, 2001.

Helm, Jürgen. "Protestant and Catholic Medicine in the Sixteenth Century? The Case of Ingolstadt Anatomy." *Medical History* 45, no. 1 (January 2001): 83–96. https://doi.org/10.1017/S0025727300067405.

Hendrix, Scott H. "Luther Against the Background of the History of Biblical Interpretation." *Interpretation: A Journal of Bible and Theology* 37, no. 3 (July 1983): 229–239. https://doi.org/10.1177/002096438303700302.

Hildegard. *Hildegard of Bingen: On Natural Philosophy and Medicine, Selections from Cause et Cure.* Translated by Margret Berger. Library of Medieval Women. D. S. Brewer, 1999.

Hill, Latoya, Samantha Artiga, and Anthony Damico. "Health Coverage by Race and Ethnicity, 2010–2022." *KFF* (blog), January 11, 2024. https://www.kff.org/racial-equity-and-health-policy/issue-brief/health-coverage-by-race-and-ethnicity/.

Hoffman, Bengt R. *Luther and the Mystics: A Re-Examination of Luther's Spiritual Experience and His Relationship to the Mystics.* Augsburg, 1976.

Hoffman, Bengt R. *The Theologia Germanica of Martin Luther.* The Classics of Western Spirituality. Paulist Press, 1980.

Hoffman, Bengt R. *Theology of the Heart: The Role of Mysticism in the Theology of Martin Luther.* Lutheran University Press, 2003.

Huizinga, Johan. *The Autumn of the Middle Ages.* Translated by Rodney J. Payton and Ulrich Mammitzsch. University of Chicago Press, 1997.

Iwu, Chinedu Anthony, Pius Ositadinma, Victor Chibiko, Ugochukwu Madubueze, Kenechi Uwakwe, and Uche Oluoha. "Prevalence and Predictors of COVID-19 Vaccine Hesitancy among Health Care Workers in Tertiary Health Care Institutions in a Developing Country: A Cross-Sectional Analytical Study." Edited by Francesco Chirico. *Advances in Public Health* 2022 (March 22, 2022): 1–9. https://doi.org/10.1155/2022/7299092.

Jackson, Mark. *The Oxford Handbook of the History of Medicine.* Oxford University Press, 2011.

Karant-Nunn, Susan C. *The Reformation of Feeling: Shaping the Religious Emotions in Early Modern Germany.* Oxford University Press, 2010.

Karant-Nunn, Susan C., and Merry E. Wiesner-Hanks, eds. *Luther on Women: A Sourcebook.* Cambridge University Press, 2003.

Kärkkäinen, Veli-Matti. *One with God: Salvation as Deification and Justification.* Unitas Books. Liturgical Press, 2004.

Karlstadt, Andreas, Martin Luther, and Ronald J. Sider, eds. *Karlstadt's Battle with Luther: Documents in a Liberal-Radical Debate.* Wipf and Stock, 2001. Previously published by Augsburg Fortress Press, 1978.

Kessler, Martin. *Das Karlstadt-Bild in Der Forschung.* Beiträge zur Historischen Theologie 174. Mohr Siebeck, 2014.

Kibre, Pearl. "The Faculty of Medicine in Paris, Charlatanism, and Unlicensed Medical Practices in the Later Middle Ages." *Bulletin of the History of Medicine* 27, no. 1 (February 1953): 1–20.

Kieckhefer, Richard. *Magic in the Middle Ages*. Cambridge University Press, 2000.

Kittelson, James M. *Luther the Reformer: The Story of the Man and His Career*. Augsburg Publishing House, 1986.

Klemm, David E., and William Schweiker. *Religion and the Human Future: An Essay on Theological Humanism*. Wiley-Blackwell, 2008.

Koerner, Joseph Leo. *The Reformation of the Image*. University of Chicago Press, 2004.

Kolb, Robert. *Martin Luther as Prophet, Teacher, Hero: Images of the Reformer, 1520–1620*. Texts and Studies in Reformation and Post-Reformation Thought. Baker Books; Paternoster Press, 1999.

Kolb, Robert. "Luther's Theology of the Cross Fifteen Years after Heidelberg: Luther's Lectures on the Psalms of Ascent." *Journal of Ecclesiastical History* 61 (2010): 69–85.

Kolb, Robert, Timothy J. Wengert, and Charles P. Arand, eds. *The Book of Concord: The Confessions of the Evangelical Lutheran Church*. Fortress Press, 2000.

Kuhn, Thomas S. *The Structure of Scientific Revolutions*. 3rd ed. University of Chicago Press, 1996.

Larchet, Jean-Claude. *The Theology of Illness*. St. Vladimir's Seminary Press, 2002.

Leclercq, Jean. *The Love of Learning and the Desire for God*. Fordham University Press, 1961.

Lewis, Margaret Brannan. *Infanticide and Abortion in Early Modern Germany*. The Body, Gender and Culture 19. Routledge, Taylor & Francis Group, 2016.

Lindberg, Carter. "'There Should Be No Beggars Among Christians:' Karlstadt, Luther, and the Origins of Protestant Poor Relief." *Church History* 46 (1977): 313–334.

Lindberg, Carter. *Beyond Charity: Reformation Initiatives for the Poor*. Fortress Press, 1993.

Lindberg, Carter. "Luther on Poverty." *Lutheran Quarterly* 15, no. 1 (Spring 2001): 85–102.

Lindemann, Mary. *Medicine and Society in Early Modern Europe*. 2nd ed. New Approaches to European History. Cambridge University Press, 2010.

Löcher, Kurt. *Martin Luther und die Reformation in Deutschland: Ausstellung zum 500. Geburtstag Martin Luthers [im Germanischen Nationalmuseum*

Nürnberg, vom 25. Juni bis 25. September 1983]. Kataloge des Germanischen Nationalmuseums. Insel Verlag, 1983.

Lockwood, Michael. *The Unholy Trinity: Martin Luther Against the Idol of Me, Myself, and I.* Concordia Publishing House, n.d.

Loewenich, Walther von. *Luther's Theologia Crucis.* Kaiser, 1954.

Lohse, Bernhard. *Martin Luther's Theology: Its Historical and Systematic Development.* Fortress Press, 1999.

Lomperis, Ekaterina N. "Many Healings of the Woman with the Flow of Blood." *Religions* 14, no. 4 (April 3, 2023): 479. https://doi.org/10.3390/rel14040479.

Louis, Gabriel Reuben. "Response to Dr. Wonsuk Ma's 'Towards an Asian Pentecostal Theology.'" *Cyberjournal for Pentecostal-Charismatic Research* (July 1998). http://www.pctii.org/cyberj/cyberj4/louis.html.

Luther, Martin. *Sermon von Ablass und Gnade* [Sermon on indulgences and grace]. Edited by Howard Jones, Martin Kessler, Henrike Lähnemann, and Christina Ostermann. Reprinted with corrections. Treasures of the Taylorian: Series one, Reformation pamphlets, Volume 2. Taylor Institution Library, 2018.

Luther, Martin. *Fleeing Plague: Medieval Wisdom for a Modern Health Crisis.* Introduction and notes by Anna Marie Johnson. Fortress Press, 2023.

Lysaught, M. Therese. "Medicine as Friendship with God: Anointing the Sick as a Theological Hermeneutic." *Journal of the Society of Christian Ethics* 29, no. 1 (2009): 171–191.

Ma, Wonsuk, Robert P. Menzies, and Russell P. Spittler, eds. *The Spirit and Spirituality: Essays in Honour of Russell P. Spittler.* Journal of Pentecostal Theology 24. T & T Clark International, 2004.

Macchia, Frank D. *Justified in the Spirit: Creation, Redemption, and the Triune God.* Pentecostal Manifestos. Eerdmans, 2010.

Mack, Arien. *Death in American Experience.* Schocken Books 409. Schocken Books, 1973.

Margolis, Howard. *Paradigms & Barriers: How Habits of Mind Govern Scientific Beliefs.* University of Chicago Press, 1993.

Marshall, Peter, and Alexandra Walsham, eds. *Angels in the Early Modern World.* Cambridge University Press, 2006.

Martin Luther Und Die Reformation in Deutschland. Exhibition Catalog. Germanisches Nationalmuseum, 1983.

Marty, Martin E. *Martin Luther: A Life.* Penguin Lives. Penguin Books, 2008.

Mattox, Mickey Leland. *Defender of the Most Holy Matriarchs: Martin Luther's Interpretation of the Women of Genesis in the Enarrationes in Genesin, 1535–45.* Studies in Medieval and Reformation Thought 92. Brill, 2003.

Maurer, Wilhelm. *Luther Und Die Schwärmer*. Lutherisches Verlagshaus, 1952.

Maxfield, John A. *Luther's Lectures on Genesis and the Formation of Evangelical Identity*. Sixteenth Century Essays & Studies 80. Truman State University Press, 2008.

May, William F. *The Physician's Covenant: Images of the Healer in Medical Ethics*. 2nd ed. Westminster John Knox Press, 2000.

McGinn, Bernard. *Presence of God: History of Western Christian Mysticism*. 7 vols. Crossroad, 1991.

McGinn, Bernard. *The Varieties of Vernacular Mysticism (1350–1550)*. Vol. 5 of *The Presence of God: A History of Western Christian Mysticism*. Crossroad, 2012.

McGrath, Alister E. *Luther's Theology of the Cross: Martin Luther's Theological Breakthrough*. 2nd ed. Wiley-Blackwell, 2011.

McKim, Donald K., ed. *The Cambridge Companion to Martin Luther*. Cambridge Companions to Religion. Cambridge University Press, 2003.

Merkel, Ingrid, and Allen G. Debus, eds. *Hermeticism and the Renaissance: Intellectual History and the Occult in Early Modern Europe*. Folger Shakespeare Library. Associated University Presses, 1988.

Miller, Donald E., and Tetsunao Yamamori. *Global Pentecostalism: The New Face of Christian Social Engagement*. University of California Press, 2007.

Nelson, Derek R., and Paul R. Hinlicky, eds. *The Oxford Encyclopedia of Martin Luther*. Oxford University Press, 2017.

Nestingen, J. A. "Luther in the Front of the Text: The Genesis Commentary." *Word and World* 14 (1994): 186–194.

Noble, Bonnie. *Lucas Cranach the Elder: Art and Devotion of the German Reformation*. University Press of America, 2009.

Numbers, Ronald L., and Darrel W. Amundsen. *Caring and Curing: Health and Medicine in the Western Religious Traditions*. Macmillan, 1986.

Oakley, Francis. "The Absolute and Ordained Power of God in Sixteenth- and Seventeenth-Century Theology." *Journal of the History of Ideas* 59, no. 3 (July 1998): 437–461. https://doi.org/10.1353/jhi.1998.0027.

Oberman, Heiko Augustinus. *The Harvest of Medieval Theology: Gabriel Biel and Late Medieval Nominalism*. Harvard University Press, 1963.

Oberman, Heiko Augustinus. *Forerunners of the Reformation: The Shape of Late Medieval Thought*. Rinehart and Winston, 1966.

Oberman, Heiko Augustinus. "'Iustitia Christi' and 'Iustitia Dei': Luther and the Scholastic Doctrines of Justification." *Harvard Theological Review* 59, no. 1 (1966): 1–26.

Oberman, Heiko Augustinus. *Die Reformation: Von Wittenberg Nach Genf*. Vandenhoeck & Ruprecht, 1986.

Oberman, Heiko Augustinus. *Luther: Man Between God and the Devil.* Translated by Eileen Walliser-Schwarzbart. Yale University Press, 1990.

Oberman, Heiko Augustinus. *The Dawn of the Reformation: Essays in Late Medieval and Early Reformation Thought.* T&T Clark, 1992.

Ogilvie, Sheilagh C. *A Bitter Living: Women, Markets, and Social Capital in Early Modern Germany.* Oxford University Press, 2003.

Origen. "An Exhortation to Martyrdom." In *Selected Writings: An Exhortation to Martyrdom; Prayer; First Principles: Book IV; Prologue to the Commentary on the Song of Songs; Homily XXVII on Numbers.* Classics of Western Spirituality Series. Paulist Press, 1979.

Ozment, Steven, ed. *The Reformation in Medieval Perspective.* Quadrangle Books, 1971.

Ozment, Steven. *Mysticism and Dissent: Religious Ideology and Social Protest in the Sixteenth Century.* Yale University Press, 1973.

Ozment, Steven. *The Age of Reform, 1250–1550: An Intellectual and Religious History of Late Medieval and Reformation Europe.* Yale University Press, 1980.

Ozment, Steven E., and Lucas Cranach. *The Serpent and the Lamb: Cranach, Luther, and the Making of the Reformation.* Yale University Press, 2011.

Park, Katharine. *Secrets of Women: Gender, Generation, and the Origins of Human Dissection.* Zone Books, 2006. Distributed by MIT Press.

Parsons, Talcott, Renee C. Fox, and Victor M. Lidz. "The 'Gift of Life' and Its Reciprocation." In *Death in American Experience*, edited by Arien Mack. Schocken Books, 1973.

Payne, Leah. *Gender and Pentecostal Revivalism.* Palgrave Macmillan, 2015. https://doi.org/10.1057/9781137494672.

Pelikan, Jaroslav, and Helmut T. Lehmann, eds. *Luther's Works.* 55 vols. Concordia Publishing Houseand Fortress Press, 1955.

Pelikan, Jaroslav, and Martin Luther. *Luther the Expositor: Introduction to the Reformer's Exegetical Writings.* Companion Volume. Concordia Publishing House, 1959.

Pelters, Britta, and Barbro Wijma. "Neither a Sinner nor a Saint: Health as a Present-Day Religion in the Age of Healthism." *Social Theory & Health* 14, no. 1 (February 2016): 129–148. https://doi.org/10.1057/sth.2015.21.

Pew Research Center. "Global Christianity—A Report on the Size and Distribution of the World's Christian Population." In *Christian Movements and Denominations* (blog), December 19, 2011. https://www.pewresearch.org/religion/2011/12/19/global-christianity-movements-and-denominations/.

Porterfield, Amanda. *Healing in the History of Christianity.* Oxford University Press, 2005.

Pozen, Alexis, and David M. Cutler. "Medical Spending Differences in the United States and Canada: The Role of Prices, Procedures, and Administrative Expenses." *INQUIRY: The Journal of Health Care Organization, Provision, and Financing* 47, no. 2 (May 2010): 124–134. https://doi.org/10.5034/inquiryjrnl_47.02.124.

Raymond of Capua. *The Life of St. Catherine of Siena.* Translated by George Lamb. Harvill Press, 1960.

Rittgers, Ronald K. *The Reformation of Suffering: Pastoral Theology and Lay Piety in Late Medieval and Early Modern Germany.* Oxford University Press, 2012.

Rittgers, Ronald K., and Vincent Evener, eds. *Protestants and Mysticism in Reformation Europe.* St Andrews Studies in Reformation History. Brill, 2019.

Robinson, James. *Divine Healing: The Holiness-Pentecostal Transition Years, 1890–1906: Theological Transposition in the Transatlantic World.* Pickwick Publications, 2013.

Roper, Lyndal. *Oedipus and the Devil: Witchcraft, Sexuality, and Religion in Early Modern Europe.* Routledge, 1994.

Roper, Lyndal. *The Holy Household: Women and Morals in Reformation Augsburg.* Repr. Oxford Studies in Social History. Oxford University Press, 2001.

Roper, Lyndal. "Martin Luther's Body: The 'Stout Doctor' and His Biographers." *The American Historical Review* 115, no. 2 (April 2010): 351–384. https://doi.org/10.1086/ahr.115.2.351.

Roper, Lyndal. *Martin Luther: Renegade and Prophet.* Random House, 2016.

Rublack, Ulinka, ed. *Gender in Early Modern German History.* Past and Present Publications. Cambridge University Press, 2002.

Saak, Eric Leland. *High Way to Heaven: The Augustinian Platform between Reform and Reformation, 1292–1524.* Studies in Medieval and Reformation Thought 89. Brill, 2002.

Saak, Eric Leland. *Luther and the Reformation of the Later Middle Ages.* Cambridge University Press, 2017.

Sawday, Jonathan. *The Body Emblazoned: Dissection and the Human Body in Renaissance Culture.* Routledge, 2006.

Schäfer, Peter, and Hans Kippenberg, eds. *Envisioning Magic: A Princeton Seminar and Symposium.* Brill, 1997.

Schreiner, Susan Elizabeth. *Are You Alone Wise? The Search for Certainty in the Early Modern Era*. Oxford Studies in Historical Theology. Oxford University Press, 2011.

Schiefelbein-Guerrero, Kyle K. "Healing Rites for a Post-Pandemic World." *CrossAccent* (Summer 2020): 50–59.

Schumann, Friedrich Karl von. *Gottesglaube und Anfechtung bei Luther*. Deichert'sche Verlagsbuchhandlung, 1938.

Shuman, Joel, and Brian Volck. *Reclaiming the Body: Christians and the Faithful Use of Modern Medicine*. Brazos Press, 2006.

Sider, Ronald J. *Andreas Bodenstein von Karlstadt: The Development of His Thought, 1517–1525*. Studies in Medieval and Reformation Thought 11. Brill, 1974.

Sigerist, Henry E. "Bedside Manners in the Middle Ages; the Treatise *de Cautelis Medicorum* Attributed to Arnald of Villanova." *Quarterly Bulletin of the Northwestern University Medical School* 20, no. 1 (1946): 136–143.

Sirovich, Brenda E., Daniel J. Gottlieb, H. Gilbert Welch, and Elliott S. Fisher. "Regional Variations in Health Care Intensity and Physician Perceptions of Quality of Care." *Annals of Internal Medicine* 144, no. 9 (May 2, 2006): 641. https://doi.org/10.7326/0003-4819-144-9-200605020-00007.

Skinner, Jonathan S., Douglas O. Staiger, and Elliott S. Fisher. "Is Technological Change in Medicine Always Worth It? The Case of Acute Myocardial Infarction: Waste and Inefficiency Are Not Inevitable By-Products of Technological Growth." *Health Affairs* 25, no. Suppl1 (January 2006): W34–47. https://doi.org/10.1377/hlthaff.25.w34.

Smith, Christian, and Melinda Lundquist Denton. *Soul Searching: The Religious and Spiritual Lives of American Teenagers*. Oxford University Press, 2009.

Smoller, Laura A. "Of Earthquakes, Hail, Frogs, and Geography: Plague and the Investigation of the Apocalypse in the Later Middle Ages." In *Last Things: Death and the Apocalypse in the Middle Ages*. University of Pennsylvania Press, 2000.

Soergel, Philip M. *Miracles and the Protestant Imagination: The Evangelical Wonder Book in Reformation Germany*. Oxford University Press, 2012.

Solberg, Mary M. *Compelling Knowledge: A Feminist Proposal for an Epistemology of the Cross*. State University of New York Press, 1997.

Steiger, Johann Anselm. *Medizinische Theologie: Christus Medicus und Theologia Medicinalis bei Martin Luther und im Luthertum der Barockzeit*. Studies in the History of Christian Traditions 121. Brill, 2005.

Steinmetz, David C. *Misericordia Dei: The Theology of Johannes von Staupitz in Its Late Medieval Setting*. E. J. Brill, 1968.

Steinmetz, David C. *Luther and Staupitz: An Essay in the Intellectual Origins of the Protestant Reformation*. Duke University Press, 1980.

Steinmetz, David C. *Luther in Context*. 2nd ed. Baker Academic, 2002.

Suk, Tae Jun. "The Theology of Martin Luther between Judaism and Roman Catholicism: A Critical-Historical Evaluation of Luther's Concept of Idolatry." PhD diss., Drew University, 1999.

Sulmasy, Daniel P. *The Healer's Calling: A Spirituality for Physicians and Other Healthcare Professionals*. Paulist Press, 1997.

Sulmasy, Daniel P. *A Balm for Gilead: Meditations on Spirituality and the Healing Arts*. Georgetown University Press, 2006.

Sumption, Jonathan. *Pilgrimage: An Image of Mediaeval Religion*. Rowman & Littlefield, 1976.

Swanson, Robert Norman. *Religion and Devotion in Europe, c. 1215–c. 1515*. Cambridge University Press, 1995.

Tacke, Andreas, ed. *Lucas Cranach, 1553/2003: Wittenberger Tagungs-Beiträge anlässlich des 450. Todesjahres Lucas Cranachs des Älteren*. Leipzig, 2003.

Tanner, Norman P., ed. *Decrees of the Ecumenical Councils*. Sheed & Ward; Georgetown University Press, 1990.

Thagard, Paul. *Conceptual Revolutions*. Princeton University Press, 1993.

Thomas, Keith. *Religion and the Decline of Magic: Studies in Popular Beliefs in Sixteenth and Seventeenth-Century England*. Scribner, 1971.

Thompson, John Lee. *John Calvin and the Daughters of Sarah: Women in Regular and Exceptional Roles in the Exegesis of Calvin, His Predecessors and His Contemporaries*. Travaux d'Humanisme et Renaissance, CCLIX. Librairie Droz, 2014.

Tu, Jack V., Chris L. Pashos, C. David Naylor, Erluo Chen, Sharon-Lise Normand, Joseph P. Newhouse, and Barbara J. McNeil. "Use of Cardiac Procedures and Outcomes in Elderly Patients with Myocardial Infarction in the United States and Canada." *New England Journal of Medicine* 336, no. 21 (May 22, 1997): 1500–1505. https://doi.org/10.1056/NEJM199705223362106.

Vajta, Vilmos. *Luther on Worship*. Muhlenberg Press, 1954.

Vanderpool, Harold Y. "The Religious Features of Scientific Medicine." *Kennedy Institute of Ethics Journal* 18, no. 3 (September 2008): 203–234. https://doi.org/10.1353/ken.0.0199.

Vauchez, André. "Saints and Pilgrimages: New and Old." In *The Cambridge History of Christianity*, edited by Miri Rubin and Walter Simons. Cambridge University Press, 2009. https://doi.org/10.1017/CHOL9780521811064.023.

Vauchez, André, Jean Birrell, and André Vauchez. *Sainthood in the Later Middle Ages*. Cambridge University Press, 2005.

Volf, Miroslav. "Materiality of Salvation: An Investigation in the Soteriologies of Liberation and Pentecostal Theologies." *Journal of Ecumenical Studies* 26, no. 3 (1989): 447–467.

Vulpe, Simona-Nicoleta, and Sorina Vasile. "Unvaccinated, Just Like Everybody Else: Vaccine Hesitancy in a Romanian Religious Community." *European Review of Applied Sociology* 16, no. 26 (June 1, 2023): 16–24. https://doi.org/10.2478/eras-2023-0003.

Wardlaw, Margaret P. "American Medicine as Religious Practice: Care of the Sick as a Sacred Obligation and the Unholy Descent into Secularization." *Journal of Religion and Health* 50, no. 1 (March 2011): 62–74. https://doi.org/10.1007/s10943-010-9320-4.

Warnke, Martin. *Cranachs Luther: Entwürfe für ein Image*. Originalausg. Kunststück. Fischer, 1984.

Wear, Andrew, Roger Kenneth French, and Iain M. Lonie, eds. *The Medical Renaissance of the Sixteenth Century*. Cambridge University Press, 1985.

Webster, Charles, ed. *Health, Medicine, and Mortality in the Sixteenth Century*. Cambridge Monographs on the History of Medicine. Cambridge University Press, 1979.

Wennberg, John E., Kristen Bronner, Jonathan S. Skinner, Elliott S. Fisher, and David C. Goodman. "Inpatient Care Intensity and Patients' Ratings of Their Hospital Experiences." *Health Affairs* 28, no. 1 (January 2009): 103–112. https://doi.org/10.1377/hlthaff.28.1.103.

Westhelle, Vítor. *The Scandalous God: The Use and Abuse of the Cross*. Fortress Press, 2006.

White, Peter. "Pentecostal Spirituality in the Context of Faith and Hope Gospel (Prosperity Preaching): African Pentecostal Response to the COVID-19 Pandemic." *Dialog* 61, no. 2 (June 2022): 148–155. https://doi.org/10.1111/dial.12727.

Whitford, David M., ed. *Martin Luther in Context*. Cambridge University Press, 2018.

Wiesner-Hanks, Merry E. *Women and Gender in Early Modern Europe*. 3rd ed. New Approaches to European History 41. Cambridge University Press, 2008.

Wilkinson, John. *The Medical History of the Reformers: Luther, Calvin and Knox*. Handsel Press, 2001.

Willcoxon, Nicole. "Older Adults Sacrificing Basic Needs Due to Healthcare Costs." *Gallup.com*, June 15, 2022. https://news.gallup.com/poll/393494/older-adults-sacrificing-basic-needs-due-healthcare-costs.aspx.

Willcoxon, Nicole. "Majorities Rate Cost, Equity of U.S. Healthcare Negatively." *Gallup.com*, October 6, 2022. https://news.gallup.com/poll/402191/majorities-rate-cost-equity-healthcare-negatively.aspx.

Williams, George Huntston. *The Radical Reformation*. 3rd ed., rev. and expanded. Sixteenth Century Essays & Studies 15. Truman State University Press, 2000.

Williams, Joseph W. *Spirit Cure: A History of Pentecostal Healing*. Oxford University Press, 2013.

Wolff, Jens. *Metapher und Kreuz: Studien zu Luthers Christusbild*. Mohr Siebeck, 2005.

Wolgast, Eike. *Die Einführung der Reformation und das Schicksal der Klöster im Reich und in Europa*. Quellen und Forschungen zur Reformationsgeschichte, Band 89. Gütersloher Verlagshaus, 2014.

Wunder, Heide. *He Is the Sun, She Is the Moon: Women in Early Modern Germany*. Translated by Thomas Dunlap. Harvard University Press, 1998.

Zachman, Randall C. "The Idolatrous Religion of Conscience." In *The Assurance of Faith: Conscience in the Theology of Martin Luther and John Calvin*. Fortress Press, 1993.

Zurlo, Gina A., Todd M. Johnson, and Peter F. Crossing. "World Christianity and Mission 2021: Questions about the Future." *International Bulletin of Mission Research* 45, no. 1 (January 2021): 15–25. https://doi.org/10.1177/2396939320966220.

INDEX